Praise for *The Official Ubuntu Book*, *Fifth Edition*

This book is the perfect companion for users new to Linux and Ubuntu. It covers the basics in a concise and well-organized manner. General use is covered separately from troubleshooting and error-handling, making the book well suited both for the beginner as well as the user that needs extended help.

—Thomas Petrucha, Austria Ubuntu User Group

I have recommended this book to several users who I instruct regularly on the use of Ubuntu. All of them have been satisfied with their purchase and have even been able to use it to help them in their journey along the way.

—Chris Crisafulli, Ubuntu LoCo Council,
Florida Local Community Team

This text demystifies a very powerful Linux operating system . . . in just a few weeks of having it, I've used it as a quick reference a half dozen times, which saved me the time I would have spent scouring the Ubuntu forums online.

—Darren Frey, Member, Houston Local User Group

The Official Ubuntu Book

Fifth Edition

Barnes & Noble Special Edition

The Official Ubuntu Book

Fifth Edition

Barnes & Noble Special Edition

Benjamin Mako Hill
Matthew Helmke
Corey Burger

**With Jonathan Jesse,
Kyle Rankin, and Jono Bacon**

PRENTICE
HALL

Upper Saddle River, NJ • Boston • Indianapolis • San Francisco
New York • Toronto • Montreal • London • Munich • Paris • Madrid
Capetown • Sydney • Tokyo • Singapore • Mexico City

Visit us on the Web: informit.com/ph

Library of Congress Control Number: 2010928480

ISBN-13: 978-0-13-708131-8
ISBN-10:   0-13-708131-6
Text printed in the United States on recycled paper at RR Donnelley in Crawfordsville, Indiana.
First printing, June 2010

This book is dedicated to the Ubuntu community. Without your tireless hard work and commitment, none of this would be possible.

Contents at a Glance

Contents

Foreword to the First Edition

IT'S A SMALL CELEBRATION for me to write this foreword—almost exactly two years after the first meeting of a small group of free software professionals that turned into the Ubuntu project. A celebration because two years ago none of us would have predicted that our dream would spawn several million CDs, three or four million enthusiastic users, hundreds of commitments of support from companies large and small, a minor prime time television reference, and now *The Official Ubuntu Book*.

The dream that brought us together can be simply expressed:

> To build a world-class operating system for ordinary desktop computer users, that is genuinely free and freely available, that is immediately useful, and that represents the very best that the free software world can achieve today.

In setting out to build a platform for "ordinary desktop computer users," I had no idea that I would have the privilege of meeting and working with so many *extra*ordinary desktop computer users. Some of those extraordinary individuals are the authors of this book, people who both understand the importance of the free software movement and have the talent to have been real contributors to its success. Others make up the backbone of the Ubuntu community—the small but dedicated army of a few hundred people that works to produce a new release of Ubuntu every six months. They are at the heart of a network that reaches out through the global free software community—through the world of Debian, an extraordinary project in its own right and without which Ubuntu could not exist, and on out to the thousands of projects, large and small, that produce the code and documentation that we pull together and call *Ubuntu*.

While this huge extended community can often appear to be fractured and divided along infinitesimal ideological lines, we are all broadly in agreement about four key ideas, and it is those ideas that are central to the Ubuntu promise:

- That our software should not come with a license fee. That we should be able to share our software, modify it, and then share our modifications, too.
- That this free software should be the best version available, including regular security updates, and not a tease for a better, commercial product.
- That full-scale, high-quality commercial support from local and global companies should be available for this free platform.
- That this software should be usable in as many languages as possible and usable by as many people as possible regardless of disability.

The 17 of us who met in London two years ago come from a very wide variety of countries and backgrounds, but we all agreed that the goal of producing a platform that could live up to that promise was a worthy one, one that we would devote ourselves to wholeheartedly.

For several months we worked quietly. We wanted to come to the world not only with a manifesto but also with a clear demonstration of work done toward our goals, something that people could test and comment on. We had no name (though industry insiders called us the "Super-Secret Debian Startup"), and, as a result, we hosted most of our work at www.no-name-yet.com. We were looking for a name that could express the beauty of the free software community development process—collaboration, interdependence, sharing, standing gently on the shoulders of giants, and reaching for lofty goals. The only word that comes close to that, of which I'm aware, is the African word *ubuntu*. It is found in many forms in many different African languages. And so we adopted it as the name of our project.

We knew that our first release would have blemishes—warts—and gave it the codename "The Warty Warthog." We called ourselves "the warthogs" and coordinated our work on the #warthogs IRC channel. Today, for better or worse, that's turned into a tradition of codenames such as "Breezy

Badger" and "Dapper Drake." As lighthearted as they sound, these code-names come to embody the spirit of our community as it works toward a particular release. This next one—Dapper—is exactly that: a man emerging from youth, professional, bold, confident, and energetic. This is our first release that is designed to meet the needs of large organizations as much as developers and engineers. In the same way, the Ubuntu community has moved from being something of a rebellion against the "Linux establishment" to a strong and professionally organized group.

What Makes Ubuntu So Popular?

First, this is the time for free software to come to the forefront, and Ubuntu is very much the beneficiary of the vast amount of work that has gone into building up a huge body of work in the GNU/Linux world. That work has been underway for nearly 30 years, in one form or another, but Ubuntu is one way in which it is suddenly becoming "visible" to the non-specialist computer user. We are in the middle of a great overturning of the industry status quo. The last time that happened, in the mid-1990s, was when the world suddenly found itself connected to itself—by the Internet. Every major company, especially those in the field of technology, had to examine itself and ask the question, "How do we adapt to an Internet world?" Today, every major technology company has to ask itself the question, "How do we adapt to a free software world?"

I would speculate and say that Ubuntu represents an idea whose time has come. We did not invent the free software movement—that honor goes to Richard Stallman and many others who had a vision far more profound at a time when it was hard to see how it could ever become reality. But Ubuntu has perhaps the honor of bringing that vision to a very wide audience in a form that we can all appreciate. I hope that the real visionaries—those who have led the way—will appreciate the decisions and the choices we make in bringing you this project. Some will take exception—I know Linus prefers KDE to GNOME, for example, so he's likely to be more of a fan of Kubuntu than Ubuntu. But in general, the ideas that others have had, the principles of the free software movement, are well expressed in Ubuntu.

Second, Ubuntu is a project on which you can have a real impact. It has the benefit of deep and reliable financial backing and a corporate team to give it muscle, but it is in every regard an open project, with participation at the highest levels by true volunteers. We work in a fishbowl—our meetings take place online, in a public forum. That can be tricky. Building an operating system is a fast-paced business full of compromise and tough decisions in the face of little information. There are disagreements and dirty laundry, and mistakes are made. (I should know; some of them are mine. You should hear the one about the Warty Warthog desktop artwork.) The transparency of our environment, however, means that we can count on having robust conversations about our options—all of them, even the ones the core team would never have dreamed up. It also means that mistakes are identified, discussed, and ultimately addressed faster than they would be if we lived and worked behind closed doors. You get a better platform as a result.

We work hard as a community to recognize the contributions of all sorts of individuals—advocates, artists, Web forum moderators, channel operators, community event organizers, writers, translators, people who file and triage bugs . . . whatever your particular interest or talent, we will find a way to integrate your contribution.

Perhaps most important is the way our approach to community differentiates Ubuntu from other free software projects with similar vision. We try to do all of this in a way that recognizes that disagreements are important but prevents those disagreements from creating deep divides in our community. Our code of conduct may not be perfect, but it reminds each of us to remember the meaning of the word *ubuntu*—that each of us has our best impact *through* the relationships we maintain with one another. Finding common ground and maintaining healthy communication are more important for us as a community in the long run than a particular technical decision or the specific choice of words with which to translate "File" into Spanish. Our community governance structures—our Technical Board and Community Council—exist to ensure that debates don't become personal and that decisions can be taken after all sides have been heard.

If you are a software professional or curious about Linux, this book and this platform are an excellent choice. You will learn about the world of Ubuntu and, indirectly, Debian and GNU/Linux. These are great foundations for working with the tools that I believe will come to define the "standard," the everyday computing base upon which we build our homes and offices.

I once heard a proprietary software vendor say, "Linux is more expensive because skilled Linux professionals are more costly." This is true. It means, of course, that Linux skills are more valuable! It won't be true forever because the world of Linux is expanding so rapidly that sooner or later we will have to accept a position in the mainstream, and that takes off some of the "geek points" associated with being part of the "future of technology." But right now, without a doubt, being ahead of the curve on Linux and on Ubuntu is the right place to be. If you're this far into this foreword, you are clearly going to make it. ;-)

It's difficult for me to speculate on what the future might hold for the Ubuntu project. I know that I along with many others are loving the opportunity to be at the center of such an exciting initiative and are committed to seeing where it leads us over the coming years. I believe that it will become a pervasive part of our everyday computing environment, so I would like to help make sure that we don't make too many mistakes along the way! Please, come and join us in the fishbowl to help ensure we do a very, very good job.

—Mark Shuttleworth
Ubuntu Founder
April 2006

Preface

AS WE WRITE THIS, it has been several years since we penned the first edition of *The Official Ubuntu Book*. Over that time, we have seen Ubuntu continue its explosive growth. Updating this book drives this fact home in striking ways. For example, the number of users and posts in the Ubuntu Forums has nearly doubled since the last edition of this book a year ago. Again. The number of officially supported flavors of Ubuntu have been added to. Again. Once again, we feel blessed that *The Official Ubuntu Book* has been able to benefit from, and perhaps in a small way even *contribute* to, that success. Ultimately, that success paved the way for several subsequent editions, and now the fifth edition of the book that you're reading now.

In the process, this book, like Ubuntu, continues to mature. Our job as authors, like that of the Ubuntu developers, now involves more updating and polishing than it used to. Distributed under a free license, a once-risky book on a once-risky operating system is, just a few short years later, as close to a sure thing as an author, publisher, and if we have done our job well, a reader, could hope for.

And yet with success comes responsibility to our readers and to our users with high expectations. Ubuntu's success is built in part of maturity and excellence, and it cannot sacrifice these qualities if it will succeed. We cannot either. Our job as writers is complicated because we need to accurately reflect and represent both while catering to an increasing and increasingly diverse group of users.

As we've noted in the prefaces to previous editions of this book, being *Official* has carried with it a set of rights and responsibilities. Our book's title means that we must attempt to reflect and represent the whole Ubuntu community. While we, as authors, are expected to put ourselves into the book, it is understood that it can never be to the detriment of the values, principles, technologies, or structures of the Ubuntu community.

Doing this has been complicated as Ubuntu has grown. In each edition, we have added new information, because the Ubuntu community has grown to include new projects. In each revision of this book, we have needed to add to the list of related projects, tools, and community initiatives. As the Ubuntu community grows, it is impossible to give a complete accounting of what Ubuntu has to offer. Creating a summary requires some hard decisions. At the end of the day, we are constrained by page count and our own limited schedules.

Meanwhile, as with earlier editions, we needed to write this book about a new release of Ubuntu while that version was under active development and was being redesigned, rethought, and rebuilt. Every day, Ubuntu grows in different, unpredictable ways, and this growth has increased exponentially with the size of the community and the diversity of the userbase. Our book's development process had to both match and track this process as our content was crafted, rewritten, adjusted, and allowed to mature itself.

As in the previous edition, the contributors to this book go well beyond those listed on the book's cover. Invisible to most readers, dozens of members of the community left their mark on different parts of the text of this book. Although this degree of participation led to a writing process that was as hectic, and at times frustrating, as the process that builds Ubuntu, we hope we can remind readers of the level of quality that this process inspires in our book's subject. In the places where we achieve this, we have earned our book's title. With that goal in mind, we look forward to future versions of Ubuntu and editions of this book wrought through the same community-driven process.

Acknowledgments

SPECIAL THANKS TO Mark Shuttleworth, Jane Silber, and Billy Cina for all their efforts to get this book out into the world for both new and veteran Ubuntu users. Thanks also to Victor Ferns, director of Canonical, Ltd., for his attention to the project. Many people at Canonical, including Marcus Haslam, Iain Farrell, Ivanka Majic, Tom Macfarlane, and Jorge O. Castro, provided immeasurable assistance in the production of this book.

We reached into the Ubuntu community for a top group of reviewers, each of whom greatly contributed to the strength of the manuscript, including Amber Graner and Joe Barker. Our thanks extend back to this group of reviewers for help with the previous editions: Alan Pope, Jonathan Riddell, Oliver Grawet, Dennis Kaarsemaker, Matthew East, Quim Gil, Dinko Korunic, Abhay Kumar, Jaldhar Vyas, and Richard Weideman. Also, Scott Ritchie provided valuable assistance with the Wine information.

And finally, we appreciate the efforts of the Prentice Hall team, including Debra Williams Cauley, Carol Lallier, Kim Arney, Linda Begley, Richard Evans, Kim Boedigheimer, Mark Taub, John Fuller, and Elizabeth Ryan.

About the Authors

Benjamin Mako Hill is a Seattle native working out of Boston, Massachusetts. Mako is a long-time free software developer and advocate. He was part of the founding Ubuntu team, one of the first employees of Canonical, Ltd., and coauthor of *The Official Ubuntu Server Book*. In addition to some technical work, his charge at Canonical was to help grow the Ubuntu development and user community during the project's first year. Mako is currently a fellow at the MIT Center for Future Civic Media, and a researcher and Ph.D. candidate at the MIT Sloan School of Management. Mako has continued his involvement with Ubuntu as a member of the Community Council governance board, through development work, and through projects such as this book.

Matthew Helmke has been an Ubuntu user since April 2005 and an Ubuntu Member since August 2006. He serves on the Ubuntu Forum Council, providing leadership and oversight of the Ubuntu Forums, as well as on the Ubuntu regional membership approval board for Europe, the Middle East, and Africa. He has written articles about Ubuntu for *Linux+* and *Linux Identity* magazines, along with books and articles on this and other topics. He recently closed his consulting business in Morocco and began a Master's degree program at the University of Arizona in Tucson, Arizona.

Corey Burger lives in Victoria, British Columbia, and is a long-term user and contributor to Ubuntu. A founder of the Ubuntu Canada group and former member of the Community Council, he has been involved with Ubuntu since its first release. Corey is currently a geography student and has most recently worked for a Canadian Linux company. He also contributes to OpenStreetMap and works to promote Ubuntu on Vancouver Island. Corey speaks regularly about Ubuntu, OpenStreetMap, and open source to a wide variety of audiences.

Jonathan Jesse is a full-time Microsoft Windows consultant specializing in IT lifecycle management products. Beginning with the Hoary Hedgehog release, he joined the Ubuntu Documentation Team by proofreading and submitting patches to the mailing list, then worked on the Kubuntu documents. Currently, Jonathan is involved in working on bugs for the Kubuntu Team, the Ubuntu Wiki, and the Laptop Testing Team. Ubuntu and Kubuntu have given Jonathan a way to give back to the community without having to be a developer, and he encourages everyone to come help him out.

Kyle Rankin is a senior systems administrator for Quinstreet, Inc.; the current president of the North Bay Linux Users' Group; the author of *Knoppix Hacks*, *Knoppix Pocket Reference*, *Linux Multimedia Hacks*, and *Ubuntu Hacks*; and he has contributed to a number of other O'Reilly books. Kyle is also a columnist for *Linux Journal* and has had articles featured in *PC Magazine*, *TechTarget*, and other publications.

Jono Bacon (www.jonobacon.org) is the community leader for Ubuntu. Previously, he was a consultant for the United Kingdom's government-funded OpenAdvantage (www.openadvantage.org) center in England, where he worked with businesses, educational and charitable organizations, and individuals to help them move to open source software and open standards. He is the cocreator of the popular LugRadio podcast (www.lugradio.org).

Introduction

WELCOME to *The Official Ubuntu Book, Fifth Edition*!

In recent years, the Ubuntu operating system has taken the open source and IT world by storm. From out of nowhere, the Little Operating System That Could has blossomed into a full-featured desktop and server offering that has won over the hearts of users everywhere. Aside from the strong technical platform and impressive commitment to quality, Ubuntu also enjoys success because of its sprawling community of enthusiastic users who have helped to support, document, and test every millimeter of the Ubuntu landscape.

In your hands you are holding the official, authorized guide to this impressive operating system. Each of the authors selected to work on this book has demonstrated a high level of technical competence, an unbridled commitment to Ubuntu, and the ability to share this knowledge in a simple and clear manner. These authors gathered together to create a book that offers a solid grounding to Ubuntu and explains how the many facets and features of Ubuntu work.

About This Book

At the start of every book, on every bookshelf, in every shop, is a paragraph that sums up the intentions and aims for the book. We have one very simple, down-to-earth aim: to make the Ubuntu experience even more pleasant for users. The Ubuntu developers and community have gone to great lengths to produce an easy-to-use, functional, and flexible operating system for doing, browsing, and creating all kinds of interesting things. This book augments that effort. With such an integrated and flexible operating system, this guide acts as a tour de force for the many things you can do with Ubuntu.

The Scope of the Book

With so much to cover, we had our work cut out to write a book that could cover the system in sufficient detail. However, if we were to write in depth about every possible feature in Ubuntu, you would need to buy a new bookcase to store the sheer amount of content.

Part of the challenge in creating *The Official Ubuntu Book* was selecting the topics and content that can be covered within a reasonably sized book. We have identified the most essential content and written only about it. These chosen topics not only include installation, use of the desktop, applications, multimedia, system administration, and software management, but also include a discussion of the community, online resources, and the philosophy behind Ubuntu and open source software. As a bonus, we decided to squeeze in a chapter full of useful troubleshooting recipes that you can use when you need to troubleshoot problems, and we expanded our discussion of projects related to Ubuntu that will be of interest to you. We believe this book provides an ideal one-stop shop for getting started with Ubuntu.

The Menu

Here is a short introduction to each chapter and what it covers.

- Chapter 1—Introducing Ubuntu: This spirited introduction describes the Ubuntu project, its distribution, its development processes, and some of the history that made it all possible.

- Chapter 2—Installing Ubuntu: We walk through the installation process one step at a time to clearly describe how anyone interested may begin using Ubuntu on their own computer.

- Chapter 3—Using Ubuntu on the Desktop: This is an informative and enjoyable introductory tour of the Ubuntu desktop, the applications included, and ways to configure and customize your desktop.

- Chapter 4—Gaining Greater Proficiency: We explore some of the advanced ways to use Ubuntu, including managing the system. These features are not vital if you want to use the computer only as a simple tool, but once you learn how to install and manage software, use hardware devices and printers, interact with remote computers, use the terminal, and run some Windows programs under Ubuntu, you will find your overall experience even more rewarding and enjoyable.

- Chapter 5—The Ubuntu Server: This introduction to Ubuntu Server installation and administration includes coverage of command-line package management, basic security topics, and advanced installer features like logical volume management and RAID.

- Chapter 6—More Applications for Ubuntu: Here we discuss some of the most interesting and useful options from among the software packages available for Ubuntu but not installed by default. These quality programs are interesting and useful, but either there is not enough space to include them on the installation CD or they are without as wide of an audience as those programs preinstalled for everyone.

- Chapter 7—The Ubuntu Community: The Ubuntu community is larger and more active than many people realize. We discuss many of its facets, including what people like you do to build, promote, distribute, support, document, translate, and advocate Ubuntu—and we tell you how you can join in the fun.

- Chapter 8—Using Kubuntu: The most popular spin-off project from Ubuntu is Kubuntu. This chapter provides a solid introduction and primer for getting started.

- Chapter 9—Mobile and Netbook Editions: There is an exciting modification of Ubuntu designed for installation and use on netbooks, the small computers created for portability and long battery life that are taking the tech world by storm.

- Chapter 10—Ubuntu-Related Projects: There are a number of Linux distributions based on Ubuntu that you will find interesting and possibly useful. We discuss some of these as well as projects that are integral to the creation of Ubuntu, such as Launchpad and Bazaar.

- Chapter 11—Introducing the Ubuntu Forums: For hundreds of thousands of people, the Ubuntu Forums have provided the first glimpse of and interaction with the greater Ubuntu community. Especially for new users, this has become the most important venue for support. We explore the forums and the people, history, and processes that have built them.

- Chapter 12—Ubuntu One: We have included as a special bonus for this Barnes & Noble edition both this chapter about the new Ubuntu One cloud storage and Music Store services and a series of introductory how-to videos on the DVD showing new users how to get started with and use Ubuntu to perform common tasks.

- Appendix—Welcome to the Command Line: You can begin to take advantage of the power and efficiency of the command line with the clear, easy-to-use examples in our brief introduction.

The Ubuntu team offers several installation options for Ubuntu users, including CDs for desktop, alternate install, and server install. These three CD images are conveniently combined onto one DVD included in the back of this book, allowing you to install Ubuntu for different configurations from just one disk. There is also an option to test the DVD for defects as well as a memory test option to check your computer.

The first boot option on the DVD, Start or Install Ubuntu, will cover most users' needs. For more comprehensive information, check the Help feature by selecting F1 on the boot menu. You can also refer to Chapter 2, which covers the Ubuntu installation process in detail.

You can find the DVD image, the individual CD images (for those who don't have a DVD drive), and Kubuntu and Edubuntu images on www. ubuntu.com/download.

This Barnes & Noble Special Edition also includes a bonus DVD with helpful screencast lessons demonstrating the basics of Ubuntu use plus an extra chapter about the exciting new Ubuntu One cloud storage, both free and paid versions, and the Ubuntu One Music Store.

When viewing the bonus DVD using Ubuntu, a copy of Firefox 3.5 or later will allow Linux users to view the screencasts in a native/free format on their desktops. Go to the folder titled "For Linux Users." The file "ubuntu_ book_linux.html" contains a simple HTML5-based player for the Ogg Theora/Vorbis videos. In the rare case that a problem is encountered, a recent copy of Totem Movie Player, mplayer, or vlc should be able to play the ".ogv" files directly.

CHAPTER 1

Introducing Ubuntu

- A Wild Ride
- Free Software, Open Source, and GNU/Linux
- A Brief History of Ubuntu
- What Is Ubuntu?
- Ubuntu Promises and Goals
- Canonical and the Ubuntu Foundation
- Ubuntu Subprojects, Derivatives, and Spin-offs
- Summary

THIS CHAPTER INTRODUCES THE Ubuntu project, its distribution, its development processes, and some of the history that made it all possible. If you are looking to jump right in and get started with Ubuntu, turn right away to Chapter 2, Installing Ubuntu. If you are interested in first learning about where Ubuntu comes from and where it is going, this chapter provides a good introduction.

A Wild Ride

In April 2004 Mark Shuttleworth brought together a dozen developers from the Debian, GNOME, and GNU Arch projects to brainstorm. Shuttleworth asked the developers if a better type of operating system (OS) was possible. Their answer was "Yes." He asked them what it would look like. He asked them to describe the community that would build such an OS. That group worked with Shuttleworth to come up with answers to these questions, and then they decided to try to make the answers a reality. The group named itself the Warthogs and gave itself a six-month deadline to build a proof-of-concept OS. The developers nicknamed their first release the Warty Warthog with the reasonable assumption that their first product would have its warts. Then they got down to business.

It's fulfilling, particularly for those of us who were privileged to be among those early Warthogs, to see the progress made by this project over the years. We had a strong beginning when, far from being warty, the Warty Warthog surpassed our most optimistic expectations and *everyone's* predictions. Within six months, Ubuntu was in the Number 1 spot on several popularity rankings of GNU/Linux distributions. Ubuntu has demonstrated the most explosive growth of any GNU/Linux distribution in recent memory and had one of the most impressive first years and continued growth of any free or open source software project in history.

It is staggering to think that after so few years, *millions* of individuals are using Ubuntu. As many thousands of these users give back to the Ubuntu community by developing documentation, translation, and code, Ubuntu improves every day. As many thousands of these users contribute to a thriving advocacy and support community—both online and in their local communities—Ubuntu's growth remains unchecked. Ubuntu subprojects, a list of efforts that includes Kubuntu, Ubuntu Netbook Edition, Ubuntu Studio, and other projects, are extending the reach and goals of the Ubuntu project into new realms.

Meanwhile, millions of pressed Ubuntu CDs have been shipped at no cost to universities, Internet cafés, computer shops, and community centers around the world. You can find Ubuntu's familiar human-colored background and title bars almost anywhere people use computers. The authors have personally seen strangers running Ubuntu on trains in Spain, in libraries in Boston, in museums in Croatia, in high schools in Mexico, and in many more places too numerous to list here.

Over the years, Ubuntu has continued to mature. The public took even more notice of Ubuntu beginning with the release of Ubuntu 6.06 LTS, the first polished release with long-term support for both desktops and servers, and followed by a new release every six months and a new LTS release every two years up to the current 10.04 LTS. With these releases, Ubuntu has proven it intends to stick around for the long term while also improving consistently and on a predictable schedule. Even with this maturation, the project maintains its youthful vigor, its ambitious attitude, its commitment to its principles, and its community-driven approach. As the project ages, it is proving that it can learn from its failures as well as its successes and that it can maintain growth without compromising stability. We've come a long way—and we're still only getting started.

Free Software, Open Source, and GNU/Linux

While thousands of individuals have contributed in some form to Ubuntu, the project has succeeded only through the contributions of many thousands more who have indirectly laid the technical, social, and economic groundwork for Ubuntu's success. While introductions to free software, open source, and GNU/Linux can be found in many other places, no introduction of Ubuntu is complete without a brief discussion of these concepts and the people and history behind them. It is around these concepts and within these communities that Ubuntu was motivated and born. Ultimately, it is through these ideas that it is sustained.

Free Software and GNU

In a series of events that have almost become legend through constant repetition, Richard M. Stallman created the concept of free software in 1983.
Stallman grew up with computers in the 1960s and 1970s, when computer
users purchased very large and extremely expensive mainframe computers, which were then shared among large numbers of programmers. Software was, for the most part, seen as an add-on to the hardware, and every
user had the ability and the right to modify or rewrite the software on his
or her computer and to freely share this software. As computers became
cheaper and more numerous in the late 1970s, producers of software
began to see value in the software itself. Producers of computers began to
argue that their software could be copyrighted and was a form of intellec-
tual property much like a music recording, a film, or a book's text. They
began to distribute their software under licenses and in forms that
restricted its users' abilities to use, redistribute, or modify the code. By the
early 1980s, restrictive software licenses had become the norm.

Stallman, then a programmer at MIT's Artificial Intelligence Laboratory,
became increasingly concerned with what he saw as a dangerous loss of
the freedoms that software users and developers had previously enjoyed.
He was concerned with computer users' ability to be good neighbors and
members of what he thought was an ethical and efficient computer-user
community. To fight against this negative tide, Stallman articulated a
vision for a community that developed liberated code—in his words, "free
software." He defined free software as software that had the following four
characteristics—labeled as freedoms 0 through 3 instead of 1 through 4 as
a nod to computer programming tradition and a bit of an inside joke:

- The freedom to run the program for any purpose (freedom 0)

- The freedom to study how the program works and adapt it to your
  needs (freedom 1)

- The freedom to redistribute copies so you can help your neighbor
  (freedom 2)

- The freedom to improve the program and release your improvements
  to the public so that the whole community benefits (freedom 3)

Access to source code—the human-readable and modifiable blueprints of any piece of software that can be distinguished from the computer-readable version of the code that most software is distributed as—is a prerequisite to freedoms 1 and 3. In addition to releasing this definition of free software, Stallman created a project with the goal of creating a completely free OS to replace the then-popular UNIX. In 1984, Stallman announced this project and called it GNU—also in the form of common programmer humor, a recursive acronym that stands for "GNU's Not UNIX."

Linux

By the early 1990s, Stallman and a collection of other programmers working on GNU had developed a near-complete OS that could be freely shared. They were, however, missing a final essential piece in the form of a kernel—a complex system command processor that lies at the center of any OS. In 1991, Linus Torvalds wrote an early version of just such a kernel, released it under a free license, and called it Linux. Linus's kernel was paired with the GNU project's development tools and OS and with the graphical windowing system called X. With this pairing, a completely free OS was born—free both in terms of price and in Stallman's terms of freedom.

All systems referred to as Linux today are, in fact, built on the work of this collaboration. Technically, the term *Linux* refers only to the kernel. Many programmers and contributors to GNU, including Stallman, argue emphatically that the full OS should be referred to as GNU/Linux in order to give credit not only to Linux but also to the GNU project and to highlight GNU's goals of spreading software freedom—goals not necessarily shared by Linus Torvalds. Many others find this name cumbersome and prefer calling the system simply Linux. Yet others, such as those working on the Ubuntu project, attempt to avoid the controversy altogether by referring to GNU/Linux only by using their own project's name.

Open Source

Disagreements over labeling did not end with discussions about the naming of the combination of GNU and Linux. In fact, as the list of contributors to GNU and Linux grew, a vibrant world of new free software projects sprouted up, facilitated in part by growing access to the Internet. As this community grew and diversified, a number of people began to notice an unintentional side effect of Stallman's free software. Because free software was built in an open way, *anyone* could contribute to software by looking through the code, finding bugs, and fixing them. Because software ended up being examined by larger numbers of programmers, free software was higher in quality, performed better, and offered more features than similar software developed through proprietary development mechanisms. It turned out that in many situations, the development model behind free software led to software that was *inherently better* than proprietary alternatives.

As the computer and information technology industry began to move into the dot-com boom, one group of free software developers and leaders, spearheaded by two free software developers and advocates—Eric S. Raymond and Bruce Perens—saw the important business proposition offered by a model that could harness volunteer labor or interbusiness collaboration and create intrinsically better software. However, they worried that the term *free software* was problematic for at least two reasons. First, it was highly ambiguous—the English word *free* means both gratis, or at no cost (e.g., free as in free beer), and liberated in the sense of freedom (e.g., free as in free speech). Second, there was a feeling, articulated most famously by Raymond, that all this talk of freedom was scaring off the very business executives and decision makers whom the free software movement needed to impress in order to succeed.

To tackle both of these problems, this group coined a new phrase—open source—and created a new organization called the Open Source Initiative. The group set at its core a definition of open source software that overlapped completely and exclusively with both Stallman's four-part definition of free software and with other community definitions that were also based on Stallman's.

One useful way to understand the split between the free software and open source movements is to think of it as the opposite of a schism. In religious schisms, churches separate and do not work or worship together because of relatively small differences in belief, interpretation, or motivation. For example, most contemporary forms of Protestant Christianity agree on *almost* everything but have separated over some small but irreconcilable differences. However, in the case of the free software and open source movements, the two groups have fundamental disagreements about their motivation and beliefs. One group is focused on freedom, while the other is focused on pragmatics. Free software is most accurately described as a social movement, while open source is a development methodology. However, the two groups have no trouble working on projects hand in hand.

In terms of the motivations and goals, open source and free software diverge greatly. Yet in terms of the software, the projects, and the licenses they use, they are completely synonymous. While people who identify with either group see the two movements as being at odds, the Ubuntu project sees no conflict between the two ideologies. People in the Ubuntu project identify with either group and often with both. In this book, we may switch back and forth between the terms as different projects, and many people in the Ubuntu community identify more strongly with one term or the other. For the purposes of this book, though, either term should be read as implying the other unless it is stated otherwise.

A Brief History of Ubuntu

There was a time when writing a history of Ubuntu may have seemed premature. However, the last several years have been busy ones for Ubuntu. With its explosive growth, it is difficult even for those involved most closely with the project to track and record some of the high points. Importantly, there are some key figures whose own history must be given to fully understand Ubuntu. This brief summary provides some of the high points of Ubuntu's history to date and the necessary background knowledge to understand where Ubuntu comes from.

Mark Shuttleworth

No history of Ubuntu can call itself complete without a history of Mark Shuttleworth. Shuttleworth is, undeniably, the most visible and important person in Ubuntu. More important from the point of view of history, Shuttleworth is also the originator and initiator of the project—he made the snowball that would eventually roll on and grow to become the Ubuntu project.

Shuttleworth was born in 1973 in Welkom, Free State, in South Africa. He attended Diocesan College and obtained a business science degree in finance and information systems at the University of Cape Town. During this period, he was an avid computer hobbyist and became involved with the free and open source software community. He was at least marginally involved in both the Apache project and the Debian project and was the first person to upload the Apache Web server, perhaps the single most important piece of server software on GNU/Linux platforms, into the Debian project's archives.

Seeing an opportunity in the early days of the Web, Shuttleworth founded a certificate authority and Internet security company called Thawte in his garage. Over the course of several years, he built Thawte into the second largest certificate authority on the Internet, trailing only the security behemoth VeriSign. Throughout this period, Thawte's products and services were built and served almost entirely from free and open source software. In December 1999, Shuttleworth sold Thawte to VeriSign for an undisclosed amount that reached into the hundreds of millions in U.S. dollars.

With his fortune made at a young age, Shuttleworth might have enjoyed a life of leisure—and probably considered it. Instead, he decided to pursue his lifelong dream of space travel. After paying approximately US$20 million to the Russian space program and devoting nearly a year to preparation, including learning Russian and spending seven months training in Star City, Russia, Shuttleworth realized his dream as a civilian cosmonaut aboard the Russian Soyuz TM-34 mission. On this mission, Shuttleworth spent two days on the Soyuz rocket and eight days on the International Space Station, where he participated in experiments related to AIDS and genome research. In early May 2002, Shuttleworth returned to Earth.

In addition to space exploration and a slightly less impressive jaunt to Antarctica, Shuttleworth has played an active role as both a philanthropist and a venture capitalist. In 2001, Shuttleworth founded The Shuttleworth Foundation (TSF)—a nonprofit organization based in South Africa. The foundation was chartered to fund, develop, and drive social innovation in the field of education. Of course, the means by which TSF attempts to achieve these goals frequently involves free software. Through these projects, the organization has been one of the most visible proponents of free and open source software in South Africa and even the world. In the venture capital area, Shuttleworth worked to foster research, development, and entrepreneurship in South Africa with strategic injections of cash into start-ups through a new venture capital firm called HBD, an acronym for "Here Be Dragons." During this period, Shuttleworth was busy brainstorming his next big project—the project that would eventually become Ubuntu.

The Warthogs

There has been no lack of projects attempting to wrap GNU, Linux, and other pieces of free and open source software into a neat, workable, and user-friendly package. Mark Shuttleworth, like many other people, believed that the philosophical and pragmatic benefits offered by free software put it on a course for widespread success. While each had its strengths, none of the offerings were particularly impressive as a whole. Something was missing from each of them. Shuttleworth saw this as an opportunity. If someone could build *the* great free software distribution that helped push GNU/Linux into the mainstream, he would come to occupy a position of strategic importance.

Shuttleworth, like many other technically inclined people, was a huge fan of the Debian project (discussed in depth later in this chapter). However, many things about Debian did not fit with Shuttleworth's vision of an ideal OS. For a period of time, Shuttleworth considered the possibility of running for Debian project leader as a means of reforming the Debian project from within. With time, though, it became clear that the best way to bring GNU/Linux to the mainstream would not be from within the Debian project—which in many situations had very good reasons for being the way it was. Instead, Shuttleworth would create a new project that worked in symbiosis with Debian to build a new, better GNU/Linux system.

To kick off this project, Shuttleworth invited a dozen or so free and open source software developers he knew and respected to his flat in London in April 2004. It was in this meeting (alluded to in the first paragraphs of this introduction) that the groundwork for the Ubuntu project was laid. By that point, many of those involved were excited about the possibility of the project. During this meeting, the members of the team—which would in time grow into the core Ubuntu team—brainstormed a large list of the things that *they* would want to see in their ideal OS. The list is now a familiar list of features to most Ubuntu users. Many of these traits are covered in more depth later in this chapter. The group wanted

- Predictable and frequent release cycles
- A strong focus on localization and accessibility
- A strong focus on ease of use and user-friendliness on the desktop
- A strong focus on Python as the single programming language through which the entire system could be built and expanded
- A community-driven approach that worked with existing free software projects and a method by which the groups could give back as they went along—not just at the time of release
- A new set of tools designed around the process of building distributions that allowed developers to work within an ecosystem of different projects and that allowed users to give back in whatever way they could

There was consensus among the group that actions speak louder than words, so there were no public announcements or press releases. Instead, the group set a deadline for itself—six short months in the future. Shuttleworth agreed to finance the work and pay the developers full-time salaries to work on the project. After six months, they would both announce their project and reveal the first product of their work. They made a list of goals they wanted to achieve by the deadline, and the individuals present took on tasks. Collectively, they called themselves the Warthogs.

What Does *Ubuntu* Mean?

At this point, the Warthogs had a great team, a set of goals, and a decent idea of how to achieve most of them. The team did not, on the other hand, have a name for the project. Shuttleworth argued strongly that they should call the project Ubuntu.

Ubuntu is a concept and a term from several South African languages, including Zulu and Xhosa. It refers to a South African ideology or ethic that, while difficult to express in English, might roughly be translated as "humanity toward others," or "I am what I am because of who we all are." Others have described ubuntu as "the belief in a universal bond of sharing that connects all humanity." The famous South African human rights champion Archbishop Desmond Tutu explained ubuntu in this way:

> A person with ubuntu is open and available to others, affirming of others, does not feel threatened that others are able and good, for he or she has a proper self-assurance that comes from knowing that he or she belongs in a greater whole and is diminished when others are humiliated or diminished, when others are tortured or oppressed.

Ubuntu played an important role as a founding principle in post-apartheid South Africa and remains a concept familiar to most South Africans today.

Shuttleworth liked the term *Ubuntu* as a name for the new project for several reasons. First, it is a South African concept. While the majority of the people who work on Ubuntu are not from South Africa, the roots of the project are, and Shuttleworth wanted to choose a name that represented this. Second, the project emphasizes relationships with others and provides a framework for a profound type of community and sharing—exactly the attitudes of sharing, community, and collaboration that are at the core of free software. The term represented the side of free software that the team wanted to share with the world. Third, the idea of personal relationships built on mutual respect and connections describes the fundamental ground rules for the highly functional community that the Ubuntu team wanted to build. *Ubuntu* was a term that encapsulated where the project came from, where the project was going, and how the project planned to get there. The name was perfect. It stuck.

Creating Canonical

In order to pay developers to work on Ubuntu full time, Shuttleworth needed a company to employ them. He wanted to pick some of the best people for the jobs from within the global free and open source communities. These communities, inconveniently for Shuttleworth, know no national and geographic boundaries. Rather than move everyone to a single locale and office, Shuttleworth made the decision to employ these developers through a virtual company. While this had obvious drawbacks in the form of high-latency and low-bandwidth connections, different time zones, and much more, it also introduced some major benefits in the particular context of the project. On one hand, the distributed nature of employees meant that the new company could hire individuals without requiring them to pack up their lives and move to a new country. More important, it meant that *everyone* in the company was dependent on IRC, mailing lists, and online communication mechanisms to do their work. This unintentionally and automatically solved the water-cooler problem that plagued many other corporately funded free software projects—namely, that developers would casually speak about their work in person and cut the community and anyone else who didn't work in the office out of the conversation completely. For the first year, the closest thing that Canonical had to an office was Shuttleworth's flat in London. While the company has grown and now has several offices around the world, it remains distributed and a large number of the engineers work from home. The group remains highly dependent on Internet collaboration.

With time, the company was named Canonical. The name was a nod to the project's optimistic goals of becoming the canonical place for services and support for free and open source software and for Ubuntu in particular. *Canonical*, of course, refers to something that is accepted as authoritative. It is a common word in the computer programmer lexicon. It's important to note that being canonical is like being standard; it is not coercive. Unlike holding a monopoly, becoming the canonical location for something implies a similar sort of success—but *never* one that cannot be undone, and *never* one that is exclusive. Other companies will support Ubuntu and build operating systems based on it, but as long as Canonical is doing a good job, its role will remain central.

What Is Ubuntu?

The Warthogs' goal and Canonical's flagship project is Ubuntu. If you've gotten this far, you already have some idea of what that means. That said, this section offers a little bit of background that is helpful in understanding exactly *what* Ubuntu is and what its goals are.

What Is a Distribution?

It's clear to most people that Ubuntu is an OS. The full story is a little more complex. Ubuntu is what is called a distribution of GNU/Linux—a *distro* for short. Understanding exactly what that means requires, once again, a little bit of history. In the early days of GNU and Linux, users needed a great deal of technical knowledge. Only geeks needed to apply. There were no Linux operating systems in the sense that we usually use the term—there was no single CD or set of disks that one could use to install. Instead, the software was dozens and even hundreds of individual programs, each built differently by a different individual, and each distributed separately. Installing each of the necessary applications would be incredibly time consuming at best. In many cases, incompatibilities and the technical trickery necessary to install software made getting a GNU/Linux system on a hard disk prohibitively difficult. A great deal of knowledge of configuration and programming was necessary just to get a system up and running. As a result, very few people who were not programmers used these early GNU/Linux systems.

Early distributions were projects that collected all of the necessary pieces of software from all of the different places and put them together in an easier-to-install form with the most basic configuration already done. These distributions aimed to make using GNU/Linux more convenient and to bring it to larger groups of users. Today, almost nobody uses GNU/Linux without using a distribution. As a result, distribution names are well known. Ubuntu is such a project. Other popular distros include Red Hat and Fedora, Novell's SUSE, Gentoo, and of course Debian.

Most distributions contain a similar collection of software. For example, they all contain most of the core pieces of GNU and a Linux kernel. Almost all contain the X Window System and a set of applications on top of it that may include a Web browser, a desktop environment, and an office suite. While distributions started out distributing only the core pieces of the OS, they have grown to include an increasingly wide array of applications as well. A modern distribution includes all of the software that "comes with an OS," that is, several CDs or DVDs containing anything that most users might want and that the distribution is legally allowed to distribute.

Ubuntu, like other contemporary distros, offers a custom installer, a framework including software and servers to install new software once the system has been installed, a standard configuration method through which many programs can be configured, a standard method through which users can report bugs in their software, and much more. Frequently, distributions also contain large repositories of software on servers accessible through the Internet. To get a sense of scale, Ubuntu includes more than 30,000 pieces of software on its central servers—each piece of software is customized slightly and tested to work well with all of the other software on the system. That number grows daily.

What's important to realize is that the creators of distributions do not, for the most part, write or create the applications you use. The Ubuntu team did not write Linux, and it did not write GNU—although individuals on the team have contributed to both projects. Instead, the Ubuntu team takes GNU, Linux, and many thousands of other applications and then tests and integrates them to be accessible under a single installer. Ubuntu is the glue that lets you take a single CD, install hundreds of separate pieces of software, and have them work together as a single, integrated desktop system. If you were to pick up a CD of another distribution such as Debian, Red Hat, or Novell, the software installed would be nearly identical to the software in Ubuntu. The difference would be in the way the software is installed, serviced, upgraded, and presented and the way it integrates with other pieces of software on the system.

An Ecosystem of Distributions

Many hundreds of GNU/Linux distributions are in active use today. A quick look at Distrowatch's database (distrowatch.com) demonstrates the staggering number and growth of distributions. One of the first GNU/Linux distributions was called Softlanding Linux System, or SLS. For a number of reasons, a programmer named Patrick Volkerding thought he could improve on SLS. Because SLS was free software, Volkerding had the freedom to make a derivative version of SLS and distribute it. Volkerding did just this when he took SLS's code and used it as the framework or model upon which to create his own variant called Slackware. Subsequently, Slackware became the first widely successful GNU/Linux distribution and is maintained to this day.

With time, the landscape of GNU/Linux distribution has changed. However, the important role of derivation that made Slackware possible has remained fully intact and is still shaping this landscape. Today, the hundreds of GNU/Linux distributions serve a multitude of users for a myriad of purposes: There are distributions specially designed for children, for dentists, and for speakers of many of the world's languages. There are distributions for science, for business, for servers, for PDAs, for nonprofit organizations, for musicians, and for countless other groups.

Despite this diversity, the vast majority of derivatives can be traced back to one of two parent distributions: Red Hat and Debian. While it is not necessary to understand the details of how these projects differ, it's useful to know that Red Hat and Debian offer two compelling, but frequently different, platforms. Each project has strengths and weaknesses. For almost every group making a Linux-based OS, one of these projects acts as square one (with a few notable exceptions, such as the Gentoo project).

However, while the process of deriving distributions has allowed for a proliferation of OS platforms serving a vast multiplicity of needs, the derivative process has, historically, been largely a one-way process. New distributions based on Red Hat—Mandriva and Novell's SUSE, for example—begin with Red Hat or a subset of Red Hat technology and then customize and diverge. Very few of these changes ever make it back into Red Hat and, with time, distributions tend to diverge to the point of irreconcilable incompatibility. While the software that each system includes remains largely consistent across all distributions, the way that it is packaged, presented, installed, and configured becomes increasingly differentiated. During this process, interdistribution sharing and collaboration grow in difficulty.

This growing divergence indicates a more general problem faced by distribution teams in getting changes upstream. Frequently, the users of GNU/Linux distributions find and report problems in their software. Frequently, distribution teams fix the bugs in question. While sometimes these bugs are in changes introduced by the distribution, they often exist in the upstream version of the software and the fix applies to *every* distribution. What is not uncommon, but is unfortunately *much* less frequent, is for these bug fixes to be pushed upstream so that all distributions and users get to use them. This lack of collaboration is rarely due to malice, incompetence, or any tactical or strategic decision made by developers or their employers. Instead, tracking and monitoring changes *across* distributions and in relation to upstream developers is complicated and difficult. It's a fact of life that sometimes changes fall on the floor. These failures are simply the product of distribution-building processes, policies, and tools that approach distributions as products in and of themselves—not processes within an ecosystem.

Like many other distributions, Ubuntu is a derivative of Debian. Unlike the creators of many derivatives, the Ubuntu community has made it one of its primary goals to explore the possibility of a better derivation process with Debian, with Debian and Ubuntu's common upstreams (e.g., projects such as Linux or GNU), and with Ubuntu's *own* derivatives. A more in-depth discussion of Debian can help explain how Ubuntu positions itself within the free software world.

The Debian Project and the Free Software Universe

Debian is a distribution backed by a volunteer project of over 1,000 official members and many more volunteers and contributors. It has expanded to encompass around 23,000 packages of free and open source applications and documentation. Debian's history and structure make it very good at certain things. For example, Debian has a well-deserved reputation for integrated package management and access to a large list of free software applications. However, as a voluntary and largely nonhierarchical organization, Debian had a challenging time providing frequent and reliable releases, corporate support and liability, and a top-down consistency.

Each new distribution exists for a reason. Creating a new distribution, even a derivative, is far from easy. In large part, Ubuntu exists to build off of the many successes of the Debian project while solving some of the problems it struggles with. The goal is to create a synthetic whole that appeals to users who had previously been unable or unwilling to use Debian.

In building off the great work of the Debian project, as well as GNU, Linux, and other projects that Debian is built on, the Ubuntu team wanted to explore a new style of derivation that focused on a tighter interproject relationship within an ecosystem of different developers. While Ubuntu tries to improve and build on Debian's success, the project is in no way trying to replace Debian. On the contrary, Ubuntu couldn't exist without the Debian project and its large volunteer and software base, as well as the high degree of quality that Debian consistently provides. This symbiotic relationship between Ubuntu and Debian is mirrored in the way that both Ubuntu and Debian depend heavily on projects such as GNU and Linux to produce great software, which they can each package and distribute. The Ubuntu project sets out explicitly to build a symbiotic relationship with both Debian and their common "upstream."

The relationship between Ubuntu and Debian has not been simple, straightforward, or painless and has involved patience and learning on both sides. While the relationship has yet to be perfected, with time it has improved consistently, and both groups have found ways to work together that seem to offer major benefits over the traditional derive-and-forget model. It is through a complex series of technological, social, and even political processes—many of which are described in the rest of this chapter—that Ubuntu tries to create a better way to build a free software distribution.

The Ubuntu Community

By now you may have noticed a theme that permeates the Ubuntu project on several levels. The history of free software and open source is one of a profoundly effective *community*. Similarly, in building a GNU/Linux distribution, the Ubuntu community has tried to focus on an ecosystem model—an organization of organizations—in other words, a community. Even the definition of *ubuntu* is one that revolves around people interacting in a community.

It comes as no surprise then that an "internal" community plays heavily into the way that the Ubuntu distribution is created. While the Ubuntu 4.10 version (Warty Warthog) was primarily built by a small number of people, Ubuntu achieved widespread success only through contributions by a much larger group that included programmers, documentation writers, volunteer support staff, and users. While Canonical employs a core group of several dozen active contributors to Ubuntu, the distribution has, from day one, encouraged and incorporated contributions from *anyone* in the community, and rewards and recognizes contributions by all. Rather than taking center stage, paid contributors are *not* employed by the Ubuntu project—instead they are employed by Canonical, Ltd. These employees are treated simply as another set of community members. They must apply for membership in the Ubuntu community and have their contributions recognized in the same way as anyone else. All nonbusiness-related communication about the Ubuntu project occurs in public and in the community. Volunteer community members occupy a majority of the seats on the two most important governing boards of the Ubuntu project: the Technical Board, which oversees all technical matters, and the Community Council, which approves new Ubuntu members and resolves disputes. Seats on both boards are approved by the relevant community groups, developers for the Technical Board and Ubuntu members for the Community Council.

In order to harness and encourage the contributions of its community, Ubuntu strives to balance the important role that Canonical plays with the value of empowering individuals in the community. The Ubuntu project is based on a fundamental belief that great software is built, supported, and maintained only in a strong relationship with the individuals who use the software. In this way, by fostering and supporting a vibrant community, Ubuntu can achieve much more than it could through paid development alone. The people on the project believe that while the contributions of Canonical and Mark Shuttleworth have provided an important catalyst for the processes that have built Ubuntu, it is the community that brought the distribution its success to date. The project members believe that it is only through increasing reliance on the community that the project's success will continue to grow. We won't outspend the proprietary software industry. As a community, though, we are very much more than Microsoft and its allies can afford.

The nature of the Ubuntu community is described in depth in Chapter 7, which is wholly devoted to the subject. Finally, it is worth noting that, while this book is official, none of the authors are Canonical employees. This book, like much of the rest of Ubuntu, is purely a product of the project's community.

Ubuntu Promises and Goals

So far, this book has been about the prehistory, history, and context of the Ubuntu project. After this chapter, the book focuses on the distribution itself. Before proceeding, it's important to understand the goals that motivated the project.

Philosophical Goals

The most important goals of the Ubuntu project are philosophical in nature. The Ubuntu project lays out its philosophy in a series of documents on its Web site. In the most central of these documents, the team summarizes the charter and the major philosophical goals and underpinnings.

- **Our philosophy**

  Our work is driven by a philosophy of software freedom that aims to spread and bring the benefits of software to all parts of the world. At the core of the Ubuntu Philosophy are these core ideals:

  1. Every computer user should have the freedom to download, run, copy, distribute, study, share, change and improve their software for any purpose, without paying licensing fees.

  2. Every computer user should be able to use their software in the language of their choice.

  3. Every computer user should be given every opportunity to use software, even if they work under a disability.

  Our philosophy is reflected in the software we produce and included in our distribution. As a result, the licensing terms of the software we distribute are measured against our philosophy, using the Ubuntu License Policy.

  When you install Ubuntu, almost all of the software installed already meets these ideals, and we are working to ensure that every single piece of software you need is available under a license that gives you those freedoms.

  Currently, we make a specific exception for some "drivers" that are available only in binary form, without which many computers will not complete the Ubuntu installation. We place these in a restricted section of your system, which makes them easy to remove if you do not need them.

- **Free software**

  For Ubuntu, the "free" in free software is used primarily in reference to freedom and not to price—although we are committed to not charging for Ubuntu. The most important thing about Ubuntu is that it confers rights of software freedom on the people who install and use it. These freedoms enable the Ubuntu community to grow and to continue to share its collective experience and expertise to improve Ubuntu and make it suitable for use in new countries and new industries.

Quoting the Free Software Foundation's "What Is Free Software," the freedoms at the core of free software are defined as

▪ The freedom to run the program for any purpose

▪ The freedom to study how the program works and adapt it to your needs

▪ The freedom to redistribute copies so you can help others

▪ The freedom to improve the program and release your improvements to the public so that everyone benefits

▪ **Open source**

Open source is a term coined in 1998 to remove the ambiguity in the English word *free*. The Open Source Initiative described open source software in the Open Source Definition. Open source continues to enjoy growing success and wide recognition.

Ubuntu is happy to call itself open source. While some refer to free and open source as competing movements with different ends, we do not see free and open source software as either distinct or incompatible. Ubuntu proudly includes members who identify with both movements.

Here, the Ubuntu project makes explicit its goals that every user of software should have the freedoms required by free software. This is important for a number of reasons. First, it offers users all of the practical benefits of software that runs better, faster, and more flexibly. More important, it gives every user the capability to transcend his or her role as a user and a consumer of software. Ubuntu wants software to be empowering and to work in the ways that users want it to work. Ubuntu wants all users to have the ability to make sure it works for them. To do this, software *must* be free, so Ubuntu makes this a requirement and a philosophical promise.

Of course, the core goals of Ubuntu do not end with the free software definition. Instead, the project articulates two new but equally important goals. The first of these, that all computer users should be able to use their computers in their chosen languages, is a nod to the fact that the majority of the world's population does not speak English, while the vast majority of software interacts only in that language. To be useful, source code comments, programming languages, documentation, and the texts and menus in computer programs must be written in *some* language. Arguably, the world's most international language is a reasonably good choice. However, there is no language that everyone speaks, and English is not useful to the majority of the world's population that does not speak it. A computer can be a great tool for empowerment and education, but *only* if the user can understand the words in the computer's interface. As a result, Ubuntu believes that it is the project's—and community's—responsibility to ensure that *every* user can easily use Ubuntu to read and write in the language with which he or she is most comfortable.

The ability to make modifications—a requirement of free software and of Ubuntu's first philosophical point—makes this type of translation possible. This book is a case in point. While it helps explain Ubuntu only to the relatively small subset of the world that already speaks English, the choice to write this book in English was made to enable it to have the widest impact. More important, it is distributed under a Creative Commons license that allows for translation, modification, and redistribution. The authors of this book cannot write this book in all of the world's languages—or even more than one of them. Instead, we have attempted to eliminate unnecessary legal restrictions and other barriers that might keep the community from taking on the translation work. As a result, the complete text of the several editions have been translated into other languages like German, Japanese, Polish, and Spanish.

Finally, just as no person should be blocked from using a computer simply because he or she does not know a particular language, no user should be blocked from using a computer because of a disability. Ubuntu must be accessible to users with motor disabilities, vision disabilities, and hearing disabilities. It should provide input and output in a variety of forms to account for each of these situations and for others. A significant percentage of the world's most intelligent and creative individuals also have disabilities. Ubuntu's usefulness should not be limited when it can be inclusive. More important, Ubuntu wants to welcome and to be able to harness the ability of these individuals as community members to build a better and more effective community.

Conduct Goals and Code of Conduct

If Ubuntu's philosophical commitments describe the *why* of the Ubuntu project, the Code of Conduct (CoC) describes Ubuntu's *how*. Ubuntu's

CoC is, arguably, the most important document in the day-to-day operation of the Ubuntu community and sets the ground rules for work and cooperation within the project. Explicit agreement to the document is the only criterion for becoming an officially recognized Ubuntu activist—an Ubuntero—and is an essential step toward membership in the project. Signing the Ubuntu Code of Conduct and becoming an Ubuntu member is described in more depth in Chapter 7.

The CoC covers "behavior as a member of the Ubuntu Community, in any forum, mailing list, wiki, Web site, IRC channel, install-fest, public meeting, or private correspondence." The CoC goes into some degree of depth on a series of points that fall under the following headings.

- Be considerate.
- Be respectful.
- Be collaborative.
- When you disagree, consult others.
- When you are unsure, ask for help.
- Step down considerately.

Many of these headings seem like common sense or common courtesy to many, and that is by design. Nothing in the CoC is controversial or radical, and it was never designed to be.

More difficult is that nothing is easy to enforce or decide because acting considerately, respectfully, and collaboratively is often very subjective. There is room for honest disagreements and occasional hurt feelings. These are accepted shortcomings. The CoC was not designed to be a law with explicit prohibitions on phrases, language, or actions. Instead, it aims to provide a constitution and a reminder that considerate and respectful discussion is *essential* to the health and vitality of the project. In situations where there is a serious disagreement on whether a community member has violated or is violating the code, the Community Council—a body that is discussed in depth in Chapter 7—is available to arbitrate disputes and decide what action, if any, is appropriate.

Nobody involved in the Ubuntu project, including Mark Shuttleworth and the other members of the Community Council, is above the CoC. The CoC is *never* optional and *never* waived. In fact, the Ubuntu community has also created a Leadership Code of Conduct (LCoC), which extends and expands on the CoC and describes additional requirements and expectations for those in leadership positions in the community. Of course, in no way was either code designed to eliminate conflict or disagreement. Arguments are at least as common in Ubuntu as they are in other projects and online communities. However, there is a common understanding within the project that arguments should happen in an environment of collaboration and mutual respect. This allows for *better* arguments with *better* results—and with less hurt feelings and fewer bruised egos.

While they have been sometimes incorrectly used as such, the CoC and LCoC are not sticks to be wielded against an opponent in an argument. Instead, they are useful points of reference upon which we can assume consensus within the Ubuntu community. Much more frequently, if a group in the community feels a member is acting in a way that is out of line with the code, the group will gently remind the community member, often privately, that the CoC is in effect. In almost all situations, this is enough to avoid any further action or conflict. Very few CoC violations are ever brought before the Community Council.

Technical Goals

While a respectful community and adherence to a set of philosophical goals provide an important frame in which the Ubuntu project works, Ubuntu is, at the end of the day, a technical project. As a result, it only makes sense that in addition to philosophical goals and a project constitution, Ubuntu also has a set of technical goals.

The first technical goal of the project, and perhaps the most important one, is the coordination of regular and predictable releases. In April 2004, at the Warthogs meeting, the project set a goal for its initial proof-of-concept release six months out. In part due to the resounding success of that project, and in larger part due to the GNOME release schedule, the team has stuck to a regular and predictable six-month release cycle and has only once chosen to extend the release schedule—by six weeks for the first LTS release to ensure it was done right—and only then after obtaining community consensus on the decision. The team then doubled its efforts and made the next release in a mere four and a half months, putting its release schedule back on track. Frequent releases are important because users can then use the latest and greatest free software available—something that is essential in a development environment as vibrant and rapidly changing and improving as the free software community. Predictable releases are important, especially to businesses, because it means that they can organize their business plans around Ubuntu. Through consistent releases, Ubuntu can provide a platform that businesses and derivative distributions can rely upon to grow and build.

While releasing frequently and reliably is important, the released software must then be supported. Ubuntu, like all distributions, must deal with the fact that all software has bugs. Most bugs are minor, but fixing them may introduce even worse issues. Therefore, fixing bugs after a release must be done carefully or not at all. The Ubuntu project engages in major changes, including bug fixes, between releases only when the changes can be extensively tested. However, some bugs risk the loss of users' information or pose a serious security vulnerability. These bugs are fixed immediately and made available as updates for the released distribution. The Ubuntu community works hard to find and minimize all types of bugs before releases and is largely successful in squashing the worst. However, because there is always the possibility that more of these bugs will be found, Ubuntu commits to supporting every release for 18 months after it is released. In the case of LTS releases such as the original LTS, Ubuntu 6.06 LTS, released in 2006, the project went well beyond even this and committed to support the release for three full years on desktop computers and for five years in a server configuration. This proved so popular with businesses, institutions, and the users of Ubuntu servers that in 2008 and 2010, Ubuntu 8.04 LTS and 10.04 LTS were released with similar three- and five-year desktop and server extended support commitments.

This bipartite approach to servers and desktops implies the third major technical commitment of the Ubuntu project: support for both servers and desktop computers in separate but equally emphasized modes. While

Ubuntu continues to be more well known, and perhaps more popular, in desktop configurations, there exist teams of Ubuntu developers focused both on server and desktop users. The Ubuntu project believes that both desktops and servers are essential and provides installation methods on every CD for both types of systems. Ubuntu provides tested and supported software appropriate to the most common actions in both environments and documentation for each. This book contains information on running Ubuntu both on the desktop and on a server. The release of 6.06 LTS with long-term support successfully helped pave the way for reliable long-term server support for Ubuntu and helped grow the now-vibrant Ubuntu server community. The 8.04 LTS release repeated this success with a more up-to-date platform, now being updated again with 10.04 LTS.

Finally, the Ubuntu project is committed to making it as easy as possible for users to transcend their role as consumers and users of software and to take advantage of each of the freedoms central to our philosophy. As a result, Ubuntu has tried to focus its development around the use and promotion of a single programming language, Python. The project has worked to ensure that Python is widely used throughout the system. By ensuring that desktop applications, text-based or console applications, and many of the "guts" of the system are written in or extensible in Python, Ubuntu is working to ensure that users need learn only one language in order to take advantage of, automate, and tweak many parts of their computer systems.

Bug #1

Of course, Ubuntu's goals are not only to build an OS that lives up to our philosophy or technical goals and to do it on our terms—although we probably would be happy if we achieved only that. Our *ultimate goal*, the one that supersedes and influences all others, is to spread our great software, our frequent releases, and the freedoms enshrined in our philosophy to as many computer users in as many countries as possible. Ubuntu's ultimate goal is not to become the most used *GNU/Linux distribution* in the world; it is to become the most widely used *OS* in the world.

The first bug recorded for Ubuntu illustrates this fact. The bug, filed by Shuttleworth and marked as severity critical, remains open today and can be viewed online at https://launchpad.net/distros/ubuntu/+bug/1. The text of the bug reads as follows.

> Microsoft has a majority market share | Non-free software is holding back innovation in the IT industry, restricting access to IT to a small part of the world's population and limiting the ability of software developers to reach their full potential, globally. This bug is widely evident in the PC industry.
>
> Steps to repeat:
>
>   1. Visit a local PC store.
>
> What happens:
>
>   2. Observe that a majority of PCs for sale have non-free software preinstalled.
>   3. Observe very few PCs with Ubuntu and free software preinstalled.
>
> What should happen:
>
>   1. A majority of the PCs for sale should include only free software such as Ubuntu.
>   2. Ubuntu should be marketed in a way such that its amazing features and benefits would be apparent and known by all.
>   3. The system shall become more and more user friendly as time passes.

Many have described Ubuntu's success in the last several years as amazing. For a new GNU/Linux distribution, the level and speed of success have been unprecedented. During this period, Ubuntu has lived up to both its philosophical and technical commitments, achieved many of its goals, and built a vibrant community of users and contributors who have accomplished monumental amounts while collaborating in a culture of respect and understanding fully in line with the Ubuntu Code of Conduct. However, Bug #1 demonstrates that the Ubuntu project will be declared a complete success only when Ubuntu's standards of freedom, technical excellence, and conduct are the norm *everywhere* in the software world.

Canonical and the Ubuntu Foundation

While Ubuntu is driven by a community, several groups play an important role in its structure and organization. Foremost among these are Canonical, Ltd., a for-profit company introduced as part of the Ubuntu history description, and the Ubuntu Foundation, which is introduced later in this section.

Canonical, Ltd.

As mentioned earlier, Canonical, Ltd. is a company founded by Mark Shuttleworth with the primary goal of developing and supporting the Ubuntu distribution. Many of the core developers on Ubuntu—although no longer a majority of them—work full time or part time under contract for Canonical, Ltd. This funding by Canonical allows Ubuntu to make the type of support commitments that it does. Ubuntu can claim that it will release in six months because releasing, in one form or another, is something that the paid workers at Canonical can ensure. As an all-volunteer organization, Debian suffered from an inability to set and meet deadlines—volunteers become busy or have other deadlines in their paying jobs that take precedence. By offering paying jobs to a subset of developers, Canonical can set support and release deadlines and ensure that they are met.

In this way, Canonical ensures that Ubuntu's bottom-line commitments are kept. Of course, Canonical does not fund all Ubuntu work, nor could it. Canonical can release *a distribution* every six months, but that distribution will be made *much* better and more usable through contributions from the community of users. Most features, most new pieces of software, almost all translations, almost all documentation, and much more are created outside of Canonical. Instead, Canonical ensures that deadlines are met and that the essential work, regardless of whether it's fun, gets done.

Canonical, Ltd. was incorporated on the Isle of Man—a tiny island nation between Wales and Ireland that is mostly well known as a haven for international businesses. Since Canonical's staff is sprinkled across the globe and no proper office is necessary, the Isle of Man seemed like as good a place as any for the company to hang its sign.

In early 2010, Mark Shuttleworth, Canonical's first CEO, stepped down, and longtime Chief Operating Officer, Jane Silber, became the new CEO. Shuttleworth retains his position as the head of the Ubuntu Community Council and Ubuntu Technical boards. He focuses his energy on product design and working with enterprise customers and partners, and leaves the day-to-day running of Canonical to Silber. Silber has been with Canonical since before the first release, and the company is expected to continue expanding and operating on its current path.

Canonical's Service and Support

While it is surprising to many users, fewer than half of Canonical's employees work on the Ubuntu project. The rest of the employees fall into several categories: business development, support and administration, and development of other projects such as Bazaar and Launchpad, which are discussed a bit later in this chapter.

Individuals involved in business development help create strategic deals and certification programs with other companies—primarily around Ubuntu. In large part, these are things that the community is either ill suited for or uninterested in as a whole. One example of business development work is the process of working with companies to ensure that their software (usually proprietary) is built and certified to run on Ubuntu. For example, Canonical worked with IBM to ensure that its popular DB2 database would run on Ubuntu and, when this was achieved, worked to have Ubuntu certified as a platform that would run DB2. Similarly, Canonical worked with Dell to ensure that Ubuntu could be installed and supported on Dell laptops and desktops as an option for its customers. A third example is the production of this book, which, published by Pearson Education's Prentice Hall imprint, was a product of work with Canonical.

Canonical also plays an important support role in the Ubuntu project in three ways. First, Canonical supports the development of the Ubuntu project. For example, Canonical system administrators keep servers up that support development and distribution of Ubuntu. Second, Canonical helps Ubuntu users and businesses directly by offering phone and e-mail support. Additionally, Canonical has helped build a large commercial Ubuntu support operation by arranging for support contracts with larger companies and organizations. This support is over and above the free (i.e., gratis) support offered by the community—this commercial support is offered at a fee and is either part of a longer-term flat-fee support contract or is pay-per-instance. By offering commercial support for Ubuntu in a variety of ways, Canonical has made a business for itself and helps make Ubuntu a more palatable option for the businesses, large and small, that are looking for an enterprise or enterprise-class GNU/Linux product with support contracts like those offered by other commercial GNU/Linux distributions.

Finally, Ubuntu supports other support organizations. Canonical does not seek or try to enforce a monopoly on Ubuntu support; it proudly lists *hundreds* of other organizations offering support for Ubuntu on the Ubuntu Web pages. Instead, Canonical offers what is called second-tier support to these organizations. Because Canonical employs many of the core Ubuntu developers, the company is very well suited to taking action on many of the tougher problems that these support organizations may run into. With its concentrated expertise, Canonical can offer this type of backup, or secondary support, to these organizations.

Bazaar and Launchpad

In addition to support and development on Ubuntu, Canonical, Ltd. funds the development of Bazaar, a distributed version control tool, and the Launchpad project. Bazaar is a tool for developing software that is used heavily in Ubuntu and plays an important role in the technical processes through which Ubuntu is forged. However, the software, which is similar in functionality to other version control systems such as CVS, Subversion, or BitKeeper, is useful in a variety of other projects as well. More important, Bazaar acts as the workhorse behind Launchpad.

More than half of Canonical's technical employees work on the Launchpad project. Launchpad is an ambitious Web-based superstructure application that consists of several highly integrated tools. The software plays a central role in Ubuntu development but is also used for the development of other distributions—especially those based on Ubuntu. Launchpad consists of the following major pieces.

- **Rosetta:**

  A Web-based system for easily translating almost any piece of free software from English into almost any language. Rosetta is named after the Rosetta Stone, which helped linguists finally crack the code of Egyptian hieroglyphics.

- **Malone:**

  The bug-tracking system that Ubuntu uses to manage and track bugs. It both tracks bugs across different versions of Ubuntu and allows the

Ubuntu community to see the status of that bug in other places, including other distributions and potentially upstream. Malone is a reference to the gangster movie musical *Bugsy Malone*.

▪ **Blueprint:**

The specification writing and tracking software that Ubuntu and a small number of other projects use to track desired features and their status and to help manage and report on release processes.

▪ **Answers:**

A simple support tracker built into Launchpad that provides one venue where users can make support requests and the community can help answer them in ways that are documented and connected to the other related functionality in Launchpad.

▪ **Soyuz:**

The distribution management part of Launchpad that now controls the processes by which Ubuntu packages are built, tested, and migrated between different parts of the distribution. Soyuz is a reference to the type of Russian rocket that took Mark Shuttleworth to space. The word *soyuz*, in Russian, means "union."

Launchpad and its components are discussed in more depth in Chapter 10. The importance of Launchpad in the Ubuntu project cannot be overstated. In addition to handling bugs, translations, and distribution building, Launchpad also handles Web site authentication and codifies team membership in the Ubuntu project. It is the place where all work in Ubuntu is tracked and recorded. Any member of the Ubuntu community and any person who contributes to Ubuntu in almost any way will, in due course, create an account in Launchpad.

The Ubuntu Foundation

Finally, in addition to Canonical and the full Ubuntu community, the Ubuntu project is supported by the Ubuntu Foundation, which was announced by Shuttleworth with an initial funding commitment of $10 million. The foundation, like Canonical, is based on the Isle of Man. The organization is advised by the Ubuntu Community Council.

Unlike Canonical, the Foundation does not play an active role in the day-to-day life of Ubuntu. At the moment, the Foundation is little more than a pile of money that exists to endow and ensure Ubuntu's future. Because Canonical is a young company, some companies and individuals found it difficult early on to trust that Canonical would be able to provide support for Ubuntu for the time frames (e.g., three to five years) that it claims it can. The Ubuntu Foundation exists to allay those fears. Time and consistency has also contributed greatly to the confidence of companies and individuals in Ubuntu, and the foundation will remain to ensure that consistency in the future.

If something unexpected were to happen to Shuttleworth or to Canonical that caused either to be unable to support Ubuntu development and maintain the distribution, the Ubuntu Foundation exists to carry on many of Canonical's core activities well into the future. Through the existence of the Foundation, the Ubuntu project can make the types of long-term commitments and promises it does.

The one activity that the Foundation can and does engage in is receiving donations on behalf of the Ubuntu project. These donations, and only these donations, are then put into action on behalf of Ubuntu in accordance with the wishes of the development team and the Technical Board. For the most part, these contributions are spent on "bounties" given to community members who have achieved important feature goals for the Ubuntu project.

Ubuntu Subprojects, Derivatives, and Spin-offs

Finally, no introduction to Ubuntu is complete without an introduction to a growing list of Ubuntu subprojects and derivatives. While Ubuntu was derived from Debian, the project has also developed a number of derivatives of its own.

First and foremost among these is Kubuntu—a version of Ubuntu that uses KDE instead of GNOME as the default desktop environment. Kubuntu is described in depth in its own chapter (Chapter 8) and so is not explored in any serious depth here. However, it is important to realize that the relationship between Kubuntu and Ubuntu is different from the relationship between Ubuntu and Debian. From a technical perspective, Kubuntu is *fully* within the Ubuntu distribution. Organizationally, the Kubuntu team works fully within Ubuntu as well.

A similar organization exists with the Edubuntu project, which aims to help develop Ubuntu so that a configuration of the distribution can be easily and effectively put into use in schools. Although the project has undergone a few changes in recent years, it remains focused on both educational and school-related software and on a Linux Terminal Server Project (LTSP) setup that allows schools to run many students' computers using one or more powerful servers and many "dumb" terminals that connect to the server and run software off it. This relatively simple technical trick translates into huge cost savings in educational settings. The Edubuntu project is discussed a bit more in Chapter 10.

The Xubuntu project is based on the lightweight window manager Xfce. Xubuntu is designed to be appropriate on older or less powerful computers with less memory or slower processors—or just for people who prefer a more responsive environment and a slimmer set of features. While started as an unofficial project, Xubuntu has enjoyed great popularity and has become integrated as an official part of the core distribution.

The Netbook Edition, until recently known as the Netbook Remix, is a variant of the Ubuntu Desktop Edition, with GNOME, but customized for the smaller screens of netbooks. Canonical employees have also been working on providing Intel's Moblin UI for Ubuntu as well.

Other derivatives exist as well, such as Ubuntu Studio and Mythbuntu. A list of officially supported and recognized derivatives is available at www. ubuntu.com/products/whatisubuntu/derivatives.

In a way, it is through these derivatives that the work and goals of the Ubuntu project come together and are crystallized. It is only through the free and open source software movements' commitment to freely accessible source code that Ubuntu could be built at all. Similarly, it is only through

Ubuntu's continued commitment to these ideals that derivatives can spring from Ubuntu. As a derivative with a view of distributions within an ecosystem, Ubuntu does not see the process of derivation as an insult or criticism. Far from it—Ubuntu thinks derivation is the highest form of compliment.

Outside of Ubuntu, Canonical's work is largely based around software projects such as Launchpad and Bazaar that are designed to facilitate precisely this sort of derivative process. This process, when practiced right, is one that describes an ecosystem of development in which *everyone* benefits—the derivative, Ubuntu, and Ubuntu's upstreams. Only through this derivative process does everyone get what they want.

Derivation, done correctly, allows groups to diverge where necessary while working together where possible. Ultimately, it leads to more work done, more happy users, and more overall collaboration. Through this enhanced collaboration, Ubuntu's philosophical and technical goals will be achieved. Through this profound community involvement, Bug #1 will be closed. Through this type of meaningful cooperation, internal and external to the project itself, the incredible growth of Ubuntu in its first four years will be sustained into the next four and the next forty.

Summary

This chapter introduced you to the phenomenon that is Ubuntu. It began with some free software and open source history and then moved on to the history of Ubuntu. It then covered the Ubuntu products, philosophy, and goals and the relationship between Canonical, Ltd. and the Ubuntu Foundation. It finished with some discussion of the various Ubuntu subprojects, derivatives, and spin-offs.

CHAPTER 2

Installing Ubuntu

- **Choosing Your Ubuntu Version**
- **Getting Ubuntu**
- **Installing from the Desktop CD**
- **Installing from the Alternate Install CD**
- **Installing from a USB Key**
- **Installing from within Windows**
- **Summary**

IF YOU ARE READING THIS, it is probably safe to assume that you have decided to give Ubuntu a try. You will find that Ubuntu is flexible and powerful not only as an operating system but also in how you evaluate and install it.

Trying Ubuntu is simple. The Ubuntu desktop CD is a special "live" CD. You can use this disk to run Ubuntu from the CD itself without Ubuntu removing or even interacting with your hard disk. This is ideal if you are already using another operating system like Windows or Mac OS X; you can try Ubuntu by running it from the CD, and you don't have to worry about it overwriting the data on your hard drive or changing any part of your current operating system unless you intentionally choose to do so.

Choosing Your Ubuntu Version

The developers behind Ubuntu have worked to make the software as easy and flexible to install as possible. They understand that people will be installing Ubuntu on computers with varying purposes (desktops, servers, laptops, and so on) and using different types of computers (PCs and Macs, 32-bit and 64-bit computers, and so on). To cater to as many people as possible, there are two Ubuntu CDs that can be used. The DVD with this book is equivalent to the downloadable desktop CD but with additional packages included for your convenience.

- **Desktop:** The desktop CD is the one recommended for *desktops* and *laptops*. With this CD, you can boot Ubuntu from the CD and, if you like it, you have the option to install it to your hard drive. Note that running from the disk without installing directly to the hard drive is the default option to help prevent accidental data loss.

- **Alternate install:** The alternate install CD is recommended for use in any scenario where the desktop version is unusable (e.g., not enough RAM) or for those with more advanced needs (e.g., automated deployments or special partitioning requirements). With this CD, you boot into an installer and then run Ubuntu when the installation is complete.

Ubuntu 10.04 officially supports two main computer types, or architectures, and a couple of additional variations:

- **i386:** This supports all Intel or compatible processors except those that require AMD64. This includes the new Apple hardware. If you are not certain which you need, use this one. It will work on either 32-bit or 64-bit systems, so it is the default choice.

- **AMD64:** If you know you are using a processor based on the AMD64 or EM64T architecture (e.g., Athlon64, Opteron, EM64T Xeon, or Core2), you should choose this version because it will be a bit more efficient on your hardware.

- **ARM:** ARM is a low-powered chip commonly found in cell phones and similar mobile devices. ARM Inc., the makers of ARM, and Canonical have an agreement to build the entire Ubuntu archive on ARM, which makes Ubuntu the first major distribution to support ARM as a standard rather than custom device–specific distribution, such as OpenWRT is for routers. For a list of the current ARM chip version being supported, please see www.ubuntu.com/products/whatisubuntu/arm.

TIP   **Where to Download**
If you lose the installation disk that accompanies this book, or if you want to use some of the other options available, such as installation from a USB drive (discussed later in the chapter), you will find what you need at help.ubuntu.com/community/GettingUbuntu.

TIP   **What about PowerPC?**
Starting with the 7.04 release, Ubuntu made Power PC an unofficial architecture.

Other Ubuntu Distributions

In addition to the official Ubuntu release, some additional distributions are based on Ubuntu but are slightly different. Here are some examples:

- **Kubuntu:** Kubuntu is Ubuntu, but instead of using the GNOME desktop, Kubuntu uses the KDE desktop. See http://kubuntu.org or Chapter 8 for more information.

- **Ubuntu Netbook Edition:** This is a custom version of the standard GNOME desktop with the addition of a custom application launcher and some other Netbook-specific configurations. See Chapter 9 for more information.

▪ **Xubuntu:** The Xubuntu distribution replaces the GNOME desktop environment with the Xfce 4 environment. Xubuntu is particularly useful for those of you who want to run Ubuntu on older hardware. See http://xubuntu.org or Chapter 10 for more information.

Edubuntu is a derivative of Ubuntu aimed at educational use and schools. To install it, you should first install the default desktop version of Ubuntu. Then use either the downloadable add-on Edubuntu CD or the Ubuntu Software Center in your Applications menu on the desktop to install the Edubuntu environment and applications. See Chapter 10 for more information.

TIP   **Downloading Edubuntu**
You may download the Edubuntu add-on CD and learn more about Edubuntu at www.edubuntu.org.

With a range of different distributions and options available, Ubuntu is flexible enough to be used in virtually all situations.

Is It Still Ubuntu?

Some of you may be reading about Kubuntu, Xubuntu, and Ubuntu Netbook Edition and wondering how different they are from the regular Ubuntu release. These distributions differ mainly in which applications and desktop interface are included. As such, they may differ quite a bit, especially in the user interface look and feel, but the underlying OS and software install system is the same.

Getting Ubuntu

Ubuntu is an entirely free OS. When you have a copy of it, you can give it to as many people as you like. This free characteristic of Ubuntu means that it is devilishly simple to get a copy. If you have a high-speed Internet connection (like DSL), then go to www.ubuntu.com/download, and select your country from the list of download sites. You can then select a desktop or alternate install CD and download it.

TIP See the upcoming Burning a CD section for details on how to create your Ubuntu CD from the file you just downloaded.

If you are willing to wait, you can get one physical Ubuntu CD mailed to you for free from https://shipit.ubuntu.com. You will need an account on the Launchpad site at https://launchpad.net/ to use the ShipIt service. If you don't have one, you will be given an opportunity to create one while you make the CD request.

You can also buy an authorized CD from a number of distributors, details of which can be found at www.ubuntu.com/getubuntu/purchase.

Burning a CD

When you download an Ubuntu CD, you download a special .iso file, which is the same size as a CD (around 650MB). This file is an "image" of the installation CD. When you burn the .iso file to the CD-ROM, you have a complete installation CD all ready to go.

TIP **Which Image?**
When you are reading about .iso files, you will often see them referred to as CD images. The term *image* here does not refer to a visual image such as a photo or picture but to an exact copy of a CD.

You need to use a CD-burning application to burn your .iso file to the CD correctly. Inside the application there should be a menu option called Burn from Disk Image or something similar. The wording and details will vary according to the program that you use to burn the image. You should select the .iso file, insert a blank CD, and after a few minutes, out will pop a fresh Ubuntu installation CD.

To give you a head start, the following subsections present instructions for burning a CD in some popular tools.

In Windows with ISO Recorder   To burn your .iso file with the freely available ISO Recorder, first go to http://isorecorder.alexfeinman.com, and then download and install ISO Recorder. To burn your image, follow these steps.

1. Insert a blank CD into your CD writer.
2. Locate the .iso file you downloaded, right-click it, and select Copy Image to CD.
3. Click Next, and the recording process begins.
4. When the image has been written, click Finish to exit ISO Recorder.

In Windows with Nero Burning ROM   To burn your image using Nero Burning ROM, follow these steps.

1. Insert a blank CD into your CD writer.
2. Start Nero Burning ROM.
3. Follow the wizard prompts, and select Data CD.
4. When the wizard finishes, click Burn Image on the File menu.
5. In the Open dialog box, select the .iso file, and then click Open.
6. In the wizard, click Burn to create the Ubuntu CD. When completed, click the Done button to exit.

In Linux with GNOME   To burn your image using Linux with GNOME, follow these steps.

1. Insert a blank CD into your CD writer.
2. In the File Browser, right-click on the file you just downloaded, and choose Write to Disk. The Write to Disk dialog box opens.
3. In the dialog box, choose your CD writer and speed, and then click on Write. The Writing Files to Disk Progress dialog box opens, and File Browser begins writing the disk.

Burning with Mac OS X   To burn your image using Mac OS X, follow these steps.

1. Load the Disk Utility application (found in your Utilities folder).
2. Insert a blank CD, and then choose Images > Burn and select the .iso file.

TIP   Use the Right Option
You need to ensure you use the Burn from Disk Image or similar option rather than just copy the .iso image onto the CD to be burned. If you just burn the file directly, you will have a CD containing the single .iso file. This won't work.

The Burn from Disk Image function takes the .iso file and restores all the original files from the installation CD onto the disk. This ensures you have a proper installation CD.

Installing from the Desktop CD

So let's assume you are playing with Ubuntu running from the desktop CD, and you decide you like it. You decide you like it so much, in fact, that you want to install it on your computer. Does this mean you need to get a separate CD and install it? Heck, no. Ubuntu lets you install to the hard disk by simply clicking a single icon and following the instructions—one disk to run them all.

If you don't already have the desktop CD running, pop it into your DVD/CD drive, and reboot your computer. If your computer does not boot from the CD, you should enter your computer's BIOS and change the boot order to ensure that your CD-ROM drive is tried first and the hard disk is tried next. Save your BIOS changes, and then restart again. The disk should boot now.

TIP   BIOS Problems
If you have problems configuring your BIOS to boot from the CD, you should consult the manual. If you don't have the manual, visit the manufacturer's Web site, and see if you can download the manual.

After a few seconds, the Ubuntu logo and boot screen appear and then you are presented with a list of languages on the left of the screen and two options on the right. Use your mouse to select your language. Then decide whether you want to Try Ubuntu 10.04, which allows you try out Ubuntu without making any changes to your computer and install it later if you decide you want to, or whether you want to Install Ubuntu 10.04, which will jump straight into the installer. Select the first option, and Ubuntu will begin to boot. After a minute or so, the Ubuntu desktop will appear, and you can use the system right away. Under this scenario, the system is running from the CD and will not touch your hard disk. Do bear in mind that because Ubuntu is running from the CD, it will run slower than if it were installed to your hard disk.

If you decide you want to install the system permanently on your computer's hard disk, you can either reboot and click on the Install Ubuntu boot menu option or you can double-click the Install icon located on the left side of the desktop. An installer application appears that walks you through the different steps to permanently install your Ubuntu system. We will run through each of these pages in turn now.

TIP   It is recommended that you back up any important files before you perform the installation. While the vast majority of Ubuntu installations can safely resize Windows partitions, installations can still result in data loss, so it is wise to be careful.

Language

The first screen you are presented with introduces you to the installation program and asks you to select your language, as shown in Figure 2-1.

Ubuntu supports a huge range of different languages. Select your language from the list, and then click Forward to continue.

Location

Now you need to tell the installer where in the world you live (Figure 2-2).

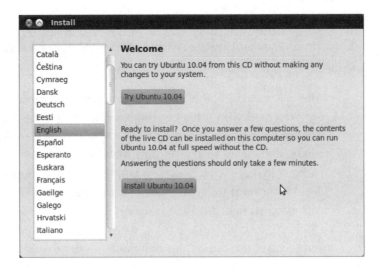

Figure 2-1 Pick your language.

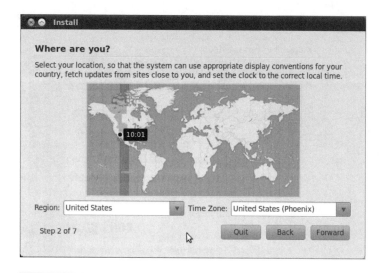

Figure 2-2 Clicking the map allows you to select a location easily.

You can select your location in one of several ways. First, you can hover your mouse over the time zone on your part of the world map to select your location. When you are happy with the time zone selection, click it, and select the city nearest to you. Alternatively, use the Selected City combo box to find the city nearest to you.

When you are done, click Forward to continue.

Configuring Your Keyboard

The next screen (shown in Figure 2-3) configures your keyboard.

The installer will suggest a keyboard option for you based on your location choice, but you may choose a different one if you desire. You can also use the box at the bottom of the window to test whether your keyboard layout works. Try typing some of the symbols on your keyboard (such as ", /, |) to make sure they work. If you press a symbol and a different one appears, you have selected the wrong keyboard layout.

Figure 2-3 Select the correct keyboard to ensure the symbols on the keys work correctly.

Disk Space

The next part of the installation process prepares your hard disk for the software. This involves creating a number of *partitions* that store the Ubuntu system and your files. Hard disks are divided into partitions. Each partition reserves a specific portion of the hard disk for use by a particular OS. As an example, you may use the entire hard disk for your new Ubuntu system, or you may share the disk so that both Windows and Ubuntu are installed. This shared scenario is known as *dual-booting*. In a dual-booting situation, your hard disk typically has Windows partitions as well as Linux partitions, and when it boots it gives you a menu so you can select whether to boot Windows or Linux.

In this part of the installer you create the partitions for your new system. This is the trickiest part of the installation and also the most dangerous. If you have existing partitions (such as a Windows installation) on the disk, it is highly recommended that you back up your important files.

TIP   Seriously, We Mean It
Really, really, really do back up any important files. If you make a mistake in this part of the installation, you could lose your files and stop your system from booting.

Deciding How You Would Like to Set Up Your Partitions Before You Create Them   If you have a clear idea of how your hard disk should be partitioned, it is easier to get everything up and running quickly.

These are the most common methods of partitioning.

- **Only Ubuntu on the disk:** If you are only installing Ubuntu on the disk and are happy to wipe the *entire disk*, your life is simple. Ubuntu can do all the work for you.

- **Dual-booting:** If you want to dual-boot your system with Windows or Mac OS X and Ubuntu, you can share the disk between your Ubuntu and Windows or Mac OS X partitions.

Regardless of whether you only install Ubuntu or you will dual-boot, you need to decide how the Ubuntu part of the disk is partitioned. Ubuntu requires at least two partitions (one for the system and one for virtual memory swap space), but you can have additional partitions if you want to. The installer tries to make things easier for you by presenting options for partitioning, as shown in Figure 2-4.

Figure 2-4 Main partitioning view

Ubuntu Only   If you are happy to erase your entire hard disk, just select the Guided—Use Entire Disk option, and click Forward. You are then asked to confirm the actions. Click Yes to continue. That's it!

Dual-Booting   Let's say you want your existing OS and Ubuntu to coexist, but you don't care about the details. Click the Guided—Resize . . . and Use Freed Space option, move the slider according to how much space you want to give each operating system, and then click Forward. You are then asked to confirm the actions. Click Yes to continue.

Manual Partitioning   In either option, installing only Ubuntu or dual-booting with an existing operating system, you may not be satisfied with the suggestions guided partitioning makes. In this case you will want to manually set the partitions. To do this, click the Manual option, and click Forward to continue. You will see the screen shown in Figure 2-5.

The main part of this screen displays available drives and configured partitions. Clicking on a drive or partition will change the actions available to you below the list. Select the relevant disk to add partitions to. The disks are listed by device name in the order they are connected within your computer.

Figure 2-5 Manual partition view

The name of the device indicates how it is connected to your computer. For example, hda is the first IDE drive, and sdb is the second SCSI or SATA drive.

Before you begin, you should prepare the disk for your partitions. If you want to completely wipe a disk, right-click on the name of the device (/dev/sda in Figure 2-5), then click New Partition Table. You'll be asked if you're sure, so click Continue. The disk is now filled with unallocated data. Now you can add your Ubuntu partitions.

To add a partition, click a free space entry in the list and then click the New button. A new window appears like that shown in Figure 2-6.

Set the values according to your requirements. The Use As combo box lets you select which one of the many filesystem types you want the partition to use. The default filesystem included with Ubuntu is ext4, and it is recommended that you use ext4 for any Ubuntu partitions. Although ext4 is a

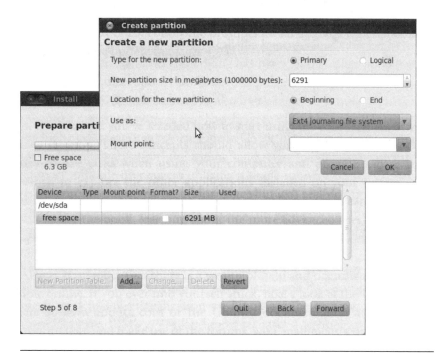

Figure 2-6 Configuring a partition

good choice for Ubuntu, you cannot read an ext4 partition in Windows. If you need to create a partition that is shared between Windows and Ubuntu, you should use the FAT32 filesystem.

Use the Mount Point combo box to select one of the different mount points, which tells Ubuntu where the partition should be used. You need to have a root partition, which has a mount point of /. Click OK to finish configuring this partition.

Once you've completed configuring all your partitions, click Forward to proceed with the installation. Please note that if you have read all of these comments on partitioning and feel a bit overwhelmed or confused, you don't need to worry. You may simply use the default settings given by the installer and all will work well.

Identification

The next step is to enter some details about you that can be used to create a user account on the computer (Figure 2-7).

Figure 2-7 This user account is also used as the main system administrator.

In the first box, enter your full name. The information from this box is used in different parts of the system to indicate who the user is behind the account.

In the next box, set a username for yourself (the installer will provide a suggestion based on your full name). Your username should be something easy to remember. Many people use either their first name or add an initial (such as jbacon or jonob). Each username on your computer must be unique—you cannot have two accounts with the same username. Usernames must begin with a lower case letter only lower case letters and numbers are permitted after that.

In the next two boxes, add a password and then confirm it. This password is used when logging in to your computer with the username that you just created. When choosing a password, follow these simple guidelines.

- Make sure you can remember your password. If you need to write it down, keep it somewhere secure. Don't make the mistake of putting the password somewhere easily accessible and known to others.

- Try not to use dictionary words such as "chicken" or "beard" when choosing a password. Try to input numbers and punctuation and to not use "real words."

- Your password should ideally be longer than six letters and contain a combination of letters, symbols, and numbers. The longer the password and the more it mixes upper and lower case letters, numbers, and symbols, the more secure it is.

Finally, add a hostname in the last box. The hostname is a single word that identifies your current machine. This is used on a local network so that you can identify which machine is which.

Believe it or not, hostnames can be great fun. Many people pick themes for their hostnames, such as superheroes, and name each computer on their network after a superhero (Superman, Batman, Spiderman, and so on). Think of a fun hostname theme you can use. For many people, this ends up being the hardest part of the install!

When you have added all the information, click Forward to continue.

Migration

Ubuntu also provides a migration assistant, which aims to ease your transition to your new OS. If a supported OS is found during installation, you will be presented with a list of accounts and the features that can be migrated. If you choose to migrate anything, you will need to provide details for the new user to whom the features will be migrated.

Finishing Up

Before the installation is completed, you are given a summary of the choices you made. Once you confirm these choices by clicking Install, the Ubuntu software will be installed on your computer. At the end of this process, you are asked to reboot your computer. You are now finished and can skip ahead to Chapter 3 to get started with using Ubuntu.

TIP   **Better Use of Your Valuable, Valuable Time**
One of the great benefits of the desktop CD installer is that while the files are being copied from the disk, you can still use the system. Instead of sitting at your computer staring at the progress bar, you can play a few games to while away the time.

Installing from the Alternate Install CD

Although the desktop CD is ideal for installing Ubuntu, you may want to use the traditional installer method to install the system. This method involves booting the alternate install CD, running through the installer, and then starting the system. This kind of installer is ideal for installation on older hardware.

To get started, put the CD in the drive, and restart your computer.

Select the Install Ubuntu option with the arrow keys, and press Enter. After a few moments, the installation process begins by asking you to choose a language. Select from the different languages by using the up and down arrow keys, and then use the Tab key to jump to the red buttons to continue through the setup.

TIP **Installing a Server**
You can obtain a third version of Ubuntu that is especially tailored for server environments. For more information about this version, see www.ubuntu.com/server, or read Chapter 5 for more details about running Ubuntu as a server.

Choosing Your Spot in the World

Next you are asked to specify your location. First you need to choose your language.

Then you need to pick which country you are in, again pressing Enter to accept your choice.

Now you need to select your keyboard layout. Keyboard layouts vary across the world to take into account the many and varied symbols and letters used in different countries. Even if you are using the typical Latin character set (as used in most European countries, America, Africa, and Australia), there are variations and additions (e.g., German umlauts). You can let Ubuntu detect your layout for you, or you can choose from a list of options. If you want your layout detected, you will be asked a series of questions until a guess can be made. If the guess is wrong, you can repeat the process. Otherwise, choose your keyboard layout from the options available.

Hardware

Next, the system will attempt to load the rest of the installer and to detect hardware. In most situations, this happens without prompting you for anything, although sometimes you might need to provide input such as choosing a primary network device. Once this is set up, your computer will also configure itself with your local network—if possible. If it cannot configure itself with a local network, it will tell you this and you'll have the option of configuring it manually or choosing to not configure it at that time. You can always come back and change things later once the installation is done.

Setting the Hostname and Time Zone

You are next asked for a hostname for the computer.

Use the text box to add your own hostname, or use the default Ubuntu hostname if required. Feel free to let your imagination go wild, and create a theme for your hostnames (such as superheroes).

After choosing a hostname, you will be asked to select your time zone. Choosing this should be a fairly straightforward operation.

Creating Partitions

The system will then read your disks to find out the current partition information. You will be asked to create or select partitions for Ubuntu to install on to. Creating partitions is the most challenging part of the installation routine. Before you partition your disk, think about how your partitions should be organized.

You are given a number of partition options:

■ Guided—Use Entire Disk

■ Guided—Use Entire Disk and Set Up LVM

■ Guided—Use Entire Disk and Set Up Encrypted LVM

■ Manual

In most cases, you probably want to use the Guided—Use Entire Disk option. This will erase everything on the hard drive in your computer and set everything up for you. The second option, Guided—Use Entire Disk and Set Up LVM, allows you to use the Logical Volume Manager (LVM). The third is identical to the second option but also employs disk encryption, which will make your data safer and more secure in some circumstances. Finally, if you want to set up specific partitions, use the Manual option.

Let's look at each of these options in turn and how they are used.

Guided—Use Entire Disk   When you select this option, your entire disk is partitioned automatically. The installer will tell you that a primary and logical partition will be created, and then it asks if you want to go ahead and create the partitions. Click Yes, and you are done.

Guided—Use Entire Disk and Set Up LVM   Configuring LVM is covered in Chapter 5.

Guided—Use Entire Disk and Set Up Encrypted LVM   Configuring LVM is identical to the previous option except that it also uses a secure encryption layer to provide additional security and protection for your data. If you choose to do this, during the process you will be asked to provide a passphrase. Be very careful to choose one that is impossible to guess and which you will also remember. You will need to use this passphrase to access your data every time you boot the computer, and if you lose or forget the passphrase, all your data will be permanently inaccessible. There is no way to recover a lost or forgotten encryption passphrase.

TIP   **Disk Encryption**
You may also decide to encrypt specific partitions manually. Simply choose "Use physical volume for encryption" in the "Use as:" option. Note: You never want to encrypt the boot partition.

Manual—Select this option if you want to create your own partitions manually. Here you can create a number of different types of partitions, set their sizes, and configure their properties. Creating these partitions is not done in the same graphical way as the live CD installer, so it is a little more complex. However, doing so is still largely a process of selecting something and pressing Enter.

Depending on your configuration (and the options you selected), you are given a number of options from which to choose:

- Configure Software RAID

- Configure the Logical Volume Manager

- Guided Partitioning

QUICK TIP   Discussion of software RAID and the Logical Volume Manager is covered in Chapter 5.

Your disk is listed below these options, and it may display a few existing partitions. If you want to delete the existing partitions, select each one, press Enter, and select Delete the Partition. When you have deleted some partitions, you should see a FREE SPACE line. The FREE SPACE line is used to create new partitions. If the disk was empty already and you don't see a FREE SPACE line, select the hard disk, and press Enter. When it asks if you want to create an empty partition table, click Yes. You should now see the FREE SPACE line.

To create a new partition, select the FREE SPACE line, and press Enter. In the next screen, click Create a New Partition, and press Enter. Now enter the size the partition should be. You can use gigabytes (GB) and megabytes (M) to indicate size. For example, 4.2GB is 4.2 gigabytes, and 100M is 100 megabytes. You can also use a percentage or just add max to use the entire disk. Add the size, and then press the Tab key to select Continue. Press Enter. You are next asked whether the partition should be primary or logical. It is likely that you will want a primary partition. Make your choice and continue.

If this is the first partition, you are asked if the partition should be at the beginning or end of the disk. It is recommended that when creating the root partition (known as /) on older computers, it should be placed at the beginning of the disk. This gets around some potential BIOS problems on older hardware. On newer computers, this is no longer a problem, and you can put the partition where you like on the disk.

On the next screen to display, you can configure some settings for the partition.

Table 2-1 describes the settings.

When the partition is configured, choose the Done Setting Up the Partition option.

You can now select FREE SPACE again (if there is free space left, of course) to create another partition. When you have finished partitioning, click the Finish Partitioning and Write Changes to Disk option.

Table 2-1 Partition Settings

Setting	Description	Example
Use as	This is the type of filesystem. For a normal Ubuntu system, ext4 is recommended.	ext4
Format the partition	This setting appears when editing an existing partition.	yes
Mount point	This specifies which part of the filesystem will live on the partition. See earlier in this chapter for details about the kind of partitions you should set up.	/
Mount options	A number of options can be passed to the mount point, although the default setting should be fine.	defaults
Label	A text label describes the partition. Usually it is set to the same value as the mount point.	/
Reserved blocks	This is the percentage of the filesystem reserved for the super-user; 5% is a good default.	5.00%
Typical usage	This option can be used to optimize how the filesystem is organized, although the standard setting is typically used.	standard
Bootable flag	Does this partition contain the kernel and bootloader? If this is the root partition (known as /), set this to *on*.	on

The system will now install the Ubuntu core to your newly partitioned disk. Depending on the speed of your computer and your CD drive, this installation could take some time.

Configuring a User

The next part of the installation routine configures a user for the computer. This user role is important because it not only can be used as a normal user but also has the ability to use sudo to perform system administrator tasks.

You are first asked to enter a full name for the user (such as Matthew Helmke). Next you are asked for a username, or one will be picked for you from your full name (such as matthew). If you want another username, enter it there. Finally, you are asked to enter a password for the user and asked to repeat the password for verification.

QUICK TIP   A good password will have at least eight characters, will use both uppercase and lowercase letters, will use at least one number, will use at least one nonletter character like & or @, will not spell a word that can be found in a dictionary, and will also be easy for you to remember while being difficult for others to guess. A modified phrase can work well, something like Gimm1e@x3ss could work well, although that one may still be a bit too obvious ("give me access" is not much better than "password").

Finishing Up

At this point, the installation routine will install the full system for you. After this, the computer will reboot, and the installation will be complete.

Installing from a USB Key

Some computers lack CD drives, especially in the recently popular Netbooks. USB keys are also more flexible, allowing you to save your files and configuration and to update the key to the latest version of Ubuntu.

As with a CD, you need to get Ubuntu onto the USB key first. Fortunately, there is an easy way to do this in Ubuntu. Under the System > Administration menu, find the USB creator tool. Upon starting, you will see a window asking for an ISO file and a few other options.

NOTE   You will need to have administrative privileges on your computer to use the USB Startup Disk Creator.

If there is an Ubuntu CD already in the CD drive, it will be automatically detected and used. If you have downloaded the ISO, click the Other button and select the ISO you want. Any mounted USB keys will be shown in the second window for you to select.

Now, you must choose whether or not to have persistence. This means that you can save your files and configuration to the USB key. Finally, click Make Startup Disk.

Another way to create a bootable USB key is to use a program called UNet-bootin, which has versions and instructions available for both Windows and Linux from unetbootin.sourceforge.net.

Once the disk has been created, you must restart your computer and boot off the USB key. This might involve holding down a key at startup to select from a boot menu or might involve changes to your computer's BIOS. Consult your manual for how to do this.

Once you are booted, your USB key will work exactly like a Live CD and allow you to use Ubuntu from the key or to install it on the computer.

NOTE   Once the size of the persistence section has been selected, it cannot be changed, so think carefully.

Installing from within Windows

Another way to install Ubuntu is to use Ubuntu Windows Installer, or Wubi. This is perhaps the easiest of all methods. Go to www.ubuntu.com/getubuntu/download-wubi and download the program and run it within Windows. Then answer the questions that come up and wait. The process can take a long time because it will download the entire installation .iso, but once finished, a dialog box will appear telling you that you need to reboot. When you do, you will find that you will boot to a menu giving you the option to boot into either Windows or Ubuntu. More detailed information is available at the link above.

Summary

Congratulations on your new Ubuntu system. Whether you used the desktop CD or the traditional alternate install CD approach to get Ubuntu on your computer, you now have a powerful, extensible, and easy-to-use OS with a huge array of available software. Unlike other operating systems, Ubuntu includes a complete end-to-end software selection with a range of tools for office productivity, system configuration, Internet access, e-mail, and more. In addition to this impressive array of desktop software, your new system also includes an incredibly powerful underlying architecture that can be heavily customized. Those of you with a fondness for code and programming will also get a kick out of the millions and millions of lines of code that are freely available and spread among the different applications included. Ubuntu also provides extensive development tools for creating desktop applications, Web applications, and more.

You are at the start of an exciting journey, so let's get going.

CHAPTER 3

Using Ubuntu on the Desktop

- Taking Your Desktop for a Ride
- Using Your Applications
- The Ubuntu File Chooser and Bookmarks
- Ubuntu in Your Language
- Customizing Ubuntu's Look and Feel
- Managing Your Files
- Ubuntu and Multimedia
- Moving to the Next Ubuntu Release
- Summary

WITH UBUNTU INSTALLED and ready to go, it's time to get started using your new desktop. The stock install of Ubuntu provides a very complete and flexible system. Unlike other operating systems, such as Microsoft Windows or Mac OS X, Ubuntu includes everything you need to get started: an office suite, media tools, a Web browser, an e-mail client, and more. Once the installation is complete, you are up and running right away without having to install any additional software. Different people use their computers in different ways, and every user has her own personal preference for look and feel. Recognizing this desire, Linux has the capability to use any one of a number of different graphical interfaces. This flexibility, combined with the ballooning popularity of Linux and open source, has resulted in literally hundreds of different graphical environments springing up, each covering these different types of users and ways of working.

Even though there is a huge range of different environments available, there are two clear leaders in KDE and GNOME. Each environment provides a good-looking, comprehensive, and easy-to-use desktop, but they differ in how that desktop is used as well as in how further personalization can take place. The KDE system aims for complete control and configurability of the desktop. Any desktop configuration options that exist are available to the user, who has easy access and can change the behavior and look of almost everything. The competing GNOME desktop takes inspiration from both Windows and Mac OS X and sets a priority on simplicity and ease of use. GNOME is also easy to customize, but the less common options are either eliminated or well hidden to prevent user overload. Luckily, Ubuntu users are blessed with the choice of either desktop, along with several others, some of which are mentioned in Chapter 10. The default desktop in Ubuntu is GNOME, and the Kubuntu distribution uses the KDE desktop. Kubuntu is covered in Chapter 8.

In this chapter, we help you get started with GNOME and show how you can use it to do the normal things you face every day with your computer and a few not-so-normal things. This includes opening and running applications, managing your files, adjusting the look and feel, using applications, managing your media, and more. Buckle up and get ready to take your shiny new desktop for a drive!

TIP   **The Ubuntu Desktop Is GNOME**

When reading about Ubuntu, you often see the terms *Ubuntu desktop* and *GNOME* used interchangeably. Both of these terms refer to the same thing—the default Ubuntu desktop is a version of GNOME itself. Of course, Ubuntu provides several other desktops, including KDE (in Kubuntu), Xfce (in Xubuntu), and a variety of others.

Taking Your Desktop for a Ride

When you start your Ubuntu system, you are presented with a list of users. Once you select your username from the list by clicking it, you are asked for a password to log in with. In the last chapter, you specified a user account when installing the system, so use that to log in. First type in your username and press Enter, then your password and press Enter.

After a few seconds you will see the Ubuntu desktop appear (Figure 3-1). The desktop has three main areas.

1. At the top of the screen is the panel. This bar contains the desktop menu options and application shortcut icons on the left side as well as the notification area on the right side. You use this bar to load applications and to see the status of certain activities on your system. The panel is always visible when you use your desktop.

2. The large middle part of the screen, located under the panel, is the desktop. This part of the screen is normally covered by the applications that you use, but you can also put icons and shortcuts on the desktop, too.

3. The bottom part of the screen is called the taskbar. This area displays a rectangle for each open application, just like in Windows.

You may have noticed that, unlike other operating systems, there are no icons on the desktop. The reason for this is that desktop icons typically get covered by applications, and, as such, you can't get at them. If you need to start applications, you typically use the Applications menu or the shortcuts.

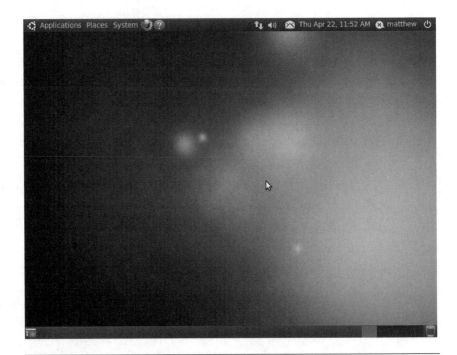

Figure 3-1 The Ubuntu desktop is simple, uncluttered, and . . . beautiful.

TIP   **Device Icons**
Although there are no application icons on the desktop, when you plug in USB devices such as portable music players, keyring drives, or digital cameras, a device icon will appear on the desktop.

Starting Applications and Finding Things

Starting applications is simple. Just click on the Applications menu on the left side of the panel. Inside this menu are a number of submenus for different types of applications. Hover your mouse over each category, and then click the application you want to load. As an example, click on Applications > Games > Mahjongg.

When applications are loaded, the window border has three buttons on the top on the left-hand side:

- **Left button (red button with a black X):** This button closes the application.

- **Middle button (white button with a gray ˅):** This minimizes the application, taking it off of your screen, and puts it in the taskbar for easy access when you need it again.

- **Right button (white button with a gray ∧):** This is used to maximize the window to take up the full desktop area.

Every application that is in use has an entry in the taskbar at the bottom of the screen. You can click these entries to minimize or restore the application to or from the taskbar, and you can right-click to see some other options.

Finding Your Files and Folders

When using your computer, you often need to save and open files and folders, move them around, and perform other tasks. The Places menu contains a bunch of entries, including those listed here, to access different parts of your computer and the network.

- **Home Folder:** Your home folder is used to store the files and work for each user who is logged in. This is the most important folder on the system, and you can think of it as the equivalent of My Documents in Windows—virtually everything you save lives here. Each user has a separate home folder.

- **Desktop:** The Desktop folder is inside your home folder and contains files that visually appear on your desktop as icons. If you drag a file onto your desktop, it will appear in the Desktop folder. Similarly, moving a file out of this folder or deleting it will remove it from your desktop.

- **Computer:** Clicking this item displays the different drives attached to your computer as floppy drives, CD/DVD drives, and USB keys or sticks. This is the equivalent of the My Computer icon in Windows.

- **Network:** This option accesses all networked and shared devices, such as file servers or printers, that are available on your local network. This is the equivalent of the Network Neighborhood or Network Places in various versions of Windows.

- **Connect to Server:** Click this to run a wizard to create a connection to a network server. You can use this to add an icon to the desktop that, when clicked, provides a list of remote files in the desktop file manager. You can then treat this window like any other file manager window and drag files back and forth. This is really useful for copying files to other computers.
- **Search for Files:** Use this to search for files on your computer.
- **Recent Documents:** Click this submenu to display the most recently used documents.

Configuring Your System

The third and final menu, System, is used to configure and customize your system, access help, and report problems. Inside the menu are a few options, including these:

- **Preferences:** This submenu contains items for customizing the look and feel of your desktop. Each of these settings applies only to the desktop of a user who is logged in. If you log in as another user, the settings change to that user's preferences.
- **Administration:** This submenu is used to configure systemwide settings such as networking, users, printing, and more. To use these menu items, your account must have system administrator privileges, and you must know and use your password.
- **Help and Support:** With this you can access the Ubuntu Help Center, which provides documentation and guides for your Ubuntu desktop.
- **About GNOME:** Here you have a simple, animated document with information and links about GNOME.
- **About Ubuntu:** This brings up a detailed document, with links, that helps users learn more about Ubuntu.

TIP   **Feel the Power**

When you installed Ubuntu, you were asked for a username and password for the system. That first user account (and its password) has access to not just your normal user account but also the all-powerful Administration features. Therefore, when you access the menu options while using this account and are asked for a password, just enter this user account's password to use those features.

This feature applies only to the user account created during installation. If you add other users, you need to explicitly allow them access to Administration options.

Adding Additional Users

Many computers these days are used by more than one person. Rather than forcing everyone to use the same desktop settings or making the computer less secure by allowing everyone who uses it to have access to administrative functions, it is easy and recommended to create an account for every person who will use the computer. This allows each user to customize how the computer works and looks without interfering with anyone else's preferences, and it grants the administrator privileges that prevent others from accessing functions that may affect everyone or even damage the installation if used incorrectly.

Adding a new user is done by clicking System > Administration > Users and Groups. In the dialog box that appears, there is a list of current users. At the bottom of the list, select Add to create a new user account, as in Figure 3-2.

A password is required to make changes to users and groups, and only those users with administrative access are able to do so. You must now provide a name for the new user as well as a short name that will be used by that user to log in. Click OK, and in the next dialog box, enter a password for that user, confirm the password by entering it a second time, and click OK again. Voila, our new user account is created. You may also have a password

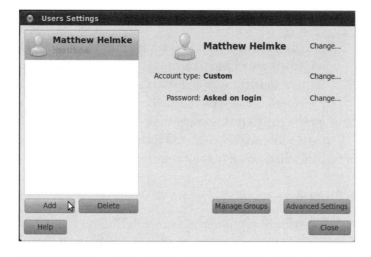

Figure 3-2 The User Settings dialog

generated randomly or allow the user to log in without a password. This last option is not generally a good idea but can be useful. For example, if the users are small children who are not expected to perform administrative tasks, the children could have an account that automatically logs in at boot time, and the administrator would have an additional account, accessed by a password, to perform changes and updates when necessary.

Finally, now that the account is created, we may customize its settings. Highlight the username in the list, and click the Change button at the right next to Account Type for a speedy way to give the user administration privileges. The Advanced Settings button from the lower right corner of the dialog box may be used to set contact information for the user, change the account's user privileges (for example, giving access to administrative and several other functions that are not available through the quick change option), and even change the location of the account's home directory. Be careful when using this power because an account can be damaged or rendered inaccessible if things are not done properly.

Shortcut Icons

On the panel are a number of shortcut icons next to the menus. These small icons are always visible and can be single-clicked to gain immediate access to your favorite applications. Ubuntu comes with several stock shortcuts on the panel, but you are welcome to add your own or remove the defaults as you like.

Adding your own icon is as simple as finding the application you want to add in the menu and then dragging it to the panel. You can then right-click the new shortcut icon and select Move to move it to the desired spot on the panel. You can also do this in the menu by right-clicking on a specific program's entry and choosing the option to have a launcher for the program to be added to the panel. You may have to click to unlock the item from the panel first, which may be done from the same menu.

Applets

One simple yet powerful feature in Ubuntu is the ability to run small programs called *applets* on the panel. These small programs are useful for a variety of tasks and provide quick and easy access via the panel.

To add an applet, right-click the panel and select Add to Panel. The window shown in Figure 3-3 pops up. Select one of the many applets, and click Add. When the applet appears on the panel, you can press the middle mouse button (or the left and right buttons together) to move it around.

The Notification Area

In the right-hand part of the top panel is the notification area and the clock. The notification area is similar to the Windows system tray in that it provides a series of small icons that indicate something specific. A good example of this is Network Manager, which looks after your network connections—both wired and wireless—for you.

You can adjust the notification area items by right-clicking them to view a context menu. Some icons (such as the volume control) allow you to left-click on them to view them. As an example, try clicking the little speaker icon and adjusting the slider.

QUICK TIP   Left-click the volume icon and select Sound Preferences to access a large number of sound settings. These settings configure the speakers, microphone, line-in, any other sound card inputs or outputs, and more.

Figure 3-3 Ubuntu comes bundled with a selection of applets.

Three applets are installed by default: the previously mentioned sound applet, the indicator applet, and the network manager applet. The indicator applet tells the user when something needs attention on the desktop and provides quick access to communication options like Empathy, Evolution, and Gwibber with a left-click (more on these later in the chapter). The network manager applet (Figure 3-4) gives easy access to networking controls.

Network Manager

Network Manager is a network interface created to help you manage your network devices and connections and is accessed using the network manager applet. The goal is to make networking "just work" easily and without requiring users to know how to hand-configure the settings (although that is still available for those who want to do so). A left-click of the mouse on the applet shows you the dialog box and enables quick changes between network types. It even provides an easy way to set up access through a virtual private network (VPN), such as many of us are required to use to access files from work or school securely. A right-click lets you enable or disable both wired and wireless networking, enable or disable notifications, see information about your current connection, and edit connections quickly and easily (Figure 3-5).

Figure 3-4 The network manager applet, left-clicked to show available wireless networks

Figure 3-5 The network manager applet, right-clicked to show connections menu

The Clock

Next to the notification area is the clock. Click on the clock to view a calendar. Later, when you use Evolution, items that are added to your calendar appear in the clock applet too. Instead of opening up Evolution to find out when your dentist appointment is, just click on the clock to see it immediately. More information about Evolution is contained later in this chapter.

QUICK TIP   Customize your clock by right-clicking it and selecting Preferences.

The Taskbar

The taskbar sits at the bottom of the screen. This small bar is always visible and indicates which applications are currently open. In addition to this, the taskbar also sneaks in a few other handy little features.

To the far left of the taskbar is the Hide/Show Desktop button. Clicking this button hides all of your open applications and shows the desktop. Clicking it again redisplays them. This button is useful when you need to quickly access something on your desktop.

Next to this button is the applications area, which shows each of the currently open applications. For each application, an entry is added, and you can right-click it to view a context menu. This menu can also be used to minimize, maximize, resize, close, and otherwise control applications.

QUICK TIP   You can switch between multiple applications in Ubuntu just like in Windows by pressing Alt-Tab. When you press this key combination, a small window appears that can be used to switch between active applications.

To the right of the applications area are two small rectangles called the workspaces. Each of these rectangles represents another screen in which you can view an application. As an example, you may be using your Web browser and e-mail client while talking to your friends in a chat client on the first desktop and working on a document on the second desktop. You can then just click each virtual desktop to switch to it to access your different applications. Another useful tip applies when you're moving applications between virtual desktops—if you have an application on the first desktop, just right-click the charcoal-colored window or the taskbar entry, select Move to Another Workspace, and pick the relevant workspace number. The menu also has Move to Workspace Left and Move to Workspace Right options. This makes moving applications between your workspaces quite simple.

QUICK TIP   Although Ubuntu has only two workspaces configured by default, you can have as many—or few—as you like. To configure them, right-click on one of the workspaces in the bottom right-hand corner of your screen, and select Preferences from the menu.

To the right of the workspaces is the trash. Files dragged onto this icon or right-clicked and "moved to trash" are destined to be deleted. To fully delete these files, right-click the trash and select Empty Trash.

TIP   **Usability and the Ubuntu Desktop**
Throughout the development of the Ubuntu desktop, great care and attention have gone into usability. As an example, the four corners of the screen are established as areas that are simple to access—you don't need to carefully mouse over the area and can instead just throw your mouse to the corner. This is why each corner has an important feature. It makes accessing each feature that little bit easier.

Ubuntu is filled with tiny usability improvements such as this that help make it as intuitive and powerful as possible. Canonical has created a collective project called Ayatana to spearhead this development, which has already produced the lovely indicator applet and is working on greater refinements and features. More on Ayatana can be found at https://wiki.ubuntu.com/Ayatana.

Shutting Down Your Computer and Logging Out

Now that you're becoming acquainted with Ubuntu, you'll want to keep using it as long as possible, but there will always come a time when you have no choice but to leave your computer and go do something else. As you have already seen, Ubuntu is extremely flexible, and this area is no exception. Click the icon in the top right of the screen to see the various options (shown in Figure 3-6) for ending your current computing session.

A number of options are available upon logout; however, the choices presented to you will depend on your installation (e.g., Suspend may not be available).

Figure 3-6 Ahh, the possibilities. . . .

- ▣ **Lock Screen:** This option locks the screen, which is useful when you need to use the bathroom or grab some lunch. It locks the computer and asks for your password to reenable the desktop.

- ▣ **Guest Session:** This option lets you allow someone else to use your computer while keeping you logged in but your data and account secure by giving the guest a limited desktop to work with temporarily and requiring your password to return to your desktop.

- ▣ **Switch from . . .:** Your username will be listed here. This option takes you to the login screen and lets you switch between logged in users without logging anyone out. It also requires each specific user's password to access his or her account.

- ▣ **Log Out:** This option lets you log out of the current session and go back to the main login screen.

- ▣ **Sleep:** If your computer supports it, this option will be included in the list, and you can click it to save the current state of your system in RAM. The next time your computer is turned on, the desktop will be resumed. This option continues to use battery power but only a minimal amount.

- ▣ **Restart:** Click this to restart the computer.

- ▣ **Shut Down:** Click this to shut down your computer.

Using Your Applications

Now that you have become familiar with the desktop, let's explore some of the many applications included on your new system. By default, Ubuntu comes with a wide range of popular and established applications to listen to music, watch videos, create documents, browse the Web, manage your appointments, read your e-mail, create images, and much more. These applications have been vetted by the developers to ensure they are the best-of-breed Linux applications available.

Although Ubuntu includes a range of software applications, it is likely you will want to install extra applications and explore other available software. Fortunately, the Ubuntu system is built on a powerful foundation that makes software installation as simple as pointing and clicking in the Ubuntu Software Center, covered in depth in Chapter 4. Just browse through the different categories and check the applications to install. Click the Apply button, and the application is downloaded and installed for you.

This tool provides a simple way to access a limited core set of popular applications, but there are actually more than 30,000 packages available to your Ubuntu system. Software installation is discussed in detail in Chapter 4.

TIP   **Another Way to Run Applications**
Although you will most typically start your applications by selecting them from the Applications menu, you can also press Alt+F2 (on Mac hardware, use Fn+Alt+F2) to bring up a box where you can type in the name of an application and run it.

Browsing the Web with Firefox

Firefox is the default Ubuntu Web browser and provides you with a simple, safe, and powerful browsing experience. Firefox is developed by Mozilla and has become one of the most successful open source projects in the world and continues to garner huge popularity. With hundreds of millions of downloads and rapidly increasing browser share, Firefox has been an unparalleled success.

QUICK TIP   You can learn more about Mozilla and Firefox, as well as their other software products, at www.mozilla.org.

Fire up Firefox by clicking its icon (the first one next to the System menu) on the panel or by selecting Applications > Internet > Firefox Web Browser. Before long, you'll be presented with the main Firefox window (Figure 3-7).

The Firefox window looks similar to most Web browsers and includes the usual back, forward, reload, and stop buttons, an address bar, and some menus. These familiar-looking elements help you become acquainted with Firefox, and if you have used Internet Explorer, Opera, Chrome, or Safari before, you are sure to pick it up in no time.

Navigating your way around the Internet is no different in Firefox than in any other browser—just type the Web address into the address bar and press Enter. Firefox also has a few nice features that make it easy to access your favorite sites. As an example, if you want to visit the Ubuntu Web site, you can just enter www.ubuntu.com (leaving off all that http:// nonsense). Alternatively, you can just type in "Ubuntu," and Firefox will do the equivalent of going off to Google, entering "Ubuntu" as the search term, and taking you to the first result for the search. This feature is incredibly handy for popular sites that are likely to be at the top of the search results page.

Figure 3-7 The Firefox interface is sleek but extensible.

TIP   The search box next to the address bar can be used to do searches. By default, these searches are on Google. To do a Google search, just type in your search term and press Enter. You can also click the down arrow next to the Google logo and select from a variety of other sites to search, including sites like Amazon.com and Wikipedia.

This search box can be used to search just about anything. To add more search engines, click the small icon and then select Manage Search Engines.

Bookmarking Your Favorite Sites   To bookmark the page you are viewing, click Bookmarks > Bookmark This Page or click Ctrl+D. In the dialog box that pops up, use the combo box to select the folder to store the bookmark in. You also have the option to add "tags" to your bookmark, which are like keywords that can be used to sort and search for your bookmarks in the future. When you have finished naming and tagging your bookmark, click Done to save the bookmark.

Save Time with Live Bookmarks   Firefox also includes a special feature called *live bookmarks* that automatically grabs content from a Web site without your needing to visit it. As an example, go to http://fridge.ubuntu.com (a popular Ubuntu news site), and you will see a small orange icon—which indicates that this site has a feed available—on the right side of the address bar. Click this orange square, and you will be taken to a new page that previews the feed and gives you the option of what you would like to use to subscribe to it. Use the default option (Live Bookmarks), and click Subscribe Now. A dialog box will pop up. Use the default values provided and click OK. A new toolbar button is added, and when you click on it, a list of the items from the Web site are displayed. Each time you start Firefox, it will quietly go away and update this list so that you don't need to visit the site yourself. The "Latest Headlines" toolbar entry is an example of this.

TIP   **If You Liked the Fridge**
You may also like Planet Ubuntu at http://planet.ubuntu.com. This site collects the personal blogs of a number of different Ubuntu developers and other community members. Planet Ubuntu gives a unique insight into what the developers are working on and/or interested in.

Bolt It On, Make It Cool   Although Firefox is already a powerful and flexible Web browser, it can be extended even further using special plug-in extensions. These extensions cover not only typical browsing needs but also other more specialized extras that extend the browser itself.

To install normal Web plug-ins, just visit a site that requires the plug-in. A yellow bar will appear at the top of the page, indicating that you are missing a plug-in necessary to fully take advantage of the page you are visiting. Click the Install Missing Plug-ins button to grab the required plug-in. For example, Ubuntu does not come with the Macromedia Flash plug-in because it does not live up to Ubuntu software freedom requirements. As a result, you will have the option to install either Macromedia Flash or the free software version Gnash if you want to use Flash.

To extend the browser itself with additional features, go to https://addons. mozilla.org and browse for an extension that you are interested in. When you find something you would like to install, click the Install link. A dialog box will pop up asking you to confirm the installation. Click Install Now. Your new extension will now download and install automatically. Typically, this requires a restart of Firefox, and then your extension is available.

TIP   **Be Careful Where You Download**
It is recommended that you download extensions only from http://addons.mozilla.org. If you do need to install an extension from another site, make sure it is a site you trust. Otherwise, the extension may contain unsafe software, viruses, or spyware.

Creating Documents with OpenOffice.org

Included with Ubuntu is a full office suite called OpenOffice.org. This office software comes by default with applications for word processing, working with spreadsheets, and presentations. Adding other features, such as the ability to create and manipulate databases, work with drawings, and more, are easily installed later. The suite provides an extensive range of functionality, including reading and writing Microsoft Office file formats, and can also export documents as Web pages, PDF files, and even animations.

Let's give OpenOffice.org a whirl by creating a letter with it. Start Open-Office.org word processor by selecting it from the Applications > Office menu. When it has loaded, you will be presented with the interface shown in Figure 3-8.

If you have used a word processing program before, many of the common interface elements, such as the buttons for setting font type and size, bold, italic, underline, and alignment, look and behave the same. The OpenOffice.org developers have designed the suite to be easy to migrate to if you have used a program like Microsoft Office before. After a few minutes playing with OpenOffice.org, you will be confident that you can find the functions you need.

Start your letter by first choosing a nice font. In the font combo box, you should see Liberation Serif (which is a free-as-in-liberty font similar to Times) selected as the default. You can click the box and choose another if you prefer, such as the lovely DejaVu Sans font. Change the font size by clicking the combo box to the right of the font box and selecting 10 as the

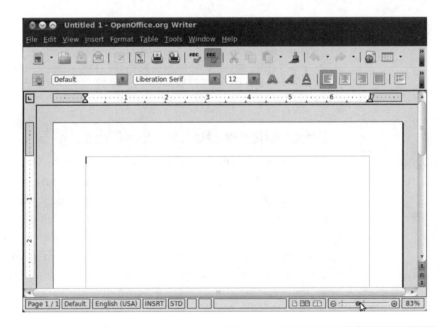

Figure 3-8 OpenOffice.org looks similar to Microsoft Office and is therefore quite simple to adjust to.

size. With the cursor on the left side of the page, add your home address to the letter.

Now press Enter to leave a blank line under the address, and click the Align Right toolbar button (the icon looks like some lines aligned to the right). If you are unsure of what a button does, hover your mouse over it to pop up a tool tip. Now add to your letter the address of the recipient.

Press Enter again to leave a blank line, and type the main body of the letter. Feel free to use the bold, italic, and underline buttons to add emphasis to your words. You can also use other toolbar buttons to add items such as bullet points and numbered lists and to change the color of the font. If you want to add features such as graphics, tables, special characters, and frames, click the Insert menu and select the relevant item. You can customize each item added to the page by right-clicking the item and using the options shown in the context menu.

When your letter is complete, you can save it by selecting File > Save, by clicking the floppy disk toolbar icon, or by pressing Ctrl-S. The default file format used by OpenOffice.org is the OpenDocument Format. This file format is an official open standard and is used across the world. The file format is slightly different for different types of applications (.odt for word processor files, .ods for spreadsheets, and so on), but each format provides an open standard free from vendor lock-in. You can also save in a variety of other formats, including the default formats for Microsoft Office.

TIP   **Vendor Lock-In?**

In the proprietary software world, it is common for each application to have its own closed file format that only the vendor knows how to implement. When a person uses the software to create documents, the closed format means that only that specific tool can read and write the format. As long as you want to access your documents, you need that tool. This is known as vendor lock-in.

To combat this problem, the OpenOffice.org suite (and the vast majority of other open source applications) uses an open file format that is publicly documented. In fact, the format is a published standard under ISO/IEC 26300:3006. This means that other applications can implement the OpenDocument file format, and you can be safe in the knowledge that your documents will always be available and you are not locked in to any specific tool.

Another useful feature wedged into OpenOffice.org is the capability to save your documents in the Adobe PDF format. PDF files have been increasingly used in the last few years and are useful for sending people documents that they should not change (such as invoices). PDF files provide a high-quality copy of the document and are well supported across all operating systems. This makes PDFs ideal for creating catalogs, leaflets, and flyers. To save a document as a PDF file, click the PDF button on the main toolbar (next to the printer icon). Click the button, enter a filename, and you are done. Simple.

Connecting with Empathy and Gwibber and the Indicator Applet

Empathy is a chat program that can interact with Google Talk, AIM, Windows Live, and many other chat programs. It has audio and video capability as well. You can get started by left-clicking the indicator applet (it looks like an envelope) on the top panel and choosing Chat. You will then be given an opportunity to enter your account information for various services and to begin communicating.

Gwibber, listed in this menu as Broadcast, is accessible from the same location and can be set up to allow you to integrate online services like Flickr, Twitter, identi.ca, and Facebook into your desktop for even easier access to what is happening in your social networks. Open it, enter your account information as directed, and you can begin to interact with all your circles from one location on your desktop.

On the top panel, you may have noticed your username with a speech balloon icon next to it. This location gives you a convenient place to mark yourself available for chat or away, update your information for social accounts that use either Empathy or Gwibber, and use your Ubuntu One services.

Ubuntu One

Ubuntu One is an online cloud storage application that is free for any Ubuntu user. This enables any user to create an Ubuntu One account and store up to 2GB on remote servers (more space is available for a fee) that may be accessed from anywhere. The service is built in to the Ubuntu desktop and, once activated, integrates smoothly. You can get started configuring your account from the menu at System > Preferences > Ubuntu One. More information is available at one.ubuntu.com.

Managing Your E-mail and Calendars with Evolution

Evolution is modeled around the all-in-one personal information management tool. Within Evolution you can read your e-mail, manage your schedule, store contact details, organize to-do lists, and more in a single place. This makes Evolution useful for both businesspeople and regular users who want easy access to this information.

Setting Up Your E-Mail Account   To use Evolution to read your e-mail, you need to find out the following settings for connecting to your e-mail server (you can get these details from your ISP or system administrator):

- Your type of e-mail server (such as POP or IMAP)
- Your mail server name (such as mail.chin.com)
- Your mail account's username and password
- Authentication type (typically by password)
- Your outgoing mail server type (typically SMTP)
- Your outgoing mail server name

To use Evolution for just the calendar function, you need to go to the indicator applet (looks like an envelope) in the notification area on the top panel and click on Set Up Mail. In a few seconds, the Evolution Setup Assistant window will pop up. Here are the necessary steps:

1. On the Welcome screen, click the Forward button.

2. Next, you may restore your e-mail from a backup, but since we are doing a fresh setup, click the Forward button.

3. On the Identify screen, enter your full name and e-mail address in the appropriate boxes. Under Optional Information, you should uncheck the Make this my default account box. Then click the Forward button.

4. In the Receiving Email dialog box under Configuration > Server, just add your name. You can add your name under Username as well. Then click the Forward button.

5. On the Receiving Options screen, click the Forward button.

6. On the Sending Email and Server Configuration screen, add your name here as you did in earlier steps.

7. In the Account Management dialog box, just click the Forward button.

8. On the Done screen, click the Forward button.

9. Finally, once Evolution opens, click New Icon (looks like a clock), and from the drop-down menu, select Calendar.

10. When the New Calendar window pops up, you can pick which type of calendar you want to use. Note: If you don't already have another type of calendar, just leave the Type as CalDAV, then fill in the name—this will be the name of your calendar. Pick the color you want your events to show up as, then click Mark as default calendar.

If you are using Google calendar, you can also add this function to your calendar. All the steps are the same, but when you get to step 10 to add a new calendar, you need to choose Google as the type of calendar. Then fill in the name you want to use for the calendar, choose the color, and mark it as your default calendar. You probably want to copy the contents locally, too, in case you need to access it when you do not have Internet access. When you click Google, you will see a Username field show up under Name. Your username should be your gmail name, but without the "@gmail.com." Once you enter your username, click on Retrieve List. You will be prompted to enter your gmail password. Enter it. When the Enter Password window goes away, you should see a list of calendars that you have linked to your Google calendars. If you have more than one Google calendar you want to add, then just pick which one will be your default calendar. Repeat step 10 for each calendar you want to add.

TIP   Evolution and Webmail
You can't use Evolution to read Webmail such as Yahoo! Mail or Hotmail unless you configure your Webmail to allow POP access and to use SMTP to send e-mail. Consult your Webmail provider for more details on if and how you can access the mail with a local client like Evolution.

Load Evolution by clicking the envelope and clock shortcut icon from the panel (hover your mouse over the shortcuts to see what they are) or by clicking Applications > Internet > Evolution Mail. When the application loads, you are taken through a wizard to set up your e-mail server (as shown in Figure 3-9).

Click Forward to continue the setup, and after choosing to not restore from a backup, you will be asked for your identity. Fill in your e-mail address in the E-Mail Address box, and add the optional information if you want to. The additional details are not essential for using Evolution. Click Forward to continue.

You are next asked to choose what kind of e-mail server you have from the drop-down box. When you make your selection, some additional settings are displayed. Fill in the server name and the username. You may need to adjust the Security and Authentication Type settings, but for most accounts the default settings should be fine. Click Forward to continue.

Figure 3-9 Setting up Evolution is simple as long as you know the details for your mail server.

The next page configures some options for receiving your e-mail. None of these options are essential, although you may want to check the first box to automatically check for new mail. Click Forward to continue. The next screen configures the settings for sending e-mail. In the combo box select the Server Type (typically SMTP) and add the server name to the Server box. Click Forward to continue.

In the next screen, enter a name to describe the account. The default entry (your e-mail address) is fine, but you may want to add something more meaningful such as "Work E-Mail" or "Home E-Mail." When you have added this, click Forward to continue. Finally, select your location from the map. If you click on your area of the world, the map will zoom in. Once you have done this, click Apply to complete the process and close the wizard.

With the wizard completed, the main Evolution interface will appear, as shown in Figure 3-10.

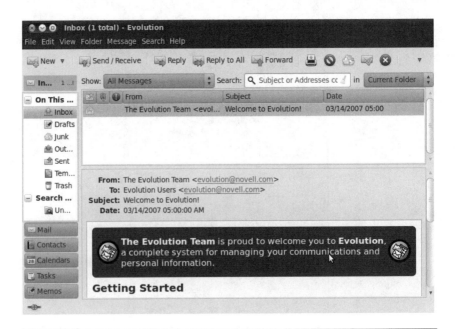

Figure 3-10 Those of you who have used Microsoft Outlook should find the interface very similar.

On the left sidebar you can see a number of buttons to access the mail, contacts, calendars, memos, and tasks components in Evolution. When you click each button, the interface adjusts to show you the relevant information about that component.

Working with Your E-Mail   Inside the e-mail component you can see the e-mail folders in the left panel and the list of messages in the top pane. When you click on a message, it is displayed in the bottom pane, where you can read it. With your new account set up, you will first want to go and grab the e-mail from your mail server. Click Send/Receive, and the mail is retrieved from your server and any unsent mail is sent.

TIP   **Problems?**
If you cannot connect to your mail server, there may be an error in your account configuration. To edit your account settings again, click Edit > Preferences, select the account from the list, and click Edit.

With your messages loaded, new e-mails are shown in bold in the top pane. Move through the different e-mails using the up and down arrow keys, and each message will be displayed. You can reply to a message by clicking the Reply or Reply To All toolbar buttons. New e-mails can be created by clicking the New toolbar button. By default, new e-mails and replies are sent automatically when you click the Send button in the compose window. This way you don't need to click the Send/Receive button to deliver them.

Managing Your Calendar   Inside calendar mode, Evolution provides another convenient way to manage your schedule, add new events, and view your calendar in different ways. When you click the Calendars button to switch to this mode, you can see the timetable for today as well as the month view. The month view shows a couple of months in which the bold dates have events.

You can add two types of events to your calendar.

- **Meetings:** These are events with a specific group of people.
- **Appointments:** These are general events.

To add a new appointment, navigate to the date you require using the calendar, then right-click a time slot in the day view, and select New Appointment. Alternatively, simply click the New toolbar item. In the box that pops up, fill in the Summary, Location, Time (adjusting the date if necessary), and Description boxes. You can also select which calendar the event appears on if you have multiple calendars configured.

TIP   Multiple Calendars

Evolution supports multiple calendars. This is useful if you want different calendars for different types of events such as personal and work-related activities. To create a new calendar, right-click the calendar list in the left sidebar and select New Calendar.

To add a new meeting, again find the date, right-click the day view, and select New Meeting. Inside the dialog box that pops up, you need to add the participants who are attending the meeting. You can add participants in two ways: Use the Add button if they are not in your address book, or use the Attendees button if they are in your address book.

When you click Attendees, a new dialog pops up with a list of attendees down the left. You can use the Add and Remove buttons to add contacts to (or remove them from) the different categories of Chairpersons, Required Participants, Optional Participants, and Resources. Now, you probably don't have any contacts in there, as you are just starting to use Evolution, so use the main Contacts button on the left side of the main Evolution window to add some.

You can view your calendar in lots of different ways by clicking the different toolbar buttons such as Week, Month, and List. Play with them and see which ones are most useful to you.

QUICK TIP   Remember, you can access your appointments without opening Evolution by clicking on the clock in the panel.

The Ubuntu File Chooser and Bookmarks

One area in which the GNOME developers have worked hard is in creating an intuitive and useful file chooser that is accessed in applications with File > Open. The window that pops open is called the file chooser. You may be wondering why they have spent so much time on such a small and seemingly insignificant part of the desktop. In reality, however, finding files is one of the most frustrating aspects of using computers and often involves digging through folder after folder to find what you need. Luckily, the GNOME file chooser (Figure 3-11) helps cut down much of this file hunting significantly.

The listing of files on the right-hand side is used to find the file you need, and you can click on folders in this listing to traverse deeper into your subfolders. Note how each folder is displayed above the listing in a series of buttons. You can click these buttons to easily jump back to parent folders when needed.

Aside from enabling you to manually pick files, the chooser also supports bookmarks. On the left side of the chooser is a list of devices and bookmarks labeled Places. These include your home directory (shown as your username), Desktop (the files on your desktop), and File System (the entire hard drive), as well as devices such as CD drives, floppy drives, and USB sticks.

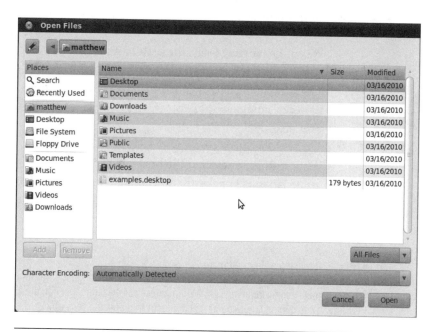

Figure 3-11 The file chooser makes it easy to find what you want.

To create your own bookmark, use the listing on the right to find the folder that you want to bookmark, single-click it, and then click Add below the Places box. You could also right-click on the file and choose Add to Bookmarks. The folder now appears in your bookmarks. Now whenever you need to access that folder, just click the bookmark! In addition to putting the bookmark in the file chooser, it is also available in other parts of the desktop, such as the Places menu and in the file manager.

Ubuntu in Your Language

When you installed Ubuntu, you were asked which language the system should use. Although this sets the initial language for the system, you may want to change the language at a later date. To do this, click System > Administration > Language Support.

Ubuntu supports a huge range of different languages, and many applications include a Translate This Application menu option in the Help menu so that all Ubuntu users can contribute translations in their language(s). If you would like to help with this effort, it is a fantastic contribution to the Ubuntu project.

When the language selector first loads, it may ask you to update your language packs. Just click Yes to continue. Inside the dialog box a number of languages are listed, each of which has a Support checkbox listed next to it. For each language that you want available on the system, check the relevant boxes.

When you have selected the boxes, click the Apply button, and the appropriate language packs are downloaded and installed. Now use the Default Language combo box to choose the new language. You need to log out and log back in for the changes to take effect.

TIP   **Choosing a New Language**
When you see the login screen, you can use the Language button to choose a language for that specific login session. When you select the language, you are asked if you want to make it the default language or use it just for that specific session.

Customizing Ubuntu's Look and Feel

Whenever we put someone in front of Ubuntu for the first time, there seems to be a uniform natural desire to tweak the look and feel of the desktop. It can be fun tweaking our desktops so they look just right, and Ubuntu has great support for all kinds of adjustments. Do you want different-looking applications with a lime green background and crazy fonts? No problem; just don't show it to anyone else....

Changing the Background

To change the background of your desktop, right-click it and select Change Desktop Background. Inside the dialog box that appears, choose your wallpaper by clicking on an image, and the desktop background will automatically change. Ubuntu comes with a limited range of preinstalled wallpapers, so it is likely that you will want to add your own wallpaper. To do this, save your wallpaper somewhere on your computer, and then use the Add Wallpaper button to select it. The new wallpaper can be selected from the list.

If you are not really a wallpaper kind of person and would prefer just a color for the background, you can use the Desktop Colors controls at the bottom of the dialog box. The combo box provides three different types of background: Solid Color, Horizontal Gradient, and Vertical Gradient. Next to the combo box, click on the color chip to select the relevant color(s).

Changing the Theme

When you are using your applications, the visual appearance of the buttons, scroll bars, widgets, and other bits and pieces are controlled by the theme. The built-in theming system can make your applications look radically different, and Ubuntu ships with a number of themes that you can try.

Choosing a New Theme   To choose a new theme, click System > Preferences > Appearance and then click on the Theme tab. Inside the tab that pops up are a number of themes that you can choose. Just click on a theme, and the desktop will be adjusted automatically. You can further customize your theme by clicking the Customize button. A new dialog box appears that has tabs for the different parts of the theme you can configure. Click each tab, and select an entry from the list to create your own perfect theme.

Installing New Themes   To install a new theme, head over to http:// art.gnome.org and find a theme that you like. You can do this directly from the Theme tab in the System > Preferences > Appearance window mentioned previously by clicking Get more themes online. You need to look for Controls and Borders when browsing under the Themes tab on the site. When you find a theme that you like, download it to your computer. Now Click System > Preferences > Appearance, and click the Install button in the Theme tab. Using the file chooser, find the theme that you just downloaded, and it will install automatically. You may now select your new theme from the list.

Configuring a Screensaver

To choose a different screensaver, click System > Preferences > Screensaver. The screensaver configuration tool then loads (Figure 3-12).

Figure 3-12   A number of screensavers are bundled with Ubuntu.

On the left side of the window is a list of available screensavers. Click on a screensaver and you will see a preview appear in the space to the right of the list. You can then use the slider to select how long the computer needs to be idle before the screensaver kicks in.

The Lock Screen When Screensaver Is Active checkbox can be selected to lock the screen when the screensaver starts and, as such, requires a user to enter the password to reactivate the desktop. This is useful if you work in an office and want to ensure that no one tampers with your computer when you are away.

Managing Your Files

Files are the primary components of any computer use, and they need to be managed, copied, moved, renamed, grouped, and loaded. Included with Ubuntu is a powerful yet simple file manager called Nautilus that integrates tightly into your desktop. You'll use it all the time even if you don't often see that name. Most often, you will see it referred to as File Browser.

File Browser makes extensive use of drag and drop. Unlike the kind of file manager used in Windows with its tree view and listing of files, File Browser displays files in a series of windows in which you can drag files around easily. For those who just can't say goodbye to the tree view, File Browser also supports that. Aside from providing a simpler user interface, File Browser also includes a number of useful features such as video and image previews, emblems, bookmarks, permissions management, and more.

You can start File Browser from a number of different places, but the easiest way to launch it is from the Places menu. Click on Places > Home Folder to load your home folder. When the folder loads, you should see something similar to what Figure 3-13 shows.

The File Browser window is split into two parts. The sidebar shows categories of information such as bookmarks, folders, emblems (more on these later), and more. In the main part of the window, you can see the subfolders and files in the current folder. By default, File Browser displays your bookmarks in the left sidebar and displays the contents of your home folder.

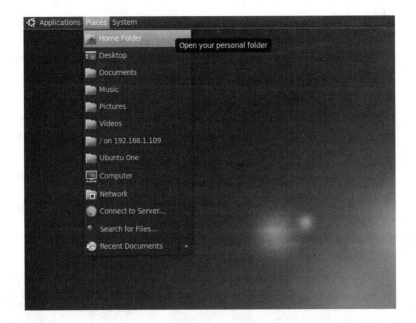

Figure 3-13 Accessing your home folder files is as simple as clicking Places > Home Folder.

So, let's play with File Browser and see what you can do with it. The first important skills to learn involve general file management. Many of the tasks you need to do can be achieved by right-clicking your file/folder and selecting the relevant option. There are also a number of options in the Edit menu.

First, create a folder by right-clicking the main part of the window and selecting Create Folder. A folder is added, and you can type in the name of it. If you change your mind about the name, rename it by right-clicking and selecting Rename. If you double-click on a folder, you can access it and perform the same operations within that folder.

QUICK TIP   Just as folders and directories are the same thing, so are folders and subfolders . . . well, almost. When we refer to subfolders, we are referring to folders contained within another folder. For example, /home is a folder, while we can refer to /home/mako as a subfolder of /home.

File Browser is also flexible in how your files are displayed. You can view the files and folders as either the default collection of icons or as a list. To switch to the list view, select View > View As List. You can also configure the organization of how your files and folders are displayed by right-clicking the main part of the window and selecting one of the options in the Arrange Items menu. Play with each of these options to see which ones work best for you.

QUICK TIP Just like in the file dialog, File Browser displays each of the different parts of the path as different buttons. As an example, /home/mako/work would have three buttons: home, mako, and work.

Selecting, Copying, and Moving Files and Folders

Copying and moving files and folders are simple tasks with File Browser and can be done in a number of different ways. To test this, create two folders called Work and Invoices in your home directory. Save some files inside each folder. You can quickly create empty files by double-clicking the folder to go into it, right-clicking, selecting Create Document > Empty File, and renaming the file to something useful. With a couple of folders now complete with files in them, let's move them around.

One method is to use two windows. Right-click the Work folder, and select Open in new window. You now have two windows open, one with the contents of Work and one with the contents of your home directory. Now copy the Invoices folder to the Work folder by clicking it and dragging it over to the second window (which shows the contents of Work). By default, dragging from one window to another copies the item.

Another option is to select what you want to copy and paste it. Selecting items can again be done in a number of ways. One method is to click each file/folder while holding down the Shift or Ctrl keys to make multiple selections. The difference between the two keys is that Shift allows you to select a number of files and folders next to each other, and Ctrl selects independent files and folders from anywhere in the folder-listing view. When you have selected what should be copied, right-click and select Cut or Copy. Cut will copy the original files but remove them, and Copy will just copy them while leaving the original files intact. Now go to the destination folder, right-click it, and select Paste. The files/folders are now added.

Using the Sidebar

The sidebar in File Browser can be changed to a variety of views that should cater to virtually all tastes. Each of these different sidebar views has a range of functions. Table 3-1 explains each one.

Although you will probably stick with one in particular, it is not uncommon to switch between options to achieve a particular task. For this reason, the flexibility provided by the range of sidebar options is useful. You can find out more about using File Browser at http://live.gnome.org/DocumentationProject/UserGuide/Nautilus, where it is referred to using its official GNOME name, Nautilus.

TIP **Drag and Drop**
If you want to put something in the Places view, drag and drop the item. The Ubuntu desktop is filled with drag-and-drop shortcuts like this. If you think something could be dragged and dropped, try it!

Table 3-1 The Different File Browser Sidebar Options

Option	Feature
Places	(Default view) Includes the devices and bookmarks in the sidebar that you typically see in the File Browser.
Information	Displays some limited information about the current folder.
Tree	Displays a tree view similar to Windows/Mac OS X. Those of you who love the way Windows/Mac OS X works may want to use this.
History	Displays a history of the folders you have clicked on.
Notes	Allows you to write notes in the sidebar that are stored in the folder. This is handy when you need to explain or make comments about the current folder.
Emblems	Lists the files and folders that have specific emblems attached.

Graphically Accessing Remote Files

Within the Ubuntu desktop, you can use the same powerful file manager to manage files that are on a remote server, either on your local network or in far-flung parts of the world via the Internet. This feature is incredibly useful when you need to transfer lots of files around, such as when you work on Web pages or need to make your work remotely available to someone else. To access these files, you can connect to the server in various ways, each of which requires a connection profile. This profile configures the connection, and you need to gather your server's settings to create it.

To set up the connection, click Places > Connect to Server, and you will see the dialog shown in Figure 3-14.

When the dialog box appears, select the type of connection from the combo box. The box then adjusts to display the settings required, and you should make sure the Name to Use for Connection box contains a descriptive name for the connection, such as "Work Server" or "Web Site." When you have added the settings, click the Connect button to continue.

An icon now appears on your desktop for the connection. Double-click the icon, and you are asked for a password to the server. Enter this password, and you are then asked if you would like to store your passwords in the keyring. The desktop keyring provides a convenient place to store all of your connection passwords, and you need to remember only the password

Figure 3-14 Access your remote server's files graphically on your desktop.

for the keyring itself. If you choose to store the password in the keyring, you are asked for a password for it. In the future, whenever you double-click the icon to access the server, you will be asked for the keyring password.

When you have been authenticated to access the server, your files appear in a file manager window, and you can use the file manager as normal.

You can also use File Browser to access Samba and NFS shared drives, FTP servers, remote ssh connections, and more by using the correct prefix in an entry in the Location box, such at ssh://accountname@192.168.1.109 to access an account on a computer at that IP address on your network via ssh. Use smb:// for Samba, nfs:// and ftp:// for those protocols.

QUICK TIP   You can learn more about the protocols File Browser can use to connect to shared storage and how to use them at http://library.gnome.org/users/user-guide/stable/gosnautilus-515. html.en.

Ubuntu and Multimedia

In recent years, multimedia has become an essential part of computing. Watching DVDs and videos and listening to CDs and music have become part and parcel of the modern desktop computer experience. These multimedia capabilities have been further bolstered by the huge popularity of legal music downloading. With a range of online stores for a variety of different types of music, it is not uncommon to listen to most of your music without ever seeing a little shiny silver disk.

Installing Codecs

Multimedia files and disks come in a variety of different types, and each type uses a special codec to compress the content to a smaller size while retaining a particular level of quality. To play this media, you need to ensure that you have the relevant codecs installed. Ubuntu now makes this easier by suggesting packages that provide a suitable codec when you open a file that isn't supported by the ones that are currently installed. Simply double-click the file you want to open, and you should be provided with a list of packages that you can install to enable support for the file you have tried to open. Select the packages that seem appropriate, and click Install.

QUICK TIP   If you double-click a file but no packages are suggested, you may need to change the package filter in the top right-hand corner to All Available Applications.

Codecs still remain a problem for open source software because of the legal restrictions placed upon them. Certain codecs (including MP3, Windows Media Format, QuickTime, and RealMedia) are proprietary and as such have restrictions placed on their use, distribution, and licensing.

Although developers in the open source community have gone away and created free implementations of some of these codecs, the licensing that surrounds them conflicts with the legal and philosophical position that Ubuntu has set. These codecs are excluded not only because they are legally dubious but also because they disagree with Ubuntu's ethic of creating a distribution that consists entirely of free software in the most free sense of the word.

QUICK TIP   If you want to find out more about installing these codecs, see https://help.ubuntu.com/community/RestrictedFormats.

To work toward resolving these problems, a number of developers are working on free codecs such as Ogg Vorbis and Ogg Theora that provide high-quality results and open licensing. The Ogg Vorbis codec is used on audio and can provide better results than MP3 at a smaller file size. The Ogg Theora codec is used for video and competes with the MPEG-4 codec. Ubuntu includes the Ogg Vorbis and Ogg Theora codecs by default, and you can encode and play back any media that uses those codecs out of the box.

Although the world would be a better place if all codecs were free, the reality is different, and many Ubuntu users still want to play media compressed with proprietary codecs. Table 3-2 shows the most typical codecs used to encode and play back media and lists their support in Ubuntu.

Table 3-2 Codec Support

Codec	File Type	Included	Supported
MP3	.MP3	No	Yes
Ogg	.ogg	Yes	N/A
Flac	.flac	Yes	N/A
Windows Media Audio	.wma	No	Yes*
Wave	.wav	Yes	N/A
MPEG-1	.mpg	No	Yes
MPEG-2	.mpg	No	Yes
Raw DV	.dv	Yes	N/A
Quicktime	.mov	No	Yes*
Windows Media Video	.wmv	No	Yes*

* These codecs involve the installation of nonfree software that may or may not be legal in your country.

Listening to Audio Files

Ubuntu includes a powerful music player called Rhythmbox to organize and play your music file collection. By default, Ubuntu will look for music in the Music directory accessible in the Places menu.

Using Rhythmbox Load Rhythmbox (Figure 3-15) by clicking on Applications > Sound & Video > Rhythmbox Music Player. The Rhythmbox window is split into a number of different panes, each displaying different details about your music collection. The left pane (Source) lets you select the source of the music, such as your media library, podcasts, and Internet radio. Each of these options has a browser pane available to display the source of the content. As an example, when you use the Library, one pane displays the artists and one displays the albums. You can use this to navigate your music.

Listening to Podcasts Podcasts are audio shows that you can subscribe to, and they are increasingly becoming the new way to listen to audio and music. When you subscribe to a podcast, each new release is automatically downloaded for you. This makes it extremely convenient to regularly listen to audio shows.

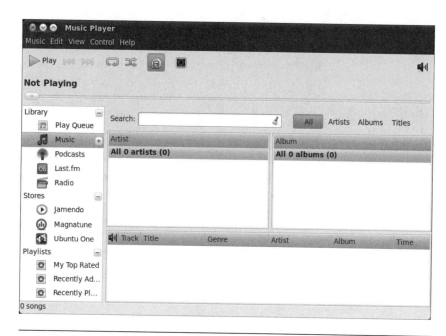

Figure 3-15 Rhythmbox is a great place to look after your music collection.

Rhythmbox has good support for Podcast feeds, and subscribing to a feed is simple. In the sidebar, right-click the Podcasts entry and click New Podcast Feed. Paste in the feed by right-clicking the box and selecting Paste. The files are automatically downloaded, and you can listen to them by double-clicking on them. Each time you start Rhythmbox, a check is made to see if any new episodes exist, and if so, they are downloaded.

NOTE   **Rhythmbox and iPods**
Rhythmbox can also read songs from your iPod—just plug it in and it will display in Rhythmbox. Rhythmbox can read from the iPod but may not be able to write to all iPods.

Playing and Ripping CDs

When you pop a CD into your CD drive, Audio CD Extractor (Sound Juicer) automatically loads to play your CD. If you are connected to the Internet, the CD is looked up on the Internet, and the album details and song titles are displayed.

Ripping Songs as Oggs   Sound Juicer is not just a CD player but a ripper too. Using a ripper you can convert the songs on the CD into files that you can play on your computer. By default, Sound Juicer rips the files in the Ogg format, which provides better sound quality than MP3 at a smaller size. By default, the ripped files are stored in the format discussed earlier, with each artist as a folder and albums as subfolders.

To rip the songs, just select the checkboxes of the songs you want ripped (by default, all songs are selected), and then click Extract. Each song is then stored in your Music folder, and the song titles are used as the names of the files.

Ripping Songs as FLACs   Sound Juicer is capable of supporting the audiophile-preferred FLAC format. Just change the output format in the program's preferences.

Ripping Songs as MP3s   Although the default Ogg support or free FLAC formats are recommended in most situations, you may prefer to rip MP3 files if you have a digital audio player that does not support Ogg or FLAC files. To do this, you need to configure Sound Juicer to enable MP3 support.

You should first use Synaptic to install the gstreamer0.10-plugins-ugly-multiverse package (see Chapter 4 for more details on installing packages). Next, in Sound Juicer, click Edit > Preferences and choose the CD Quality, MP3 (MP3 audio) profile from the Output Format options.

Buying Music

Canonical has added a special new option within Rhythmbox. You may now buy music through the Ubuntu One Music Store alongside Jamendo and Magnatune. While Jamendo and Magnatune are great sources for creative commons and other open-licensed music, for the first time, major and minor label artists will have their music available directly from within Ubuntu. These are the songs you would typically find in your local record shop or on a radio station. Music in the Ubuntu One Music Store will be encoded at a minimum of 256 kbps in MP3 format without any digital rights management (DRM). An Ubuntu One account (mentioned earlier in the chapter) is required to purchase music.

NOTE   You can learn more about the Ubuntu One Music Store at https://wiki.ubuntu.com/UbuntuOne/MusicStore.

Interacting with Photos

F-Spot is a photo management program that you may use to import your pictures, organize them, and perform basic touch-ups like removing red eye, cropping, or simple color adjustment. When F-Spot imports photos, it reads the metadata embedded in the image file and then sorts the images by date. Once done, it creates a timeline that allows you to view photos easily as a group, individually, and even as a full-screen slideshow. You can export your photos individually or in groups directly from F-Spot to well-known Web services like Flickr or Google's Picasa, to a folder, or even to a CD you could give to a friend or family member. You can find F-Spot in the menu at Applications > Graphics > F-Spot Photo Manager. More information about F-Spot is available at https://help.ubuntu.com/community/F-SpotHowto.

Watching Videos

To watch videos in Ubuntu, you need to ensure that you have the correct codecs installed. As discussed earlier, some of these codecs are available separately due to the legal implications of including them with the Ubuntu system. Although the new process for suggesting and installing codecs should cover most popular types of files, you should still refer to the Ubuntu wiki at http://wiki.ubuntu.com for details of how to install ones that are not recognized.

Using Totem   To watch videos in Ubuntu, you use the Totem media player (Figure 3-16). Load it by clicking Applications > Sound & Video > Movie Player.

To watch a video on your hard disk, click Movie > Open, and select the file from the disk.

TIP   **Another Way to Load Files into Totem**
You can also load multimedia files into Totem by double-clicking them on your desktop or in the file manager.

Figure 3-16 Totem is a simple and flexible media player.

Totem also supports video streams. To watch a stream, click Movie > Open Location, and enter the Internet address for the stream. The video feed is then loaded and displayed.

Getting DVDs to Work Ubuntu comes with DVD support for unencrypted DVDs. With the DVD industry being what it is, the majority of DVDs come encrypted, and if you want to watch them, you need to ensure that a library that can decrypt these DVDs is installed. Unfortunately, this library needs to be installed separately and is not included with Ubuntu. Refer to the Ubuntu restricted formats page at https://help.ubuntu.com/community/RestrictedFormats for details.

With the library installed, insert a disk into your computer, and Ubuntu will automatically start Totem to view the disk. Alternatively, fire up Totem, and click Movie > Play Disk to play the DVD. Totem doesn't support DVD menus but you can still use it to play a DVD.

If you are settling down to watch a movie, you may want to configure a few other settings. First click View > Aspect Ratio to select the correct aspect ratio for your screen, and then select View > Fullscreen to switch to full-screen mode. To exit full-screen mode, just move your mouse, and some on-screen controls will appear.

TIP **Control Totem with a Remote Control**
Totem supports the Linux Infrared Control (LIRC) library so you can use a remote control while watching your media.

If you want to use a remote control with your Ubuntu computer, you need to install the Linux Infrared Control (LIRC) package in Synaptic. LIRC is the library, and it supports a wide range of remote control units.

The first step is to determine which LIRC driver is required for your particular remote control. Take a look at the list of remotes on the LIRC site at www.lirc.org, or use your favorite search engine if your remote is not listed on the site.

LIRC includes a number of built-in drivers. You can see which ones are included by running the following command:

```
foo@bar:~$ lircd –driver=help
```

When you know which driver is required and you know your installed LIRC supports your hardware, you can edit the hardware.conf file in the /etc/lirc file to configure which one is used. Simply set the DRIVER line to the driver you selected. Then restart LIRC:

```
foo@bar:~$ /etc/init.d/lirc restart
```

With LIRC ready and running, you can test it by running the following command:

```
foo@bar:~$ /etc/init.d/lirc restart
```

When you press the buttons on your remote control, a code should appear. This code can be mapped to a button on your remote by editing the lircd. conf file in /etc/lirc. For more information, see http://help.ubuntu.com/ community/LIRC.

Creating Videos

PiTiVi is a movie editor that is based on the same media framework as Rhythmbox and Totem, GStreamer. As a result, it handles any video format supported by GStreamer, which makes it very powerful indeed. It has interface options ranging from the simplicity of iMovie to a more complex professional view, as in Complex View. The goal is an easy-to-use but powerful piece of software for taking your video footage from your camera and editing it, adding effects and transitions, and mixing audio to create your own personal cinematic masterpiece. More information about PiTiVi is available at www.pitivi.org. PiTiVi can be found in your menu at Applications > Sound & Video > Pitivi Video Editor.

Exploring the Ubuntu Landscape

Unlike many other operating systems, Ubuntu includes a comprehensive suite of applications right inside the system. This range of tools has been selected to allow you to install Ubuntu and get your work done, communicate with other people, read and create documents, watch and/or listen to media, and more. Unfortunately, due to space restrictions, this book can only skim over the surface of available applications.

To help remedy this a bit, here is a quick summary of many of the applications listed on the Applications menu in Ubuntu, including how to find the applications and a brief description.

- **gedit Text Editor**

  Applications > Accessories > gedit Text Editor

  This simple yet powerful text editor is ideal for editing documents, making quick notes, and programming. Included is a range of plug-ins for spell checking, statistics, file listings, and more.

▪ **Calculator**

Applications > Accessories > Calculator

For those times when you need to figure out a percentage or calculate whether you are getting a raw deal from your employer, the calculator is there. It provides a range of functionality for simple and scientific calculations.

▪ **Terminal**

Applications > Accessories > Terminal

Underpinning the desktop is an incredibly powerful command-line core. This application puts a window around a command-line interface and allows you to configure transparency, fonts, behavior, and more. Essential for the command-line junkies among you.

▪ **Quadrapassel (ex-Gnometris)**

Applications > Games > Quadrapassel

If you have too much time on your hands, a surefire way to waste it is to play this version of Tetris. If you decide that single-player Tetris is not enough, you can install gtetrinet from the Ubuntu Software Center.

▪ **Mahjongg**

Applications > Games > Mahjongg

For those of you who actually understand the rules of Mahjongg, this application provides a great implementation of the game.

▪ **Sound Recorder**

Applications > Sound & Video > Sound Recorder

If you need to record something, such as your voice for a podcast or audio message, you can use this simple tool.

▪ **System Monitor**

System > Administration > System Monitor

To get an idea of the current performance or load on your computer, click on this tool. The System Monitor lets you know which applications are running and how much memory/processing power they are using, and it also allows you to kill or restart processes that are hogging the resources.

▪ **Sudoku**

Applications > Games > Sudoku

The increasingly popular logic game arrives on Ubuntu.

▪ **Disk Usage Analyzer**

Applications > Accessories > Disk Usage Analyzer

Bits and bytes never looked so good! In case you were wondering exactly where all your disk space had gone, this will help solve the mystery.

Other Applications to Try   There are literally thousands of available packages that can be installed on your Ubuntu computer. These packages span a range of different areas, and this section highlights some of the popular ones. Software installation is covered in Chapter 4.

▪ **Inkscape**

Package to install: inkscape

Inkscape (Figure 3-17) is a drawing package for creating Scalable Vector Graphics (SVG). Ever since the SVG format was introduced, it has taken the design world by storm. SVG allows the creation of graphics that can scale to any size. Inkscape is a hugely flexible tool for creating such graphics, and a huge range of icons and artwork in open source projects are made in Inkscape.

▪ **Gimp**

Package to install: gimp

The GIMP Image Editor (Figure 3-18) is a powerful raster or bitmap graphics program that lets you draw, paint, edit images, and much more. It is similar to proprietary graphics programs and has the ability to process and create images using layers, plug-ins, and much more.

Figure 3-17 Inkscape

Figure 3-18 GIMP Image Editor

■ **Blender**

Package to install: blender

Blender (Figure 3-19) is an incredibly powerful 3D modeling, animation, rendering, and production studio. Blender amasses an impressive range of functionality for creating photorealistic scenes, animations, and real-time virtual walkthroughs. Blender is also fully scriptable in Python.

Figure 3-19 Blender

■ **Scribus**

Package to install: scribus

Scribus (Figure 3-20) lets you lay out pages graphically and create publication-ready output in PDF and Postscript formats. It is ideal for newsletters, magazines, technical documentation, and more. It supports CMYK color, Unicode text, and many graphic formats in the creation process.

■ **Bluefish Editor**

Package to install: bluefish

For those of you who want to create Web pages but prefer to write code, Bluefish Editor (Figure 3-21) is a lightweight but feature-rich editor with support for a range of languages as well as HTML and CSS.

Figure 3-20 Scribus

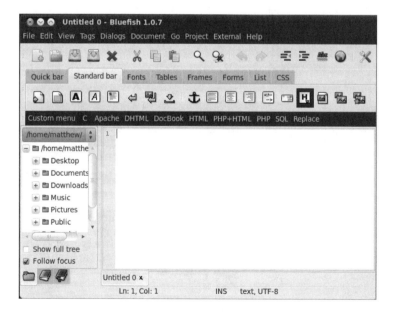

Figure 3-21 Bluefish

▪ **Tracker Search Tool**

Package to install: tracker

Have you ever tried to search your computer for a file, but couldn't remember the file's name? Tracker (Figure 3-22) was created to help in these situations by indexing the contents of your hard drive using the metadata and tags attached to your files and allowing you to search with greater precision and accuracy.

▪ **Audio CD Extractor**

Package to install: sound-juicer

Many of us have legally purchased compact disks that we would like to listen to using our computer or portable music player. Audio CD Extractor (Figure 3-23) will help you record the songs to your hard drive so you may do so. With this package installed, it is also possible to rip a CD from within Rhythmbox, making the process even more convenient.

Figure 3-22 Tracker

Figure 3-23 Sound Juicer: An audio CD extractor

Moving to the Next Ubuntu Release

So your system is up to date and current, but Ubuntu doesn't like to let the grass grow. One of the original goals for Ubuntu was to have frequent releases, and with only one notable exception (the 6.06 LTS release, which was delayed by two months), there have been six months between each release since 4.10. This book has been revised for the latest version—10.04—but another release will be along soon. Release 10.04, like the earlier 8.04 and 6.06, is a Long Term Support (LTS) version of Ubuntu, supported for three years on the desktop and five on the server. All other versions are supported for eighteen months and at the same time are superseded by a new version every six months. Essentially, if you are running the LTS version, you might not be too interested in moving to the latest and greatest until the next LTS version comes out, but if you are running a regular release version, you might be the sort of person who is more interested in the latest and greatest software updates. In either case, this is how you perform the upgrade.

Doing the Actual Upgrade

A graphical tool called Update Manager, found in the System > Administration menu, tells you when a new version of Ubuntu is available and walks you through the upgrade process. Note that if you already know or want to learn the manual method, that is fine too. Both means will achieve the same result.

When a new release is available, Update Manager will alert you, as in Figure 3-24. All you need to do is click on the Upgrade button to start the process. You will first be shown the release notes, which mention new features or any outstanding bugs. After you click on the Upgrade button on

Figure 3-24 Upgrading from Ubuntu 9.10 using Update Manager and an Internet connection

Figure 3-25 Upgrading from Ubuntu 9.10 using a 10.04 CD

this screen, the necessary changes to your software repositories are made, and then the program downloads and installs the new distribution. You may be prompted if you have changed any configuration files. After the actual installation is complete, you will be told which, if any, packages are no longer officially supported by Ubuntu (have moved to the universe repository). Last, all you need to do is restart your computer when prompted, and you will begin enjoying the new release.

You can also initiate an upgrade simply by inserting a CD that contains a newer version of Ubuntu than the one you are currently running, as shown in Figure 3-25. Follow the prompts for an upgrade experience similar to using the update manager.

Summary

In this chapter, you've learned how to start using the core features of your new desktop. These concepts should allow you to perform most of the day-to-day tasks when using your computer and provide a base from which to explore the other applications installed on your system. This solid grounding in the desktop paves the way for you to meander through the rest of the book, learning about the more advanced uses of your new system and exploring the enormous flexibility that Ubuntu provides.

Always remember that there is a wealth of help and documentation available online. If you ever find yourself stuck, take a look at the Ubuntu Web site at www.ubuntu.com or the Ubuntu documentation at http://help.ubuntu.com and make use of the forums, wiki, mailing lists, and IRC channels. Much of this is easily found in links provided for you in System > About Ubuntu in your menu.

CHAPTER 4

Gaining Greater Proficiency

- Adding and Removing Programs and Packages
- Keeping Your Computer Updated
- Adding Additional Users
- Using and Abusing Devices and Media
- Configuring a Printer in Ubuntu
- How Linux Stores and Organizes Files
- The Terminal
- Backup Strategies
- Working with Windows Programs
- Summary

AS YOU'VE SEEN SO FAR, Ubuntu is relatively straightforward to set up and use for the common day-to-day tasks. With time, though, most users want to change their software, add and experiment with other software options available in Ubuntu, install and use hardware devices like printers, access remote files, use the famous (and sometimes feared) terminal, and maybe even run some Windows programs. Ubuntu provides many ways to do each of these things. While they are a little more complex than the material covered in previous chapters, the Ubuntu community has worked hard to make them as easy as possible, and this chapter gets you started with each of them and more.

Adding and Removing Programs and Packages

While Ubuntu already includes the things most people need, sometimes you want or need something extra, such as a desktop publishing application for school or a game to pass the time. The easiest way to add these is with Ubuntu Software Center, which is extremely simple to use but has a few limitations. This section also highlights a couple of other options. Work done using one tool to add or remove software is recognized by the related tools, so it is okay to mix and match which ones you use.

Using Ubuntu Software Center

Like other tools discussed later in this chapter, Ubuntu Software Center installs software from the online Ubuntu software repositories.

To launch Ubuntu Software Center, simply click on the entry at the bottom of the Applications menu. When it is run for the first time, and occasionally afterward, it will take a few moments to initialize itself and the list of available and installed applications. Once this is complete, you will see the main screen shown in Figure 4-1.

The interface is divided into two parts. On the left are options to see what software is already installed or to get new software. If you highlight the Get Software option, the right panel provides you with a list of software categories to explore, including a Featured category that includes some of the more popular choices for software available from the Ubuntu repositories but not installed by default, as in Figure 4-2. To get more information or to

Figure 4-1 Ubuntu Software Center main screen

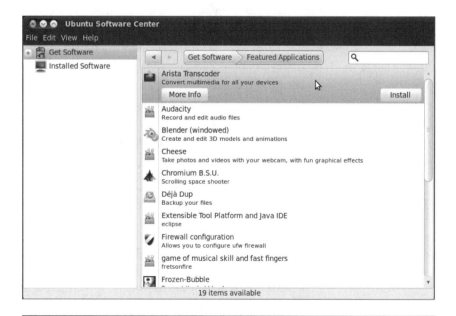

Figure 4-2 Featured applications in Ubuntu Software Center

install an item, click on the appropriate option. It really is that easy. To navigate back to the main menu, simply click the previous option from the hierarchy at the top of the pane or Get Software from the list in the left pane.

By default, Ubuntu Software Center shows all applications that are supported by Ubuntu, including those supported by community volunteers called MOTUs (more on them in Chapter 7). While using Ubuntu Software Center to install new applications from both the officially supported Ubuntu-provided repositories as well as the community repositories is perfect for most users, there are times when a more conservative approach to software choices may be appropriate. In this case, you may limit the number of applications shown from the View menu by selecting Canonical-Maintained Applications in order to see only those pieces of software that are actively watched over and updated by Canonical, the company behind Ubuntu. This is sometimes preferred in corporate environments that desire or require a stronger guarantee of support.

Terminology

You might want to know a few terms before we continue. These are words used to describe how the software gets installed on your machine as well as how the system works.

- **APT:** Advanced Package Tool, or APT, describes the entire system of online repositories and the parts that download them and install them. This is not highly visible when using graphic interface–based systems like Ubuntu Software Center but very clear when using command-line tools like apt-get or aptitude. Either way, APT is at work.

- **Repositories or software channels:** In the Ubuntu world, these giant online warehouses of software are divided between official Ubuntu repositories and unofficial ones.

- **Packages:** Applications are stored in packages that not only describe the program you want to install but also tell your package manager what the program needs to run and how to safely install and uninstall it. This makes the process of dealing with software dependencies smooth and easy for end users.

  ▪ **Dependencies:** Dependencies comprise the software that is needed as
    a foundation for other software to run. For example, APT is needed
    for Ubuntu Software Center to run because APT takes care of many
    of the details behind the scenes.

Managing Software with Synaptic

Synaptic is a powerful graphical tool called a package manager. While
Ubuntu Software Center deals with packages that contain applications,
Synaptic deals with all packages, including applications, system libraries,
and other pieces of software. Changing the system on this level is more
complicated but also allows more detailed control. For instance, you can
choose to install a specific library if you need it for a program that is not
available in a package format.

TIP **What's a Library?**
In this context, a library is a collection of software functions that may be useful to more than
one program. This collection is put into a separate package to save space by not forcing
multiple programs to include the same code but instead simply refer to the library when a
certain function the library contains is needed. It also makes updates easier, such as when a
security issue is fixed, because the programming code may be changed in one place while
benefiting all programs that use the function. Libraries streamline software support to be
more efficient.

Synaptic may be found at System > Administration > Synaptic Package Manager. Launch it and you will see the main window, as shown in Figure 4-3.

TIP **What's in a Name?**
Why the name Synaptic? *Synaptic* is a play on words, based on your brain's synapses and
the word APT.

Installing a Package   As with Ubuntu Software Center, installing packages with Synaptic is fairly easy. After you find the package you wish to
install, click the checkbox to the right of the name of the package and select
Mark for Installation. A dialog box may pop up (Figure 4-4) showing you
what dependencies need to be installed—if any—which you can accept by

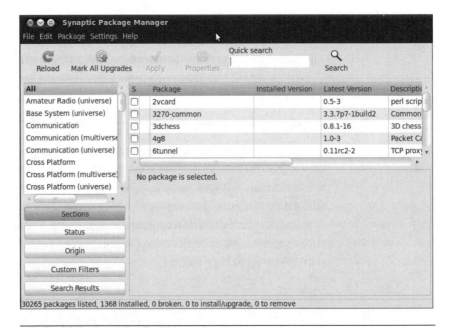

Figure 4-3 Synaptic main window

Figure 4-4 Pop-up on Mark for Installation

clicking the Mark button. After you have selected all the package(s) you wish to install, click Apply on the Synaptic toolbar to begin installation.

Removing a Package   To remove a package, click on the green box, and choose Mark for Removal. As with installing a package, you may be asked to mark additional packages for removal (Figure 4-5). These are generally packages that depend on the presence of the main package you are marking for removal. If you wish to remove all the configuration files too, choose Mark for Complete Removal. After you have selected the packages you wish to remove, click Apply on the toolbar to start the actual process of removing the package.

Finding That Package   So you are looking for a package but don't know where to start? The fastest and easiest way is to simply enter a word in the Quick Search box at the top center of the Synaptic window. You can also click the Search button on the toolbar or type Ctrl+F to launch a search dialog box. By default, the regular search looks at both the package name and the description, but it can also search just by name or a number of other fields.

If you know what section the package is in, select it in the left pane (you may need to go back to the Sections pane). Select the button in the lower left labeled Sections, and browse through the packages in that section.

In addition to Sections, there are other package listing and sorting options worth exploring that you may access using the buttons at the bottom left of the Synaptic window. Status lets you sort according to installation status. Origin sorts according to the repository from which the software was installed (or no repository for manually installed software, see the section

Figure 4-5 Pop-up on Mark for Removal

later in this chapter on installing software that is not in a repository). You can even make custom filters to aid your search.

Keeping Your Computer Updated

No operating system or piece of software is perfect. Because of this, Ubuntu developers will release security and other updates as needed. These are placed into the Ubuntu repositories and are quite easy to install.

Most of the updates to your machine will be security related. This means that the developers have found a weakness in a particular program in Ubuntu and have released a fix for it. There will also be a small number of updates to fix some critical bugs. For a home user, there is generally no reason not to install these right away, as not installing them might leave your computer open to security breaches. While Ubuntu is significantly more secure from the main concerns of some operating systems, such as fears involving viruses and spyware, no computer is perfectly secure because no software is perfect. When problems are discovered that could lead to security issues, like buffer overflows or remote exploits, they are fixed and released as quickly as possible, even if the danger is quite remote. Ubuntu developers also have a very strict policy about not putting new release versions of programs with function changes or new features into stable versions of Ubuntu. This practice keeps your system more stable by not introducing new problems.

Installing Updates

Helpfully, Ubuntu checks the Ubuntu repositories once a day to see if there are any new versions of software you have installed, and it tells you when you need to update your machine.

Ubuntu 10.04 handles package updates by launching update-manager. Users are notified of security updates on a daily basis and are also notified when new Ubuntu versions are released. Because 10.04 is an LTS release, by default it will only notify of new LTS releases, meaning that it would likely be silent until April 2012. This behavior may be changed using System > Administration > Update Manager and clicking Settings.

Learning about What Was Updated

The update window, shown in Figure 4-6, will also show you specifically what is going to be fixed. In the details pane, it will show you what got fixed and how. It might also list a CVE number. The CVE number is a unique identifier for a security vulnerability. You can look it up on http://cve.mitre.org to see what the exact flaw was. However, most people don't need to worry (and really don't care) about these details.

I Want to Install an Application That Is Not in the Repositories

Although the repositories contain a huge selection of packages, sometimes the package you need is not included. The first thing you should check is that you have enabled the additional repositories such as universe and multiverse. You can do this from your menu at System > Administration > Software Sources. In the Ubuntu Software tab, ensure that the boxes are

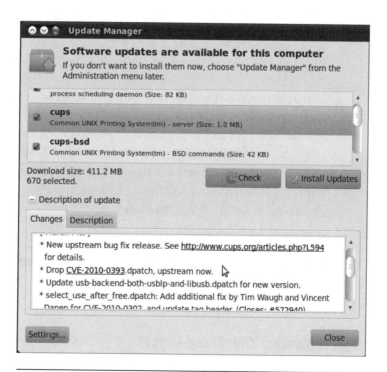

Figure 4-6 The update window

checked for main, universe, restricted, and multiverse. (See help.ubuntu.com/community/Repositories/Ubuntu for more details.)

TIP   **The Repository Run-Down**

The *universe* repository contains the thousands of packages that are part of the Debian distribution upon which Ubuntu is based. All of these packages are entirely free and supported by a community of Ubuntu contributors.

The *multiverse* repository contains a number of packages that are freely available to download but are not fully open source. If you want to run only open source software, you may not want to use this repository.

If you have enabled these extra repositories and your package is still not there, have a quick hunt around with a search engine to see if you can find a repository (known as a Debian or APT repository) for your package. If you find one, use the Repositories dialog box you have just played with to add the new repository, and then use Synaptic to install the package.

One common type of extra repository you may encounter is called a PPA, or personal package archive. There is good information available for using PPAs at https://help.launchpad.net/Packaging/PPA/InstallingSoftware .

If no repository is available, look for a Debian package (.deb) for the application, most likely available from the software company's Web site, such as Adobe does with its Reader software or Skype with its VOIP software. If you find one, download it, and double-click it to install. If no Debian package exists, look for an Autopackage. (An upcoming subsection, "I Downloaded an Autopackage, but I Don't Know How to Run It," provides details about Autopackage installation.)

Finally, if all else fails, you may need to download the source code and compile it using instructions found at https://help.ubuntu.com/community/CompilingSoftware.

Changing Your Menu Layout

Although the main Applications, Places, and System menus are logical by default, you may want to further customize them by moving entries into different submenus, not displaying certain items, and making other tweaks. All of this is easily done with the built-in menu editor.

To edit the menus, open the option at System > Preferences > Main Menu or right click on one of the menus and choose Edit Menus. Using either method, the menu editor will appear, as shown in Figure 4-7.

The menu editor is fairly intuitive. To adjust which items are shown, click on a submenu in the left-hand pane and change the Show checkbox for the items you want to show or hide. To add a new item, select the submenu the item should appear in, and then click the New Item button on the right-hand side. The box shown in Figure 4-8 will appear.

Menu items can be applications (the default), applications running in terminals, or files. Select the appropriate setting for the Type box for your menu item, or leave it as Application. Provide a name for your menu item

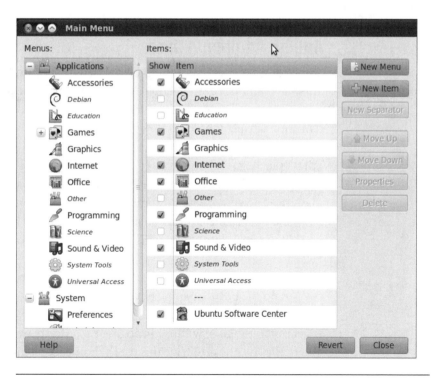

Figure 4-7 The menu editor lets you easily change the Ubuntu menus.

Figure 4-8 Feel free to add your own menu items.

in the Name box, the command to run in the Command box (or the location of your file in the Location box if you changed the type to File), and a brief description in the Comment box. You can also use the Browse button to select the application to run (or the file to open). Finally, click the default icon off to the side, and select an icon for the item. Click OK to finish adding the new menu item.

Adding Additional Users

Some computer systems end up being used by only one person, but many are shared among several people. When more than one person uses a computer system, it is always a good idea to create a unique account on the system for each person. This also gives everyone who uses the system the freedom to customize their experience without affecting the experience of other users (e.g., each user may choose her own desktop wallpaper or theme and it won't change the preferences of others). This also means that you may create accounts with administrative privileges for people you trust to make changes to the entire system and less privileged accounts for people who do not need this power. This keeps your system more secure.

To add additional users, select System > Administration > Users and Groups. In the box that appears, click the Add button in the lower left corner. In the Create New User dialog box, enter the new user's name and a short name the user will use to login (e.g., Matthew Helmke and matt). You may also choose to have this user's /home folder encrypted as it is created. After you click OK, you will have a chance to enter a password for this user or to generate a random password.

You can even click the option to not ask for a password from this user when he logs in, but we don't recommend that unless this is going to be an account without administrative privileges and will be the default for booting in a very special case, such as a computer used primarily by children with a limited account but with an administrative account used by an adult for occasional maintenance.

Once you click OK on the password box, the account will be created and listed in the Users Settings window. By default, the account created is that of a normal user. If you want to give this new user the ability to administer the system, or other privileges, highlight the user's name in the list on the left and then click Advanced Settings at the bottom right. You can change the user's contact information, privileges, and more from here.

You may also delete users, change and manage user groups and memberships, and more from this location.

If you would prefer to do this from the terminal, use the `adduser` command while logged in to an account with administrative privileges:

```
matt@laptop:~$ sudo adduser corey
```

After you enter your password, this will add a new user named `corey`. You will be asked several questions in the process. Answer them, and at the end, the account will be created.

To delete a user from the command line, use the `deluser` command in place of `adduser` in the above example. You can learn more about dealing with users from the command line in the appendix.

Using and Abusing Devices and Media

Using devices like USB memory sticks or burning CDs in Ubuntu is simple and intuitive. In the vast majority of cases, you just plug them in and they work. Each device needs to be mounted before it can be used, but Ubuntu automatically mounts it for you. The main point to remember is to always unmount the device before you remove it. Unmounting a device ensures all data has been copied to it before you pull it out.

If at any time you are unsure which devices are plugged into your computer, click Places > Computer to see a list of the drives available.

Using USB Keyring Drives

In the last few years, USB keyrings, pens, and sticks have taken over as the common method for moving files between different computers. These cheap and often high-capacity little devices offer a simple and efficient way to carry your files with you. Although they come in many different shapes and forms, they all basically work the same way in Ubuntu.

Using USB storage devices in Ubuntu is a piece of cake. Just plug them in and a moment or two later, an icon representing the device appears on your desktop. A file manager window also appears to display the contents of the device. You can interact with the device and the files as you would with the files on your hard disk. With some types of files on the drive, a helpful dialog box may appear offering to start a specific program relating to that file type for you so that you may begin working with the file(s) quickly.

When you have finished using your USB device, right-click the device icon that appeared on your desktop and select Unmount. When the icon disappears from your desktop, you can safely remove it from the USB port.

Burning CDs

Burning files is simple in Ubuntu with its built-in support for CD writers. Simply place a writable CD into the drive, and an icon appears on the desktop. Double-click the icon, and an empty file manager window appears. Now drag the files to be burned into this window. When you are ready to burn the CD, click File > Write to Disk.

A dialog box appears, and you can configure a few items before the disk is burned. Enter a name for the disk in the Disk Name box, and use the Write

Speed combo box to select the best write speed for your drive. If you have an old or unreliable CD writer, you may want to select a slower speed to prevent a burn error. Finally, click the Write Disk button to start the burn.

QUICK TIP   You can also access the burner by clicking Places > CD/DVD Burner.

Burning a CD from an Image   With more and more people downloading open source software, installation disks are often released as downloadable .iso files. When you burn these files to a CD, the files from the disk image are restored and the resulting CD looks just like a normal CD.

To burn an .iso file to a CD, simply right-click it and select Write to Disk.

TIP   **More Complex Burning**
A very useful and capable program for working with CDs and DVDs, Brasero, has been installed by default. You will find it in the menu at Applications > Sound & Video > Brasero Disc Burner. Brasero is capable of creating audio CDs, data CDs and DVDs, video project DVDs and SVCDs, burning images to disks, and copying disks.

Using Floppy Disks

They aren't seen much anymore, but you can use a floppy disk in Ubuntu. Just insert the disk in the drive. If a file manager window doesn't come up automatically, you can select Places > Computer from the menu and double-click on your floppy drive to mount it and display the files. When you have finished using the disk, right-click the floppy drive and select Unmount.

Using Digital Cameras

When you plug a digital camera into your computer, a device icon automatically appears on your desktop, and Ubuntu pops up a window asking if you want to view the photos from your camera. You can then view the photos and drag them from the photo viewer window over to a file manager window to save the photo.

The majority of digital cameras are actually just USB devices, and you can access the photos on them just like any other USB device, from within the file manager.

TIP   **Ubuntu and Digital Photography**

Ubuntu is a fantastic platform for digital photography and photo manipulation. F-Spot tool provides a complete solution for managing your photo collection and can be started by clicking on Applications > Graphics > F-Spot Photo Manager. Chapter 3 has more information on how to use F-spot.

For photo manipulation, GIMP provides a comprehensive tool and can be installed quickly from Ubuntu Software Center. Once installed, it can be found at Applications > Graphics > GIMP Image Editor.

Configuring a Printer in Ubuntu

In the Linux world, configuring a printer has traditionally been a challenge. For years, newcomers to Linux have been repeatedly challenged and even bludgeoned with scary terms, commands, and phrases that sound like a language from another planet. Users often had to edit fairly complex text files by hand and spend a good deal of time learning how to insert arcane instructions just to get a printer to work. However, things have changed with Ubuntu.

Most of the time, it is possible to add or configure a printer easily and quickly. The one caveat is that not all printer manufacturers provide Linux drivers for their devices. While the Linux community works very hard to write drivers, many times the newest printer models do not have adequate software to interact with Linux. Most printers that are older than 6 or 9 months seem to work quite well, though. You can also check before buying a printer to see what other people have experienced by looking at the list of models and the state of their drivers at http://www.openprinting.org/printers. The Linux Foundation maintains that list, which is a pretty good gauge for determining how well your model should work out of the box with Ubuntu, making this an excellent resource when shopping for new hardware as well as useful for troubleshooting when problems are encountered.

To get started installing your printer, go to System > Administration > Printing (Figure 4-9).

Selecting this option will bring up the Printers window, as shown in Figure 4-10.

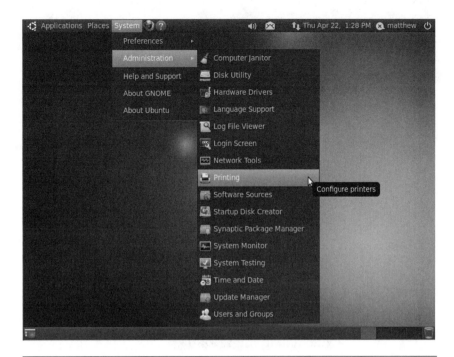

Figure 4-9 Selecting the Printing application from the System > Administration menu in Ubuntu

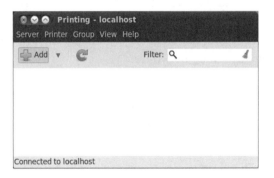

Figure 4-10 The GNOME Printers dialog box

The Printer configuration application allows you to add printers as well as modify their settings. In the upcoming example, you will add a new printer and then view its settings.

Gathering Information

The most important thing to remember when configuring a printer is to not get ahead of yourself. Before you start clicking on icons and running anything, make sure that you have completed the following steps.

1. Note the make and model of the printer. This information is usually printed clearly on the hardware itself. In our example, we add a Brother MFC-7820N.

2. Plug the printer in to your computer or to the network, and turn it on.

Launching the Wizard

Once you have properly prepared to install your printer, click on the New Printer icon. The system will then automatically search for any new connected printers and will launch a New Printer wizard, shown in Figure 4-11.

In most cases, the wizards will be able to detect an attached printer automatically and will include it in a list of devices on the left. If your printer is plugged directly into a router, it is possible for the printer Wizard to find it by selecting Find Network Printer.

Select the device with your printer's name, and then hit forward.

At this point, you will have to choose a printer manufacturer. If your printer has been automatically detected, the wizard will choose a manufacturer. Click forward.

In the next screen, you'll be asked to choose both a model and a driver. For autodetected printers, both should be automatically selected, and the default driver should work. You can always change it later. If no driver is selected, scroll through the list of options by manufacturer. Figure 4-12 shows that a driver for the Brother MFC-7820N has been selected.

Figure 4-11   Step 1, selecting a printer

Figure 4-12   Step 2, selecting a driver

Sometimes you may not find the exact model or driver for your specific printer. Generally, if the driver does not exist for your exact model, choose the closest one, and then test it. If that doesn't work, you can try other drivers intended for printers from the same manufacturer.

Click Forward to proceed with the installation. If you need to install a custom driver, click the Install Driver button. You can see this button in Figure 4-12.

Finally, you can enter a description and location for your printer, as shown in Figure 4-13. Click Apply to complete the process and set up your printer.

Mission Accomplished!

After you click Apply, you will see your printer's name under the Local Printers heading. You can click on it and then print out a test page. Do so, and make sure that the page prints correctly. If you find that the page prints well, you are finished. You can now print from the applications you

Figure 4-13 Step 3, entering printer location and description

have installed. For example, you can print from OpenOffice.org, Mozilla, or even the command line.

Remote Printing

You can also configure your Ubuntu system to send print jobs to a remote print server. If, for example, you have a Windows system with a printer attached on your network, simply choose the Network Printer radio button and specify the host name or IP address of the Windows system. You will then have to specify a connection protocol.

If your Windows system is sharing a printer, you will have to specify Samba, which is the standard way to get Linux and Windows systems to communicate with each other. You will still have to specify a print driver, as described earlier.

How Linux Stores and Organizes Files

If you have not used Linux before, the way that Linux stores and organizes files is likely to be new to you because the layout is quite different from Windows and Mac OS X.

TIP **Folders and Directories**
When reading about file management, don't get confused by the terms *folders* and *directories*—*both* words describe the same thing.

In the Windows world, each disk drive is labeled with an identifying letter such as C: for your hard disk and A: for the floppy drive. In the Linux world, however, everything is part of the same filesystem organization. As such, if you have two or three hard disks, a CD drive, and a USB stick all plugged in, they will all be part of the same folder structure.

The diagram shown in Figure 4-14 should give you an idea of how everything hangs together.

Right at the top of the tree is the root folder, referred to as /. Inside this folder are a number of special system folders, each with a specific use. As an example, the /home folder contains a number of home directories for each

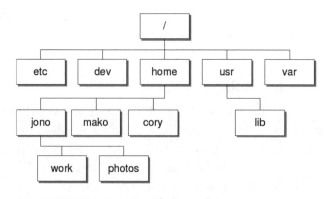

Figure 4-14 Linux filesystem organization

user on the system. As such, the mako user account has the home folder set to /home/mako.

Which Folder Does What?   The folder structure in a modern Linux distribution such as Ubuntu was largely inspired by the original UNIX foundations that were created by men with large beards. Although you don't really need to know what these folders do, since Ubuntu looks after the housekeeping for you, some of you may be interested in the more important folders. For your pleasure, we present the Linux folder hit list in Table 4-1.

Configuration Files   In Table 4-1, /etc is described as storing systemwide configuration files for your computer. Aside from these files that affect everyone, there are also configuration files for each specific user. Earlier, when you customized Ubuntu's look and feel, the settings were applied only to your current user account. So where are those settings stored?

Inside your home directory are a number of folders that begin with a dot (.), such as .gnome2 and .openoffice.org. These folders contain the configuration settings for user-specific applications. By default, these dot folders are hidden in Nautilus because you rarely need to access them. For future reference, you can view these hidden files and folders by clicking View > Show Hidden Files or by pressing Ctrl+H.

Table 4-1 Linux Folders

Folder	Use
/boot	This folder contains important files to boot the computer, including the bootloader configuration and the kernel.
/dev	Each device on your system (such as sound cards, Webcams, etc.) has an entry in this folder. Each application accesses the device by using the relevant items inside /dev.
/etc	Systemwide configuration files for the software installed on your system are stored here.
/home	Each user account on the system has a home directory that is stored here.
/lib	Important system software libraries are stored here. You should never need to delve into this world of the unknown.
/media	Media devices such as CD drives and USB sticks are referenced here when they are plugged in. More on this later.
/mnt	Other devices can be mounted too. Again, more on this later.
/opt	Optional software can be installed here. This folder is usually used when you want to build your own software. If you don't build your own software, you ignore this folder.
/proc/sys	Information about the current running status of the system is stored here.
/root	This is the home directory for the main superuser.
/bin	Software that is vital for the system to be able to boot is stored here.
/sbin	Software that should be run only by the superuser is stored here.
/usr	General software is installed here.
/var	This folder contains log files about the software on your computer.

Using Windows Files on Another Partition

For those of you who spend a considerable amount of your life on Windows partitions, you may want to be able to access these partitions from Ubuntu. This is no problem, although you will need to edit a special configuration file to do this. Luckily, you need to edit this file only once, and then everything will be set up.

Ubuntu should automatically recognize any Windows partitions you have on your computer and set them up for you; however, you may need to modify them or add your own. You should first open System > Administration > Disk Utility and write down the partition numbers and filesystem for your Windows partitions. The partition number will look something like /dev/hdb1 or /dev/sdb1, and the filesystem will be either FAT, VFAT, or NTFS.

The next step is to create some mount points. When your Windows partitions are enabled, they are accessed via a particular folder in Ubuntu. This is called a mount point. As an example, if you have a mount point as /media/win1 and on your Windows partition you want to access your Work folder, you would access it from Ubuntu as /media/win1/work.

Mount points usually live in the /media folder. Create a different mount point for each Windows partition. As an example, if you have three Windows partitions, run the following commands:

```
foo@bar:~$ sudo mkdir /media/win1
foo@bar:~$ sudo mkdir /media/win2
foo@bar:~$ sudo mkdir /media/win3
```

Now open up the following configuration file:

```
foo@bar:~$ sudo gedit /etc/fstab
```

The /etc/fstab file maps partition numbers to mount points. At the bottom of the file, add a line like this for each mount point:

```
/dev/hdb1 media/win1 vfat users,rw,owner,umask=000 0 0
```

You will need to change the partition number (the first column), mount point (second column), and filesystem (third column) for your relevant partitions.

Now reload /etc/fstab to enable the partitions:

```
foo@bar:~$ sudo mount -a
```

Some hard disk icons for the new partitions now appear.

TIP   You can find more about fstab at https://help.ubuntu.com/community/Fstab.

The Terminal

Although Ubuntu is a desktop-driven OS, the system is running on a powerful and incredibly flexible command-line core. Inspired by more than 30 years of UNIX heritage, the command-line environment present on Linux systems enables you to perform some incredibly powerful tasks by stringing together different commands in different ways.

The philosophy behind UNIX is to create a large number of small tools, each of which is designed to do one task but do it incredibly well. As a quick example to whet your appetite, there is a command called `ls` that does nothing more than list files in a folder. Although listing files is its singular function in life, it has every option imaginable for listing files.

Now, `ls` is limited by itself, but it can be combined with other commands that have equal levels of flexibility to create impressively powerful combinations. To do this, a *pipeline* is created using the | symbol to connect these different commands. Pipelines can be constructed in any number of different ways, and once the user has even a basic knowledge of what a few different commands do, stringing together a pipeline of commands can solve virtually any task you can imagine in quick and powerful ways.

It should be made 100 percent clear that using the command line is *not* an essential skill required to use Ubuntu, but it is a skill that can increase the flexibility of your computer for more advanced, customized tasks. Rather than cover the use of the terminal here, we have included an excellent introduction in the appendix.

Backup Strategies

Everyone who has used a computer for any length of time has heard the advice, "Backup, backup often, test the backups, repeat." Few people actually do it. Ignoring this advice is dangerous and can cause the loss of important documents, files, pictures, and more.

To prevent this loss, prudent computer users, regardless of operating system, will pick a method of copying their files to a safe location for storage and will use that method on a regular basis. To help you devise a strategy that best suits you, we have come up with a few options to consider. This topic is a big one, and how you deal with it is a very personal decision. Rather than give step-by-step instructions, we mention a few options to consider and leave it to you to research them further and decide on one that looks appropriate and inviting.

Some users find that the easiest thing for them to do is copy all of their files to a CD-R or DVD-R every week or two. Others buy an external hard drive and do the same thing. Either of these methods is effective and easy enough for anyone to do.

Others will look at this and think to themselves, "There has to be a better way." Perhaps they noticed that these methods require every single file to be copied every time, even if the file has not changed in ages. In these cases, an incremental backup is ideal, where the computer is told to compare the files in the original location with stored files in a backup location (like an external hard drive) and copy only new or changed files.

Several graphic user interface programs for backing up are available from the Ubuntu repositories. Each comes with a basic and useful graphic interface that is easy to figure out and use, and each is configurable to allow you to do full or incremental backups. The most commonly recommended one is Simple Backup Suite, available in Ubuntu Software Center in the System Tools section, with both a backup configuration and backup restore entry.

For those users who are a little more advanced (or a little braver) and who love the raw power available from learning a command-line program, the best two programs for backups are rar and rsync, which are both available from the Ubuntu repositories. Once they are installed, you can read the manual page and learn how to use them by typing man rar or man rsync from a terminal. They are complicated but are also fast and amazingly effective both at making the backups and restoring them.

Unfortunately, this quick mention in a small section of a very diverse chapter can only get you thinking about the need for good backups and help guide you in your search for the perfect method for you. However you decide to back up your data, we strongly encourage you not to ignore the need but to find a way to do it. If you have any questions about this or other topics, the Ubuntu community has a large number of very helpful people you can ask for help, and we recommend you start by searching or asking questions in the Ubuntu Forums at http://ubuntuforums.org/.

TIP   You can find more backup ideas and information at https://help.ubuntu.com/community/BackupYourSystem.

Working with Windows Programs

Although Linux offers an increasingly compelling platform for the desktop, some situations arise when there is just no alternative other than an application written for Windows. This is generally the case with specific business applications, some educational tools, and many games. Luckily, there is a way you can run many of these applications on your Ubuntu desktop.

For more than fifteen years, the Wine project team members have been working to create a free way to run Windows applications on Linux. While not every application works perfectly, and some don't work at all, the number of programs that do work in Wine has dramatically increased and continues to do so. However, it is recommended that you thoroughly test the applications you want to run in Wine before you use them for important work, and if you run into trouble, try consulting help resources, use virtualization to run Windows on top of Ubuntu, or search for a different application to use.

TIP   You can find some useful help resources for Wine at www.winehq.org/help/, and you can learn more about alternatives to Wine at www.winehq.org/docs/wineusr-guide/alternatives.

Install the Wine package from the System Tools section of the Ubuntu Software Center or simply double-click an .exe file, and you will be prompted to install the package. You can configure Wine at System > Preferences > Wine Applications. Your C:\ Drive will appear in your Places menu for easy access, and you will be able to uninstall Wine from the Ubuntu Software Center.

Running Applications

To run an application, simply double-click on the install .exe file. Once installed, the program should appear in your menu under Applications > Wine.

TIP   You can find even more about Wine from the Ubuntu perspective at https://help.ubuntu.com/community/Wine.

Summary

In this chapter we looked at a variety of different advanced subjects related to running and managing your Ubuntu system. Installation, removal, and upgrade of software using the Ubuntu Software Center and other options were discussed. We also looked at the installation and use of several different types of hardware devices. We perused some of the methods of accessing remote files and mentioned the powerful Ubuntu terminal and the need for learning how to back up your data regularly. Finally, we looked at a possibility of running certain programs written for Microsoft Windows under Ubuntu.

CHAPTER 5

The Ubuntu Server

- What Is Ubuntu Server?
- Installing Ubuntu Server
- Ubuntu Package Management
- Ubuntu Server Security
- Advanced Topics
- Summary

UBUNTU 4.10, LOVINGLY KNOWN AS WARTY WARTHOG, was the first public version of Ubuntu. Its installation media provided no obvious way to install the bare-bones OS without a full desktop environment. The system administrator crowds, easily irritable and feisty by nature, were greatly annoyed: They proclaimed Ubuntu was just a desktop distribution and sauntered back to their caves in contempt.

The next release of Ubuntu that came out, Hoary Hedgehog, rectified the problem and allowed for trivial installation of a minimal Ubuntu version suitable for servers. Yet the myth of Ubuntu as a purely desktop-oriented distribution stuck.

Luckily, the sentiment is just that—a myth. Ubuntu is a world-class server platform today, providing everything you'd expect from a server OS and with the human flavor that makes Ubuntu different. The dedicated hackers on the Ubuntu Server Team tend to the minutiae of hardware support and testing, mercilessly beat on the latest version of server software to make sure it's up to snuff for inclusion in the distribution, look for ways to push innovation into the server field, and are available to users like you to field feedback, questions, and cries of anguish.

That said, setting up a server is no small task. Server administrators constantly deal with complex issues such as system security, fault tolerance, and data safety, and while Ubuntu makes these issues more pleasant to deal with, they're not to be taken lightly. The aim of this chapter is thus not to teach you how to be a system administrator—we could easily fill a dozen books attempting to do that—but to give you a quick crash course. We'll also highlight the specific details that set Ubuntu Server apart from other server platforms, offer tips on some of the most common server uses, and give you pointers on where to find other relevant information.

What Is Ubuntu Server?

By far the most common reaction from users first encountering Ubuntu Server is one of utter and hopeless confusion. People are foggy on whether Ubuntu Server is a whole new distribution or an Ubuntu derivative like Kubuntu (only for servers) or perhaps something else entirely.

Let's clear things up a bit. The primary software store for Ubuntu and official derivatives is called the Ubuntu archive. The archive is merely a collection of software packages in Debian "deb" format, and it contains every single package that makes up distributions such as Ubuntu, Edubuntu, Xubuntu, Kubuntu, and Ubuntu Server. What makes Kubuntu separate from Ubuntu, then, is only the set of packages from the archive that its installer installs by default and that its CDs carry.

Ubuntu Server is no different. It depends on the very same archive as the standard Ubuntu distribution, but it installs a distinctive set of default packages. Notably, the set of packages comprising Ubuntu Server is very small. The installer will not install things such as a graphical environment or many user programs by default. But since all the packages for Ubuntu Server come from the same official Ubuntu archive, you can install any package you like later. In theory, there's nothing stopping you from transforming an Ubuntu Server install into a regular Ubuntu desktop installation or vice versa (in practice, this is tricky, and we don't recommend you try it). You can even go from running Kubuntu to running Ubuntu Server. The archive paradigm gives you maximum flexibility.

We've established that Ubuntu Server just provides a different set of default packages than Ubuntu. But what's important about that different set? What makes Ubuntu Server a server platform?

The most significant difference is a custom server kernel. This kernel employs an internal timer frequency of 100Hz instead of the desktop default of 250Hz, uses the deadline I/O scheduler instead of the desktop's CFQ scheduler, and contains a batch of other minor tweaks for virtualization, memory support, and routing. We'll spare you the OS theory: The idea is to offer some extra performance and throughput for server applications. In addition, the server kernel supports basic NUMA, a memory design used in some multiprocessor systems that can dramatically increase multiprocessing performance.

So what else is different in Ubuntu Server? Other than the server kernel and a minimal set of packages, not too much. Though Ubuntu has supported a minimal installation mode for a number of releases, spinning off Ubuntu Server into a separate product that truly stands on its own is still a young effort, but one that's moving along very quickly.

Starting with Ubuntu Server 6.06 LTS, known as Dapper Drake, Ubuntu Server offers officially supported packages for the Red Hat Cluster Suite, Red Hat's Global File System (GFS), Oracle's OCFS2 filesystem, and the Linux Virtual Server utilities: keepalived and ipvsadm. Combined with the specialized server kernel, these bits already let you use your Ubuntu Server for some heavy lifting. And there's a growing lineup of compelling features, including built-in virtualization, interoperability with Windows machines on the network through Samba, automatic version control for configuration files, support for LDAP directory services, hard drive replication over the network, and even a healthy dose of the latest buzzword—cloud computing.

Installing Ubuntu Server

So you've downloaded your Ubuntu Server CD from http://releases.ubuntu.com/10.04/ and burned it, eagerly placed it in your CD drive, and rebooted the machine to be greeted by the friendly Ubuntu menu. The first option, Install Ubuntu Server, marks the beginning of a journey toward your very own system administrator cave.

Until recently, the process of installing Ubuntu Server was identical to installing a desktop. Both installations were performed with a textual installer, a charmingly quaint combination of red and blue screens with text all over. Since then, the desktop version's installer has been replaced by a beautiful graphical environment that lets you play with a fully usable Ubuntu setup right off the install CD. But the Server CD retained its red and blue colors; because the textual installer doesn't rely on automatically detecting finicky graphics cards, it's just about certain to work on most any piece of hardware you can get your hands on. And when you're installing a server, that's worth more than all the eye candy in the world.

Here, we look at some of the advanced textual installer gadgetry that is particularly geared toward server users.

The neat stuff begins when you arrive at the partitioning section of the installer. With a desktop machine, you'd probably let the installer configure a basic set of partitions by itself and go on its merry way. But with servers, things get a bit more complicated.

A Couple of Installer Tricks

As we'll explore below, in terms of partitioning and storage, server installations can be quite a bit more complex than desktop ones. There's a small bag of useful tricks with the installer that can help when things get hairy.

The installer itself runs on virtual console 1. If you switch to console 2 by pressing Alt-F2, you'll be able to activate the console by hitting Enter and land in a minimalistic (busybox) shell. This will let you explore the complete installer environment and take some matters into your own hands if necessary. You can switch back to the installer console by pressing Alt-F1. Console 4 contains a running, noninteractive log file of the installation, which you can inspect by pressing Alt-F4. Finally, it's sometimes useful to be able to connect to another server during installation, perhaps to upload a log file or to gain access to your mailbox or other communication. By default, the shell on console 2 will not provide you with an ssh client, but you can install one by running `anna-install openssh-client-udeb` after the installer has configured the network. Now you can use the `ssh` and `scp` binaries to log in or copy data to the server of your choice.

Partitioning Your Ubuntu Server

Deciding how to partition the storage in your server is a tricky affair and certainly no exact science. Generally, it's a good idea to have at least three partitions separate from the rest of the system:

- /home: where all the user files will live

- /tmp: temporary scratch space for running applications

- /var: mail spools and log files

TIP **Partition Security and Separating Logs and Spools**
There are several options that you can turn on for specific system partitions that afford you extra security. We'll explain them later in this chapter, in the section dealing with security.

As an aside, if your server will keep extensive mail and news spools, you might want to further separate /var into partitions for /var/log and /var/spool. Having them both on the same partition might cause severe I/O congestion under heavy use.

Keeping data on separate partitions gives you, the administrator, an expansive choice of filesystems you use for particular purposes. For instance, you might choose to put /tmp on ReiserFS for its superior handling of many files in a directory and excellent performance on small files, but you might keep /home and /var on ext3 for its rock-solid robustness.

In addition, a dedicated /home partition lets you use special options when mounting it to your system, such as imposing disk space quotas or enabling extended security on user data. The reason to keep /tmp and /var separate from the rest of your system is much more prosaic: These directories are prone to filling up. This is the case with /tmp because it's a scratchpad, and administrators often give users very liberal quotas there (but have a policy, for example, of purging all user data in /tmp older than two days), which means /tmp can easily get clogged up. /var, on the other hand, stores log files and mail spools, both of which can take up massive amounts of disk space either as a result of malicious activity or due to a significant spike in normal system usage.

Becoming a system administrator means you have to learn how to think like one. If /tmp and /var are easy to fill up, you compartmentalize them so that they can't eventually consume all the disk space available on your server.

The Story of RAID

If you've got only one hard drive in your server, feel free to skip ahead. Otherwise, let's talk about putting those extra drives to use. The acronym RAID stands for redundant array of inexpensive disks, although if you're a businessperson, you can substitute the word *independent* for *inexpensive*. We forgive you. And if you're in France, RAID is short for *recherche* assistance intervention dissuasion, which is an elite commando unit of the National Police—but if that's the RAID you need help with, you're reading the wrong book. We think RAID is just a really awesome idea for data: When dealing with your information, it provides extra speed, fault tolerance, or both.

At its core, RAID is just a way to replicate the same information across multiple physical drives. The process can be set up in a number of ways, and specific kinds of drive configurations are referred to as RAID levels. These days, even low- to mid-range servers ship with integrated hardware RAID controllers, which operate without any support from the OS. If your new server doesn't come with a RAID controller, you can use the software RAID functionality in the Ubuntu kernel to accomplish the same goal.

Setting up software RAID while installing your Linux system was difficult and unwieldy only a short while ago, but it is a breeze these days: The Ubuntu installer provides a nice, convenient interface for it and then handles all the requisite backstage magic. You can choose from three RAID levels: 0, 1, and 5.

RAID 0   A so-called striped set, RAID 0 allows you to pool the storage space of a number of separate drives into one large, virtual drive. The important thing to keep in mind is that RAID 0 does not actually concatenate the physical drives—it actually spreads the data across them evenly, which means that no more space will be used on each physical drive than can fit on the smallest one. In practical terms, if you had two 250GB drives and a 200GB drive, the total amount of space on your virtual drive would equal 600GB; 50GB on each of the two larger drives would go unused. Spreading data in this fashion provides amazing performance but also significantly decreases reliability. If any of the drives in your RAID 0 array fail, the entire array will come crashing down, taking your data with it.

RAID 1   This level provides very straightforward data replication. It will take the contents of one physical drive and multiplex it to as many other drives as you'd like. A RAID 1 array does not grow in size with the addition of extra drives—instead, it grows in reliability and read performance. The size of the entire array is limited by the size of its smallest constituent drive.

RAID 5   When the chief goal of your storage is fault tolerance, and you want to use more space than provided by the single physical drive in RAID 1, this is the level you want to use. RAID 5 lets you use n identically sized physical drives (if different-sized drives are present, no more space than the size of the smallest one will be used on each drive) to construct an array whose total available space is that of $n-1$ drives, and the array tolerates the failure of any one—but no more than one—drive without data loss.

TIP   **The Mythical Parity Drive**
If you toss five 200GB drives into a RAID 5 array, the array's total usable size will be 800GB, or that of four drives. This makes it easy to mistakenly believe that a RAID 5 array "sacrifices" one of the drives for maintaining redundancy and parity, but this is not the case. Through some neat mathematics of polynomial coefficients over Galois fields, the actual parity information is striped across all drives equally, allowing any single drive to fail without compromising the data. Don't worry, though. We won't quiz you on the math.

Which RAID to Choose?   If you're indecisive by nature, the past few paragraphs may have left you awkwardly hunched in your chair, mercilessly chewing a No. 2 pencil, feet tapping the floor nervously. Luckily, the initial choice of RAID level is often a no-brainer, so you'll have to direct your indecision elsewhere. If you have one hard drive, no RAID for you. Do not pass Go, do not collect $200. Two drives? Toss them into RAID 1, and sleep better at night. Three or more? RAID 5. Unless you really know what you're doing, avoid RAID 0 like the plague. If you're not serving mostly read-only data without a care about redundancy, RAID 0 isn't what you want.

TIP   **Other RAID Modes**
Though the installer offers only the most common RAID modes—0, 1, and 5—many other RAID modes exist and can be configured after the installation. Take a look at http://en.wikipedia.org/wiki/RAID for a detailed explanation of all the modes.

Setting Up RAID

After carefully studying the last section, maybe reading a few books on abstract algebra and another few on finite field theory, you finally decided on a RAID level that suits you. Since books can't yet read your mind, we'll assume you chose RAID 1. So how do you set it up?

Back to the installer. When prompted about partitioning disks, you'll want to bravely select the last option, Manually Edit Partition Table.

Below the top two options on the screen (Guided Partitioning and Help), you'll find a list of the physical drives in your server that the Ubuntu installer detected.

TIP   **Avoiding the "Oh, No!" Moment**

We've said this before, and we'll say it again: It's very easy to mistakenly erase valuable data when partitioning your system. Since you're installing a server, however, we'll assume you're comfortable deleting any data that might already exist on the drives. If this is not the case, back up all data you care about now! We mean it.

Indented below each drive, you'll find the list of any preexisting partitions, along with their on-disk ordinal number, size, bootable status, filesystem type, and, possibly, their mount point. Using the arrow keys, highlight the line summarizing a physical drive (not any of its partitions), and hit Enter—you'll be asked to confirm replacing any existing partition table with a new one. Select Yes, and the only entry listed below that drive will be FREE SPACE. In our fictional server, we have two 80GB drives—hda and hdb—so we'd follow this process for both drives, giving each a fresh partition table. Say we've decided on a 20GB /home partition. Arrow over to FREE SPACE, hit Enter, and create the partition. Once you've entered the size for the new partition, you'll be brought to a dialog where you can choose the filesystem and mount options. Instead of plopping a filesystem on the raw partition, however, you'll want to enter the Use As dialog and set the new partition to be a physical volume for RAID.

Still with us? Now rinse and repeat for the other drive—create the exact same partition, same size, and set it as a RAID volume. When you're done, you should be back at the initial partitioning screen, and you should have an identically sized partition under each drive. At this point, choose Configure Software RAID at the top of the screen, agree to write out changes to the storage devices if need be, and then choose to create an MD (multidisk) device. After selecting RAID 1, you'll be asked to enter the number of active devices for the array. In our fictional two-drive server, it's two. The next question concerns the number of spare devices in the array, which you can leave at zero. Now simply use the spacebar to put a check next to both partitions that you've created (hda1 and hdb1), and hit Finish in the Multidisk dialog to return to the basic partitioner.

If you look below the two physical drives that you used to have there, you'll notice a brand new drive, the Software RAID device that has one partition below it. That's your future /home partition, sitting happily on a RAID array. If you arrow over to it and hit Enter, you can now configure it just as you would a real partition.

The process is the same for any other partitions you want to toss into RAID. Create identical-sized partitions on all participating physical drives, select to use them as RAID space, enter the multidisk configurator (software RAID), and finally, create an array that uses the real partitions. Then create a filesystem on the newly created array.

TIP   Array Failure and Spare Devices

When a physical drive fails in a RAID array that's running in a level that provides redundancy—such as 1 or 5—the array goes into so-called degraded mode (never verbally abuse or be cruel to your RAID arrays!). Depending on the number of devices in the array, running in degraded mode might just have performance downsides, but it might also mean that another physical drive failure will bring down the whole array and cause total data loss. To recover the array from degraded mode, you need to add a working physical drive to the system (the old one can be removed) and instruct the array to use the new device to "rebuild."

In order to minimize the amount of time an array spends in degraded mode, and to prevent having to power off the machine to insert new physical drives if the server doesn't support hot-swapping, you can put extra physical drives into the machine and flag them as hot spares, which means the system will keep them active but unused until there's a drive failure. Cold spares, as the name implies, are just extra drives that you keep around on a shelf until there's a failure, at which point you manually add them to the array.

That's it! The Ubuntu installer will take care of all the pesky details of configuring the system to boot the RAID arrays at the right time and use them, even if you've chosen to keep your root partition on an array. Now let's look at another great feature of the Ubuntu installer: logical volume management (LVM).

The Story of the Logical Volume Manager

Let's take a step back from our RAID adventure and look at the bigger picture in data storage. The entire situation is unpleasant. Hard drives are slow and fail often, and though abolished for working memory ages ago, fixed-size partitions are still the predominant mode of storage space allocation. As if worrying about speed and data loss weren't enough, you also have to worry about whether your partition size calculations were just right when you were installing a server or whether you'll wind up in the unenviable position of having a partition run out of space, even though another partition is maybe mostly unused. And if you might have to move a partition across physical volume boundaries on a running system, well, woe is you.

RAID helps to some degree. It'll do wonders for your worries about performance and fault tolerance, but it operates at too low a level to help with the partition size or fluidity concerns. What we'd really want is a way to push the partition concept up one level of abstraction, so it doesn't operate directly on the underlying physical media. Then we could have partitions that are trivially resizable or that can span multiple drives, we could easily take some space from one partition and tack it on another, and we could juggle partitions around on physical drives on a live server. Sounds cool, right?

Very cool, and very doable via LVM, a system that shifts the fundamental unit of storage from physical drives to virtual or logical ones (although we harbor our suspicions that the term *logical* is a jab at the storage status quo, which is anything but). LVM has traditionally been a feature of expensive, enterprise UNIX operating systems or was available for purchase from third-party vendors. Through the magic of free software, a guy by the name of Heinz Mauelshagen wrote an implementation of a logical volume manager for Linux in 1998. LVM has undergone tremendous improvements since then and is widely used in production today, and just as you expect, the Ubuntu installer makes it easy for you to configure it on your server during installation.

LVM Theory and Jargon Wrapping your head around LVM is a bit more difficult than with RAID because LVM rethinks the whole way of dealing with storage, which expectedly introduces a bit of jargon that you need to learn. Under LVM, physical volumes, or PVs, are seen just as providers of disk space without any inherent organization (such as partitions mapping to a mount point in the OS). We group PVs into volume groups, or VGs, which are virtual storage pools that look like good old cookie-cutter hard drives. We carve those up into logical volumes, or LVs, that act like the normal partitions we're used to dealing with. We create filesystems on these LVs and mount them into our directory tree. And behind the scenes, LVM splits up physical volumes into small slabs of bytes (4MB by default), each of which is called a physical extent, or a PE.

Okay, so that was a mouthful of acronyms, but as long as you understand the progression, you're in good shape. You take a physical hard drive and set up one or more partitions on it that will be used for LVM. These partitions are now physical volumes (PVs), which are split into physical extents (PEs) and then grouped in volume groups (VGs), on top of which you finally create logical volumes (LVs). It's the LVs, these virtual partitions, and not the ones on the physical hard drive, that carry a filesystem and are mapped and mounted into the OS. And if you're really confused about what possible benefit we get from adding all this complexity only to wind up with the same fixed-size partitions in the end, hang in there. It'll make sense in a second.

The reason LVM splits physical volumes into small, equally sized physical extents is that the definition of a volume group (the space that'll be carved into logical volumes) then becomes "a collection of physical extents" rather than "a physical area on a physical drive," as with old-school partitions. Notice that "a collection of extents" says nothing about where the extents are coming from and certainly doesn't impose a fixed limit on the size of a volume group. We can take PEs from a bunch of different drives and toss them into one volume group, which addresses our desire to abstract partitions away from physical drives. We can take a VG and make it bigger simply by adding a few extents to it, maybe by taking them from another VG, or maybe by tossing in a new physical volume and using extents from there. And we can take a VG and move it to different physical storage simply by telling it to relocate to a different collection of extents. Best of all, we can do all this on the fly, without any server downtime.

Do you smell that? That's the fresh smell of the storage revolution.

Setting Up LVM

By now, you must be convinced that LVM is the best thing since sliced bread. Which it is—and, surprisingly enough, setting it up during installation is no harder than setting up RAID. Create partitions on each physical drive you want to use for LVM just as you did with RAID, but tell the installer to use them as physical space for LVM. Note that in this context, PVs are not actual physical hard drives; they are the partitions you're creating.

You don't have to devote your entire drive to partitions for LVM. If you'd like, you're free to create actual filesystem-containing partitions alongside the storage partitions used for LVM, but make sure you're satisfied with your partitioning choice before you proceed. Once you enter the LVM configurator in the installer, the partition layout on all drives that contain LVM partitions will be frozen.

Let's look back to our fictional server, but let's give it four drives, which are 10GB, 20GB, 80GB, and 120GB in size. Say we want to create an LVM partition, or PV, using all available space on each drive, and then combine the first two PVs into a 30GB volume group and the latter two into a 200GB one. Each VG will act as a large virtual hard drive on top of which we can create logical volumes just as we would normal partitions.

As with RAID, arrowing over to the name of each drive and hitting Enter will let us erase the partition table. Then hitting Enter on the FREE SPACE entry lets us create a physical volume—a partition that we set to be used as a physical space for LVM. Once all three LVM partitions are in place, we select Configure the Logical Volume Manager on the partitioning menu.

After a warning about the partition layout, we get to a rather spartan LVM dialog that lets us modify VGs and LVs. According to our plan, we choose the former option and create the two VGs we want, choosing the appropriate PVs. We then select Modify Logical Volumes and create the LVs corresponding to the normal partitions we want to put on the system—say, one for each of /, /var, /home, and /tmp.

You can already see some of the partition fluidity that LVM brings you. If you decide you want a 25GB logical volume for /var, you can carve it out of the first VG you created, and /var will magically span the two smaller hard drives. If you later decide you've given /var too much space, you can shrink the filesystem and then simply move over some of the storage space from the first VG to the second. The possibilities are endless.

Last but not least, recent Ubuntu versions support encrypting your LVM volumes right from the installer, which is music to paranoid ears: It means you can now have full-disk encryption from the moment you install your machine. Encrypted LVM is offered as one of the "guided" options in the partitioning menu, but you can also accomplish the same result by hand.

TIP   **LVM Doesn't Provide Redundancy**

The point of LVM is storage fluidity, not fault tolerance. In our example, the logical volume containing the /var filesystem is sitting on a volume group that spans two hard drives. Unfortunately, this means that either drive failing will corrupt the entire filesystem, and LVM intentionally doesn't contain functionality to prevent this problem.

Instead, when you need fault tolerance, build your volume groups from physical volumes that are sitting on RAID! In our example, we could have made a partition spanning the entire size of the 10GB hard drive and allocated it to physical space for a RAID volume. Then, we could have made two 10GB partitions on the 20GB hard drive and made the first one also a physical space for RAID. Entering the RAID configurator, we would create a RAID 1 array from the 10GB RAID partitions on both drives, but instead of placing a regular filesystem on the RAID array as before, we'd actually designate the RAID array to be used as a physical space for LVM. When we get to LVM configuration, the RAID array would show up as any other physical volume, but we'd know that the physical volume is redundant. If a physical drive fails beneath it, LVM won't ever know, and no data loss will occur. Of course, standard RAID array caveats apply, so if enough drives fail and shut down the array, LVM will still come down kicking and screaming.

Encrypted Home and Software Selection

After you have partitioned the disk, the installer will install the base system and ask you for user information, much like with the desktop install. You'll then be asked a question you might not have seen before: Do you wish to encrypt your home directory?

If you answer in the affirmative, your account password will take on a second purpose. Rather than just allowing you to log in, it will also be used to transparently encrypt every file in your home directory, turning it into gibberish for anyone without the password. This means that if your computer gets stolen, your data remains safe from prying eyes as long as your password isn't too easy to guess. If this sounds familiar, it's because this functionality exists as FileVault on Apple's Mac OS X and is also a subset of the BitLocker system that debuted in Windows Vista. (The directory encryption system used in Ubuntu is called ecryptfs, which is a decidedly less punchy name. We're working on it.)

TIP   **Encrypted Swap and Remote Login**
If you use a swap partition, protecting your home directory isn't enough; sensitive data can get swapped out to disk in the clear. The solution is to use encrypted swap, which you can manually enable with the `ecryptfs-setup-swap` command, but this will presently take away your computer's ability to enter the hibernate power-saving mode. Suspend mode is unaffected.

Note also that encrypting your home directory makes all the data in it, including special directories such as .ssh, unavailable until after you log in. If you're logging into a machine where your home directory is encrypted and hasn't yet been unlocked, and the machine only allows SSH public key authentication, there is no way for the system to consult your authorized_keys file, and you're locked out. You can fix this by physically logging in, unmounting your encrypted home directory with `ecryptfs-umount-private`, then creating a .ssh directory in your "underlying" home directory left behind by ecryptfs. Stick your public keys into an authorized_keys file under that .ssh directory as normal, and you'll be all set to log in remotely, at which point you can use `ecryptfs-mount-private` to enter your password and unlock your actual home directory.

After the installer downloads some updated software sources, though, you will see a new menu that lists a number of common server types, including DNS, LAMP, Mail, OpenSSH, PostgreSQL, Print, and Samba servers. Select one or more of these options and the installer will automatically download the standard set of packages you will need for that server as well as perform some basic configuration of the services for you. For instance, if you wanted to install a LAMP environment, but you also wanted to make sure you could ssh into the machine from another computer, you could select both LAMP and OpenSSH server from the menu.

TIP   **Software Installer Prompts**
Depending on which servers you select, you may be asked a number of questions as the packages install. For instance, when you select the LAMP environment, the installer will recommend you choose a password for the root MySQL user.

You're Done—Now Watch Out for Root!

Whew. With the storage and software stuff out of the way, the rest of your server installation should go no differently than installing a regular Ubuntu workstation. And now that your server is installed, we can move on to the fun stuff. From this point on, everything we do will happen in a shell.

When your Ubuntu server first boots, you'll have to log in with the user you created during installation. Here's an important point that bites a number of newcomers to Ubuntu: Unlike most distributions, Ubuntu does not enable the root account during installation! Instead, the installer adds the user you've created during installation to the admin group, which lets you use a mechanism called sudo to perform administrative tasks. We'll show you how to use sudo in a bit. In the meantime, if you're interested in the rationale for the decision to disable direct use of the root account, simply run man sudo_root after logging in.

TIP   **Care and Feeding of RAID and LVM Arrays**
If you've set up some of these during installation, you'll want to learn how to manage the arrays after the server is installed. We recommend the respective how-to documents from The Linux Documentation Project at

www.tldp.org/HOWTO/Software-RAID-HOWTO.html and
www.tldp.org/HOWTO/LVM-HOWTO.

The how-tos sometimes get technical, but most of the details should sound familiar if you've understood the introduction to the subject matter that we gave in this chapter.

Ubuntu Package Management

Once your server is installed, it contains only the few packages it requires to boot and run properly plus whatever software you selected at the software select screen. In the comfort of the GNOME graphical environment on an Ubuntu desktop, we could launch Synaptic and point and click our way through application discovery and installation. But on a server, we must be shell samurai.

The Ubuntu Archive

Before we delve into the nitty-gritty of package management, let's briefly outline the structure of the master Ubuntu package archive, which we mentioned in the introduction to this chapter. Each new release has five repositories in the archive, called main, restricted, backports, universe, and multiverse. A newly installed system comes with only the first two enabled plus the security update repository. Here's the repository breakdown.

- **Main:** This includes all packages installed by default; these packages have official support.

- **Restricted:** These are packages with restricted copyright, often hardware drivers.

- **Backports:** These are newer versions of packages in the archive, provided by the community.

- **Universe:** The universe includes packages maintained by the Ubuntu community.

- **Multiverse:** The multiverse includes packages that are not free (in the sense of freedom).

The term *official support* is a bit of a misnomer, as it doesn't refer to technical support that one would purchase or obtain but speaks instead to the availability of security updates after a version of Ubuntu is released. Standard Ubuntu releases are supported for 18 months, which means that Ubuntu's parent company, Canonical, Ltd., guarantees that security updates will be provided, free of charge, for any vulnerabilities discovered in software in the *main* repository for 18 months after a release. No such guarantee is made for software in the other repositories.

Of particular note is that certain Ubuntu releases have longer support cycles. These releases are denoted by the acronym LTS (Long Term Support) in their version number. The latest Ubuntu LTS, version 10.04 (Lucid), will be supported for five years on servers.

APT Sources and Repositories

You're now aware of the structure of the Ubuntu archive, but we didn't explain how to actually modify the list of repositories you want to use on your system. In Debian package management parlance, the list of repositories is part of the list of Advanced Package Tool (APT) sources. (Keep your eyes peeled: Many of the package tools we'll discuss below begin with the prefix *apt*.) These sources tell APT where to find available packages: in the Ubuntu archive on the Internet, on your CD-ROM, or in a third-party archive.

The APT sources are specified in the file /etc/apt/sources.list. Let's open this file in an editor. (If you're not used to vim, substitute nano for it, which is an easier-to-use, beginner-friendly editor.)

```
$ vim /etc/apt/sources.list
```

The lines beginning with a hash, or #, denote comment lines and are skipped over by APT. At the top, you'll see the CD-ROM source that the installer added, and following it these two lines (or something very similar):

```
deb http://us.archive.ubuntu.com/ubuntu/ lucid main restricted
deb-src http://us.archive.ubuntu.com/ubuntu/ lucid main restricted
```

We can infer the general format of the APT sources list by looking at these lines. The file is composed of individual sources, one per line, and each line of several space-separated fields. The first field tells us what kind of a source the line is describing, such as a source for binary packages (deb) or source code packages (deb-src). The second field is the actual URI of the package source, the third names the distribution whose packages we want (lucid), and the remaining fields tell APT which components to use from the source we're describing—by default, main and restricted.

If you look through the rest of the file, you'll find it's nicely commented to let you easily enable two extra repositories: the very useful universe and the bleeding-edge backports. In general, now that you understand the format of each source line, you have complete control over the repositories you use, and while we strongly recommend against using the backports repository on a server, enabling universe is usually a good idea.

With that in mind, let's get you acquainted with some of the basic command-line package management tools on an Ubuntu system. Ubuntu inherits its package management from Debian, so if you're familiar with Debian, the utilities we'll discuss are old friends.

dpkg

Our first stop is the Debian package manager, dpkg, which sits around the lowest levels of the package management stack. Through a utility called dpkg-deb, dpkg deals with individual Debian package files, referred to as *debs* for their .deb filename extension.

dpkg is extensively documented in the system manual pages, so you can read about the various options it supports by entering man dpkg in the shell. We'll point out the most common dpkg operations: listing and installing packages. Of course, dpkg can also remove packages, but we'll show you how to do that with the higher-level tool called apt-get instead.

Listing Packages Running dpkg -l | less in the shell will list all the packages on your system that dpkg is tracking, in a six-column format. The first three columns are one letter wide each, signifying the desired package state, current package status, and error status, respectively. Most of the time, the error status column will be empty.

The top three lines of dpkg output serve as a legend to explain the letters you can find in the first three columns. This lets you use the grep tool to search through the package list, perhaps to look only at removed packages or those that failed configuration.

Installing a Package Manually

There are more than 17,000 packages in the Ubuntu archive for each release. Only a small percentage of those are officially supported, but all the other packages are still held to reasonably rigorous inclusion requirements. Packages in the Ubuntu archive are thus almost universally of high quality and are known to work well on your Ubuntu system.

Because of this, the archive should be the very first place you look when you choose to install new software. On rare instances, however, the software you want to install won't be available in the archive because it's new or because redistribution restrictions prevent it from being included. In those cases, you might have to either build the software from source code, run binaries that the vendor provides, or find third-party Ubuntu or Debian packages to install.

TIP   **Practice Safe Hex!**
That's a terrible pun. We apologize. But it probably got your attention, so follow closely: Be very, very cautious when dealing with third-party packages. Packages in the Ubuntu archive undergo extensive quality assurance and are practically certain to be free from viruses, worms, Trojan horses, or other computer pests. If you install software only from the archive, you'll never have to worry about viruses again.

With third-party packages, you just don't know what you could be installing. If you install a malicious package, you've given the package creator full control of your system. So ideally, don't install third-party packages at all. And if you must, make absolutely sure you trust the source of the packages!

Impatience is a hallmark virtue of programmers and system administrators alike, so if you were too impatient to read the warning note, do it now. This is serious business. Let's continue: Say you've downloaded a package called myspecial-server.deb. You can install it simply by typing:

```
$ sudo dpkg -i myspecial-server.deb
```

dpkg will unpack the deb, make sure its dependencies are satisfied, and proceed to install the package. Remember what we said about the root account being unusable by default? Installing a package requires administrator privileges, which we obtained by prefixing the command we wanted to execute with sudo and entering our user password at sudo's prompt.

TIP   A Quick Note on Shell Examples
In the dpkg example, the dollar sign is the standard UNIX shell symbol, so you don't need to actually type it. We'll use it in the rest of the chapter to indicate things that need to be entered in a shell. On your Ubuntu system, the shell prompt won't be just a dollar sign but will look like this:

user@server:~$

user and *server* will be replaced by your username and the hostname you gave the server during installation, respectively, and the part between the colon and dollar sign will show your working directory. A tilde is UNIX shorthand for your home directory.

apt-get and apt-cache

Now let's jump higher up in the stack. Whereas dpkg deals mostly with package files, apt-get knows how to download packages from the Ubuntu archive or fetch them from your Ubuntu CD. It provides a convenient, succinct interface, so it's no surprise it's the tool that most system administrators use for package management on Ubuntu servers.

While apt-get deals with high-level package operations, it won't tell you which packages are actually in the archive and available for installation. It knows how to get this information behind the scenes from the package cache, which you can manipulate by using a simple tool called apt-cache. Let's see how these two commands come together with an example. Say we're trying to find and then install software that lets us work with extended filesystem attributes.

Searching the Package Cache and Showing Package Information   We begin by telling apt-cache to search for the phrase "extended attributes."

```
$ apt-cache search "extended attributes"
attr - Utilities for manipulating filesystem extended attributes
libattr1 - Extended attribute shared library
libattr1-dev - Extended attribute static libraries and headers
python-pyxattr - module for manipulating filesystem extended
attributes
python2.4-pyxattr - module for manipulating filesystem extended
attributes
rdiff-backup - remote incremental backup
xfsdump - Administrative utilities for the XFS filesystem
xfsprogs - Utilities for managing the XFS filesystem
```

The parameter to apt-cache search can be either a package name or a phrase describing the package, as in our example. The lines following our invocation are the output we received, composed of the package name on the left and a one-line description on the right. It looks like the attr package is what we're after, so let's see some details about it.

```
$ apt-cache show attr
Package: attr
Priority: optional
Section: utils
Installed-Size: 240
Maintainer: Ubuntu Core Developers <ubuntu-deel-
discuss@lists.ubuntu.com>
Original-Maintainer: Nathan Scott <nathans@debian.org>
Architecture: i386
Version: 1:2.4.39-1
Depends: libattr1 (>= 2.4.4-1), libc6 (>= 2.6.1-1)
Conflicts: xfsdump (<< 2.0.0)
Filename: pool/main/a/attr/attr_2.4.39-1_i386.deb
Size: 31098
MD5sum: 84457d6edd44983bba3dcb50495359fd
SHA1: 8ae3562e0a8e8a314c4c6997ca9aced0fb3bea46
SHA256:
f566a9a57135754f0a79c2efd8fcec626cde10d2533c10c1660bf7064a336c82
```

```
Description: Utilities for manipulating filesystem extended
  attributes
  A set of tools for manipulating extended attributes on filesystem
  objects, in particular getfattr(1) and setfattr(1).
  An attr(1) command is also provided which is largely compatible
  with the SGI IRIX tool of the same name.
  .
  Homepage: http://oss.sgi.com/projects/xfs/
Bugs: mailto:ubuntu-users@lists.ubuntu.com
Origin: Ubuntu
```

Don't be daunted by the verbose output. Extracting the useful bits turns out to be pretty simple. We can already see from the description field that this is, in fact, the package we're after. We can also see the exact version of the packaged software, any dependencies and conflicting packages it has, and an e-mail address to which we can send bug reports. And looking at the filename field, the pool/main snippet tells us this is a package in the main repository.

Installing a Package   So far, so good. Let's perform the actual installation:

```
$ sudo apt-get install attr
```

apt-get will track down a source for the package, such as an Ubuntu CD or the Ubuntu archive on the Internet, fetch the deb, verify its integrity, do the same for any dependencies the package has, and, finally, install the package.

Removing a Package   For didactic purposes, we're going to keep assuming that you're very indecisive and that right after you installed the attr package, you realized it wasn't going to work out between the two of you. To the bit bucket with attr!

```
$ sudo apt-get remove attr
```

One confirmation later and attr is blissfully gone from your system, except for any configuration files it may have installed. If you want those gone, too, you'd have to instead run the following:

```
$ sudo apt-get --purge remove attr
```

Performing System Updates   Installing and removing packages is a common system administration task, but not as common as keeping the system up to date. This doesn't mean upgrading to newer and newer versions of the software (well, it does, but not in the conventional sense), because once a given Ubuntu version is released, no new software versions enter the repositories except for the backports repository. On a server, however, you're strongly discouraged from using backports because they receive a very limited amount of quality assurance and testing and because there's usually no reason for a server to be chasing new software features. New features bring new bugs, and as a system administrator, you should value stability and reliability miles over features. Ubuntu's brief, six-month development cycle means that you'll be able to get all the new features in half a year anyway. But by then they will be in the main repositories and will have received substantial testing. Keeping a system up to date thus means making sure it's running the latest security patches, to prevent any vulnerabilities discovered after the release from endangering your system.

Luckily, `apt-get` makes this process amazingly easy. You begin by obtaining an updated list of packages from the Ubuntu archive:

```
$ sudo apt-get update
```

and then you simply run the upgrade:

```
$ sudo apt-get upgrade
```

After this, `apt-get` will tell you either that your system is up to date or what it's planning to upgrade, and it will handle the upgrade for you automatically. How's that for cool?

Running a Distribution Upgrade

When a new Ubuntu release comes out and you want to upgrade your server to it, you'll use a new tool, `do-release-upgrade`. The upgrade tool will switch over your sources.list to the new distribution and will figure out what packages are needed and whether they have any known issues. After it has done this, it will ask you to confirm the update by pressing y or to view the updated packages by pressing d. If you choose to view the updates, merely type y to continue the update, as the tool will not prompt you again.

NOTE   The update process may take a couple of hours and should not be interrupted during that time.

Building Packages from Source   The Ubuntu archive, unlike Debian's, doesn't permit direct binary uploads. When Ubuntu developers want to add a piece of software to the archive, they prepare its source code in a certain way and put it in a build queue. From there it's compiled, built automatically, and—if those steps succeed—pushed into the archive.

Why go through all the trouble? Why not just have the developers build the software on their machines? They could upload binaries to the archive, bypassing the build queue, which can take hours to build software. Here's the catch: Ubuntu officially supports three hardware platforms (Intel x86, AMD64/EM64T, and PowerPC). Without the build queue, developers would have to build separate binaries of their software for each platform, which entails owning a computer running on each platform (expensive!) or creating complicated cross-compilation toolchains. And even then, sitting through three software builds is an enormous waste of precious developer time.

The build queue approach solves this problem because the automatic build system takes a single source package and builds it for all the necessary platforms. And it turns out that the approach provides you, the system administrator, with a really nifty benefit: It lets you leverage the dependency-solving power and ease of use of apt-get and apply it to building packages from source!

Now that you're excited, let's backtrack a bit. Building packages from source is primarily of interest to developers, not system administrators. In fact, as a sysadmin, you should avoid hand-built packages whenever possible and instead benefit from the quality assurance that packages in the Ubuntu archive received. Sometimes, though, you might just have to apply a custom patch to a piece of software before installing it. We'll use the attr package example, as before. What follows is what a session of building attr from source and installing the new package might look like—if you want to try it, make sure you install the dpkg-dev, devscripts, and fakeroot packages.

```
$ mkdir attr-build
$ cd attr-build
```

```
$ apt-get source attr
$ sudo apt-get build-dep attr
$ cd attr-2.4.39
```
<apply a patch or edit the source code>
```
$ dch -i
$ dpkg-buildpackage -rfakeroot
$ cd ..
$ sudo dpkg -i *.deb
```

All of the commands we invoked are well documented in the system man pages, and covering them in detail is out of the scope of this chapter. To briefly orient you as to what we did, though, here's a quick description.

1. We made a scratch directory called attr-build and changed into it.

2. `apt-get source attr` fetched the source of the attr package and unpacked it into the current directory.

3. `apt-get build-dep attr` installed all the packages required to build the attr package from source.

4. We changed into the unpacked attr-2.4.25 directory, applied a patch, and edited the package changelog to describe our changes to the source.

5. `dpkg -buildpackage -rfakeroot` built one or more installable debs from our package.

6. We ascended one directory in the filesystem and installed all the debs we just built.

This is a super-compressed cheat sheet for a topic that takes a long time to master. We left a lot of things out, so if you need to patch packages for production use, first go and read the man pages of the tools we mentioned and get a better understanding of what's going on!

aptitude

Around the highest levels of the package management stack hangs `aptitude`, a neat, colorful textual front end that can be used interchangeably with `apt-get`. We won't go into detail about `aptitude` use here; plenty of information is available from the system manual pages and the online `aptitude` help system (if you launch it as `aptitude` from the shell). It's worth mentioning, though, that one of the chief reasons some system administrators prefer `aptitude` over `apt-get` is its better handling of so-called orphan packages. Orphan packages are packages that were installed as a dependency of another package that has since been removed, leaving the orphan installed for no good reason. `apt-get` provides no automatic way to deal with orphans, instead relegating the task to the `deborphan` tool, which you can install from the archive. By contrast, `aptitude` will remove orphan packages automatically.

Tips and Tricks

Congratulations. If you've gotten this far, you're familiar with most aspects of effectively dealing with packages on your Ubuntu server. Before you move on to other topics, though, we want to present a few odds and ends that will probably come in handy to you at one point or another.

Listing Files Owned by a Package   Sometimes it's really useful to see which files on your system belong to a specific package, say, `cron`. `dpkg` to the rescue:

```
$ dpkg -L cron
```

Be careful, though, as `dpkg -L` output might contain directories that aren't exclusively owned by this package but are shared with others.

Finding Which Package Owns a File   The reverse of the previous operation is just as simple:

```
$ dpkg -S /etc/crontab
cron: /etc/crontab
```

The one-line output tells us the name of the owner package on the left.

Finding Which Package Provides a File   Both `dpkg -S` and `dpkg -L` operate on the database of installed packages. Sometimes, you might need to figure out which—potentially uninstalled—package provides a certain file. We might be looking for a package that would install the bzr binary, or /usr/bin/bzr. To do this, first install the package `apt-file` (requires the universe repository), then execute:

```
$ apt-file update
$ apt-file search /usr/bin/bzr
```

Voila! `apt-file` will tell you that the package you want is bzr, with output in the same format as `dpkg -S`.

That's it for our package management tricks—now it's time to talk about security.

Ubuntu Server Security

As a system administrator, one of your chief tasks is dealing with server security. If your server is connected to the Internet, for security purposes it's in a war zone. If it's only an internal server, you still need to deal with (accidentally) malicious users, disgruntled employees, and the guy in accounting who *really* wants to read the boss's secretary's e-mail.

In general, Ubuntu Server is a very secure platform. The Ubuntu Security Team, the team that produces all official security updates, has one of the best turnaround times in the industry. Ubuntu ships with a no open ports policy, meaning that after you install Ubuntu on your machine—be it an Ubuntu desktop or a server installation—no applications will be accepting connections from the Internet by default. Like Ubuntu desktops, Ubuntu Server uses the `sudo` mechanism for system administration, eschewing the root account. And finally, security updates are guaranteed for at least 18 months after each release (five years for some releases, like Dapper), and are free.

In this section, we want to take a look at user account administration, filesystem security, system resource limits, logs, and finally some network security. But Linux security is a difficult and expansive topic; remember that we're giving you a crash course here and leaving out a lot of things—to be a good administrator, you'll want to learn more.

User Account Administration

Many aspects of user administration on Linux systems are consistent across distributions. Debian provides some convenience tools, such as the `useradd` command, to make things easier for you. But since Ubuntu fully inherits Debian's user administration model, we won't go into detail

about it here. Instead, let us refer you to www.oreilly.com/catalog/debian/
chapter/book/ch07_01.html for the basics. After reading that page, you'll
have full knowledge of the standard model, and we can briefly talk about
the Ubuntu difference: `sudo`.

As we mentioned at the end of the installation section (You're Done—
Now Watch Out for Root!), Ubuntu doesn't enable the root, or administrator, account by default. There is a great deal of security benefit to this
approach and incredibly few downsides, all of which are documented at
the man pages for `sudo_root`.

The user that you added during installation is the one who, by default, is
placed into the admin group and may use `sudo` to perform system administration tasks. After adding new users to the system, you may add them to
the admin group like this:

```
$ sudo adduser username admin
```

Simply use `deluser` in place of `adduser` in the above command to remove a
user from the group. (Adding the `--encrypt-home` option to `adduser` will automatically set up home directory encryption for the new user.)

One thing to keep in mind is that `sudo` isn't just a workaround for giving
people root access. `sudo` can also handle fine-grain permissions, such as
saying, "Allow this user to execute only these three commands with superuser privileges."

Documentation about specifying these permissions is available in the
sudoers man page, which can be a bit daunting—feel free to skip close to
the end of it, until you reach the EXAMPLES section. It should take you
maybe 10 or 15 minutes to grok it, and it covers a vast majority of the situations for which you'll want `sudo`. When you're ready to put your new
knowledge to use, simply run:

```
$ visudo
```

Be careful here—the sudoers database, which lives in /etc/sudoers, is not
meant to just be opened in an editor because an editor won't check the syntax

for you! If you mess up the sudoer's database, you might find yourself with no way to become an administrator on the machine.

Filesystem Security

The security model for files is standardized across most UNIX-like operating systems and is called the POSIX model. The model calls for three broad types of access permissions for every file and directory: owner, group, and other. It works in exactly the same way on any Linux distribution, which is why we won't focus on it here. For a refresher, consult the man pages for chmod and chown, or browse around the Internet.

We want to actually look at securing partitions through mount options, an oft-neglected aspect of dealing with system security that's rather powerful when used appropriately. When explaining how to partition your system, we extolled the virtues of giving, at the very least, the /home, /tmp, and /var directories their own partitions, mentioning how it's possible to use special options when mounting these to the filesystem.

Many of the special mount options are filesystem-dependent, but the ones we want to consider are not. Here are the ones that interest us.

nodev A filesystem mounted with the nodev option will not allow the use or creation of special "device" files. There's usually no good reason to allow most filesystems to allow interpretation of block or character special devices, and allowing them poses potential security risks.

nosuid If you read up about UNIX file permissions, you know that certain files can be flagged in a way that lets anyone execute them with the permissions of another user or group, often that of the system administrator. This flag is called the setuid (suid) or the setgid bit, respectively, and allowing this behavior outside of the directories that hold the system binaries is often unnecessary and decreases security. If a user is able to, in any way, create or obtain a setuid binary of his or her own choosing, the user has effectively compromised the system.

noexec If a filesystem is flagged as noexec, users will not be able to run any executables located on it.

noatime   This flag tells the filesystem not to keep a record of when files were last accessed. If used indiscriminately, it lessens security through limiting the amount of information available in the event of a security incident, particularly when computer forensics is to be performed. However, the flag does provide performance benefits for certain use patterns, so it's a good candidate to be used on partitions where security is an acceptable tradeoff for speed.

Deciding which mount options to use on which partition is another fuzzy science, and you'll often develop preferences as you become more accustomed to administering machines. Here's a basic proposal, though, that should be a good starting point:

- /home: `nosuid, nodev`
- /tmp: `noatime, noexec, nodev, nosuid`
- /var: `noexec, nodev, nosuid`

System Resource Limits

By default, Linux will not impose any resource limits on user processes. This means any user is free to fill up all of the working memory on the machine, or spawn processes in an endless loop, rendering the system unusable in seconds. The solution is to set up some of your own resource limits by editing the /etc/security/limits.conf file:

```
$ sudoedit /etc/security/limits.conf
```

The possible settings are all explained in the comment within the file, and there are no silver bullet values to recommend, though we do recommend that you set up at least the `nproc` limit and possibly also the as/data/memlock/rss settings.

TIP   **A Real-Life Resource Limit Example**
Just to give you an idea of what these limits look like on production servers, here is the configuration from the general login server of the Harvard Computer Society at Harvard University:

```
*       -       as      2097152
*       -       data    131072
```

```
*      -       memlock    131072
*      -       rss        1013352
*      hard    nproc      128
```

This limits regular users to 128 processes, with a maximum address space of 2GB, maximum data size and locked-in-memory address space of 128MB, and maximum resident set size of 1GB.

If you need to set up disk quotas for your users, install the quota package, and take a look at its man page.

System Log Files

As a system administrator, the system log files are some of your best friends. If you watch them carefully, you'll often know in advance when something is wrong with the system, and you'll be able to resolve most problems before they escalate.

Unfortunately, your ability to pay close attention to the log files dwindles with every server you're tasked with administering, so administrators often use log-processing software that can be configured to alert them on certain events, or they write their own tools in languages such as Perl and Python.

Logs usually live in /var/log, and after your server runs for a while, you'll notice there are a lot of increasingly older versions of the log files in that directory, many of them compressed with gzip (ending with the .gz filename extension).

Here are some log files of note:

- /var/log/syslog: general system log

- /var/log/auth.log: system authentication logs

- /var/log/mail.log: system mail logs

- /var/log/messages: general log messages

- /var/log/dmesg: kernel ring buffer messages, usually since system bootup

Your Log Toolbox   When it comes to reviewing logs, you should become familiar with a few tools of choice. The `tail` utility prints, by default, the last ten lines of a file, which makes it a neat tool to get an idea of what's been happening last in a given log file:

```
$ tail /var/log/syslog
```

With the `-f` parameter, tail launches into follow mode, which means it'll open the file and keep showing you changes on the screen as they're happening. If you want to impress your friends with your new system administrator prowess, you can now easily recreate the Hollywood hacker movie staple: text furiously blazing across the screen.

Also invaluable are `zgrep`, `zcat`, and `zless`, which operate like their analogues that don't begin with a `z`, but on `gzip`-compressed files. For instance, to get a list of lines in all your compressed logs that contain the word "warthog" regardless of case, you would issue the following command:

```
$ zgrep -i warthog /var/log/*.gz
```

Your toolbox for dealing with logs will grow with experience and based on your preferences, but to get an idea of what's already out there, do an apt-cache search for "log files."

A Sprinkling of Network Security

Network security administration is another feature provided largely by the OS, so it's no different on Ubuntu than on any other modern Linux distribution. That means we won't cover it here but will leave you with a pointer.

The `iptables` command is the front end to the very powerful Linux firewall tables. Unfortunately, dealing with `iptables` can be rather difficult, particularly if you're trying to set up complex firewall policies. To whet your appetite, here's `iptables` in action, dropping all packets coming from a notorious time-sink domain:

```
$ sudo iptables -A INPUT -s www.slashdot.org -j DROP
```

Tutorials, how-tos, and articles about iptables are available on the Internet in large numbers, and the system man pages provide detailed information about all the possible options. Spending some time to learn iptables is well worth it because it'll let you set up network security on any Linux machine and will make it pretty easy for you to learn other operating systems' firewall systems if need be.

If you want to just manage a basic firewall on Ubuntu Server, you don't necessarily even need to venture into iptables. Ubuntu provides an excellent front-end called ufw that makes it very easy to add new firewall rules. For more information on ufw, check out the man page for that tool, or if you want a more complete reference, look at the security section of *The Official Ubuntu Server Book.*

Final Words on Security

We've barely even scratched the surface of system security in this subsection, though we've tried to give you good pointers on where to start and where to get the information you need to learn more. But let us give you some sage advice on security in general, since it's a painful truth to learn: There is no such thing as a fully secure system. Securing systems isn't about making it impossible for a breach to occur. It's about making the breach so difficult that it's not worth it to the attacker. This definition is pretty fluid because if your attacker is a bored 14-year-old sitting in a basement somewhere chewing on cold pizza, you can bet that kid will leave your system alone if it's even marginally secure. But if you're keeping around top-secret information, it's a lot more difficult to have the system be secure enough that breaking into it isn't worth it, from a cost/benefit point of view, to the attackers.

Security is also neat because, as a concept, it permeates the entire idea space of computer science. Getting really good at security requires an incredibly deep understanding of the inner workings of computer systems, which has the nonobvious advantage that if you're trying to get a deep understanding of computer systems but don't know where to start, you can start with security and simply follow the trail. Use this to your advantage! Good luck.

Advanced Topics

A single book chapter isn't the right place to go into great detail on all the features packed into Ubuntu Server. There isn't enough space, and many of the features are quite specialized. But that doesn't stop us from taking you on a whirlwind tour. Our goal here is to give just enough information to let you know what's there and interest you in finding out more about those features that may be relevant to how you use Ubuntu.

Virtualization

If there's been one buzzword filling out the server space for the past couple of years, it's *virtualization*. In August 2007, a virtualization company called VMware raised about a billion U.S. dollars in its initial public offering, and the term virtualization finally went supernova, spilling from the technology realm into the financial mainstream, and soon to CIOs and technology managers everywhere.

Fundamentally, virtualization is a way to turn one computer into many. (Erudite readers will note this is precisely the opposite of the Latin motto on the Seal of the United States, "E Pluribus Unum," which means "out of many, one." Some technologies match that description, too, like Single System Image, or SSI, grids. But if we talked about virtualization in Latin, it would be "Ex Uno Plura.") Why is it useful to turn one computer into many?

Back in the 1960s, servers were huge and extremely expensive, and no one wanted to buy more of them than they absolutely needed. It soon became clear that a single server, capable of running different operating systems at once, would allow the same hardware to be used by different people with different needs, which meant fewer hardware purchases, which meant happier customers with less devastated budgets. IBM was the first to offer this as a selling point, introducing virtualization in its IBM 7044 and IBM 704 models, and later in the hardware of its Model 67 mainframe. Since then, the industry largely moved away from mainframes and toward small and cheap rack servers, which meant the need to virtualize mostly went away: If you needed to run separate operating systems in parallel, you just bought two servers. But eventually Moore's law caught up with us, and even small rack machines became so powerful that organizations found many of them underutilized, while buying more servers (though cheap in itself) meant sizable auxiliary costs for cooling and electricity. This set the stage for virtualization to once again become vogue. Maybe you want to run different Linux distributions on the same machine. Maybe you need a Linux server side by side with Windows. Virtualization delivers.

There are four key types of virtualization. From the lowest level to highest, they are hardware emulation, full virtualization, paravirtualization, and OS virtualization. Hardware emulation means running different operating systems by emulating, for each, all of a computer's hardware in software. The approach is very powerful and painfully slow. Full virtualization instead uses a privileged piece of software called a hypervisor as a broker between operating systems and the underlying hardware, and it offers good performance but requires special processor support on instruction sets like the ubiquitous x86. Paravirtualization also uses a hypervisor but supports only executing operating systems that have been modified in a special way, offering high performance in return. Finally, OS virtualization is more accurately termed "containerization" or "zoning" and refers to operating systems that support multiple user spaces utilizing a single running kernel. Containerization provides near-native performance but isn't really comparable to the other virtualization approaches because its focus isn't running multiple operating systems in parallel but carving one up into isolated pieces.

The most widely used hardware emulators on Linux are QEMU and Bochs, available in Ubuntu as packages qemu and bochs respectively. The big players in full virtualization on Linux are the commercial offerings from VMware, IBM's z/VM, and most recently, a technology called KVM that's become part of the Linux kernel. In paravirtualization, the key contender is Xen; the Linux OS virtualization space is dominated by the

OpenVZ and Linux-VServer projects, though many of the needed inter-faces for OS virtualization have gradually made their way into the Linux kernel proper.

Now that we've laid the groundwork, let's point you in the right direction depending on what you're looking for. If you're a desktop Ubuntu user and want a way to safely run one or more other Linux distributions (including different versions of Ubuntu!) or operating systems (BSD, Windows, Solaris, and so forth) for testing or development, all packaged in a nice interface, the top recommendation is an open source project out of Sun Microsys-tems called VirtualBox. It's available in Ubuntu as the package virtualbox-ose, and its home page is www.virtualbox.org.

If you want to virtualize your server, the preferred solution in Ubuntu is KVM, a fast full virtualizer that turns the running kernel into a hypervisor. Due to peculiarities of the x86 instruction set, however, full virtualizers can work only with a little help from the processor, and KVM is no excep-tion. To test whether your processor has the right support, try:

```
$ egrep '(vmx|svm)' /proc/cpuinfo
```

If that line produces any output, you're golden. Head on over to https://help.ubuntu.com/community/KVM for instructions on installing and con-figuring KVM and its guest operating systems.

If you lack the processor support for KVM, you don't have great options. Ubuntu releases after Hardy (8.04) no longer offer kernels capable of host-ing Xen guests (dom0 kernels aren't provided, in Xen parlance), which means if you're desperate to get going with Xen, you'll have to downgrade to Hardy or get your hands quite dirty in rolling the right kind of kernel yourself, which is usually no small task.

TIP   **Point-and-Click Xen**
One Xen-related project to point out is MIT's open source XVM (not to be confused with Sun Microsystems' xVM), which is a set of tools built on top of Debian that allow users to create and bring up Xen guests through a Web browser, complete with serial console redirection, ssh access, and a variety of other goodies. MIT uses the system to offer point-and-click vir-tual machines to any MIT affiliate; the project home page is http://xvm.mit.edu.

Disk Replication

We've discussed the role of RAID in protecting data integrity in the case of disk failures, but we didn't answer the follow-up question: What happens when a whole machine fails? The answer depends entirely on your use case, and giving a general prescription doesn't make sense. If you're Google, for instance, you have automated cluster management tools that notice a machine going down and don't distribute work to it until a technician has been dispatched to fix the machine. But that's because Google's infrastructure makes sure that (except in pathological cases) no machine holds data that isn't replicated elsewhere, so the failure of any one machine is ultimately irrelevant.

If you don't have Google's untold thousands of servers on a deeply redundant infrastructure, you may consider a simpler approach: Replicate an entire hard drive to another computer, propagating changes in real time, just like RAID1 but over the network.

This functionality is called DRBD, or Distributed Replicated Block Device, and it isn't limited to hard drives: It can replicate any block device you like. Ubuntu 9.04 and newer ships with DRBD, and the user space utilities you need are in the drbd8-utils package. For the full documentation, see the DRBD Web site at www.drbd.org.

Cloud Computing

Slowly but surely overtaking virtualization as the uncontested hottest topic in IT, cloud computing is just a new term for an old idea: on-demand or "pay-as-you-go" computing. Building and managing IT infrastructure aren't the core competencies of most organizations, the theory goes, and it's hard to predict how much computing capacity you'll need at any given time: If your company store transitions from wallowing in relative obscurity to becoming an overnight Internet sensation, what do you do? Buy up a truckload of new servers, ship them overnight, and work your IT staff to a pulp to bring all this new infrastructure up in as little time as possible? In the interim, your customers are overwhelming your existing capacity and getting frustrated by the slow response times. In the worst case scenario, by the time you have the new hardware running, customer interest has ebbed away, and you're now stuck having paid for a ton of extra hardware doing nothing at all. Cloud computing is the promise of a better way. Instead of dealing with IT infrastructure yourself, why not rent only the amount of it you need at any given moment from people whose job it is to deal with IT infrastructure, like Amazon or Google?

Cloud services like Amazon's S3 and EC2 and Google's App Engine offer exactly that. And Ubuntu is getting in on the action in two ways. As this book goes to press, Ubuntu is offering a beta program wherein Ubuntu images can be deployed to existing Amazon EC2 instances, allowing you to run Ubuntu servers on Amazon's infrastructure. It is expected that this functionality will become widely available in the foreseeable future. More interestingly, Ubuntu bundles a set of software called Eucalyptus (http://eucalyptus.cs.ucsb.edu) that allows you to create an EC2-style cloud on your own hardware while remaining interface-compatible with Amazon's. Such a setup offers savvy larger organizations the ability to manage their own infrastructure in a much more efficient way and makes it possible for even small infrastructure shops to become cloud service providers and compete for business with the big boys.

Summary

If you've never administered a system before, the transition from being a regular user will be difficult, regardless of which OS you choose to learn to administer. The difficulty stems from the wider shift in thinking that's required. Instead of just making sure your room is clean, now you have to run and protect the whole apartment building. But the difficulty is also educational and rewarding. (We realize they also told you this for your theoretical physics class in college, but we are not lying.) Learning to maintain Ubuntu servers is a great choice for you because you'll benefit from a vibrant and helpful user community, and you'll be working with a top-notch OS every step of the way.

Just as we were in the final editing stages of the first edition of this book, Ubuntu founder Mark Shuttleworth took the stage with then-new Sun Microsystems CEO Jonathan Schwartz in front of an audience of 15,000 at Sun's annual JavaOne conference. In 2001, Sun's previous CEO Scott

McNealy famously compared running Linux on a mainframe to "having a trailer park in the back of your estate." But standing together in San Francisco, Schwartz and Shuttleworth announced that Sun plans to provide commercial support for Ubuntu Server on Sun's hardware. Meeting with reporters after his presentation, Schwartz called Ubuntu "one of the most important—if not *the* most important—Linux distribution out there," adding that "the odds are quite good that [Sun] will be aggressively supporting the work that Ubuntu is doing." Recent work with Sun has culminated with a version of Java shipped on Ubuntu servers and support for Sun's SPARC architecture. While it's still too early to know exactly how Sun's collaboration with Ubuntu will play out in the long term, one thing is certain after the JavaOne announcement: The industry sees Ubuntu Server as a very powerful contender in the server OS arena.

If you're a seasoned administrator who came to see what all the Ubuntu Server fuss is about, stay tuned. The project, though rock solid as far as stability goes, is still in its feature infancy, and the Server Team is working very hard at making it the best server platform out there. We're emphasizing advanced features and we're being very fussy about getting all the little details just right.

In both cases, if you're installing a new server, give Ubuntu Server a try. It's a state-of-the-art system, and we're sure you'll enjoy using it. Get in touch, tell us what to do to make it better, and lend a hand. Help us make Ubuntu rock even harder on big iron and heavy metal!

CHAPTER 6

More Applications for Ubuntu

- Creating Graphics with GIMP and Inkscape
- Desktop Publishing with Scribus
- Exploring the Future with GNOME-shell and Zeitgeist
- Getting There Faster with GNOME Do and Docky
- Summary

IN ADDITION TO THOSE INSTALLED BY DEFAULT, Ubuntu offers a wealth of other applications to help you make the most of your computer. Different people use their computers in different ways, and it is for that reason that we wanted to help you discover how to enable your Ubuntu computer to do even more.

In this chapter, we show you just a few of the thousands of additional applications that you can install on your Ubuntu system. Each section showcases one application, starting with the name of the package you need to install and what Windows/OS X equivalents might exist. This is followed by the main thrust of the chapter, which shows you how that application works and walks you through the initial steps of creation. At the end of the discussion of each application, you will find a Further Resources section to help you go from novice to expert. Let's get ready to supercharge your Ubuntu!

Creating Graphics with GIMP and Inkscape

GIMP

Package name: gimp
Windows Equivalent: Adobe Photoshop or GIMP

The GNU Image Manipulation Program, affectionately known as GIMP to its friends, is a powerful graphics package. GIMP provides a comprehensive range of functionality for creating different types of graphics. It includes tools for selecting, drawing, paths, masks, filters, effects, and more. It also includes a range of templates for different types of media such as Web banners, different paper sizes, video frames, CD covers, floppy disk labels, and even toilet paper. Yes, toilet paper.

NOTE In previous versions of Ubuntu, GIMP was installed by default, but for 10.04, it was replaced by Pitivi, a video editor. For this reason, GIMP is now included in this additional applications chapter.

Unlike Adobe Photoshop, GIMP does not place all of its windows inside a single large window; instead, GIMP has a number of separate child windows. This can be a little confusing at first for new users—especially those used to Photoshop. To get you started, let's run through a simple session in GIMP.

An Example   Start GIMP by clicking Applications > Graphics > GNU Image Manipulation Program.

When GIMP loads, you will see a collection of different windows, as shown in Figure 6-1.

Close the Tip of the Day window, and you are left with two other windows. The one on the left in the screenshot is the main tool palette. This window provides you with a range of different tools that can be used to create your images. The window on the right provides details of layers, brushes, and

Figure 6-1 GIMP does not put everything in one window like Adobe Photoshop does.

other information. GIMP provides a huge range of different windows that are used for different things, and these are just two of them.

To create a new image, click File > New. The window shown in Figure 6-2 will appear.

The easiest way to get started is to select one of the many templates. Click the Template combo box and select 640 × 480. If you click the Advanced Options expander, you can also select the color used in the image with the Colorspace box and the background fill. The Fill combo box is useful for either selecting a fill color or having a transparent background.

Click OK, and you will see your new image window (Figure 6-3).

Figure 6-2 Lots of templates are available, including one for toilet paper!

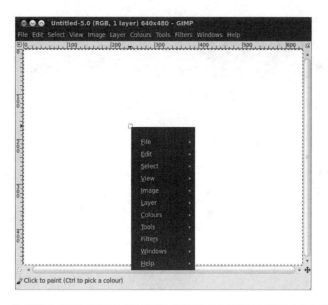

Figure 6-3 Use the right mouse button on the image to access lots of GIMP options and features.

To work on your image, use the tool palette to select which tool you want to use on the new image window. Each time you click on a tool in the palette, you see options for the tool appear at the bottom half of the palette window.

When you click the A button in the palette, it selects the text tool. At the bottom of the palette, you see the different options. Click the Font button that looks like an uppercase and a lowercase case A (like Aa) and select the Sans Bold font. Now click the up arrow on the Size box, and select the size as 60. Move your mouse over to the empty image window, and you will see the mouse pointer change to a text carat. Click in the image, and a box pops up in which you can enter the text to add to the image. Type in "Ubuntu." With the text entry still open, click the up arrow on the Size box so the text fills most of the window. As you can see, you can adjust the text while it is in the image. When you are happy with the formatting, click Close on the text entry box. Your image should look a little like Figure 6-4.

Now in the palette, click the button that has a cross with an arrow on each end. You can use this tool to move the text around. Click the black text, and move the mouse.

Figure 6-4 Ubuntu comes with a range of attractive fonts for use in your images.

Let's now add an effect filter. GIMP comes with a range of different filters built in. You can access these by right-clicking the image and selecting the Filters submenu.

For our image, right-click the image and select Filters > Blur > Gaussian Blur. In the Horizontal and Vertical boxes, select 5 as the value. Click OK, and the blur is applied to your text. Anything in GIMP can be undone by clicking Edit > Undo or typing Ctrl+Z. Your image should now look like Figure 6-5.

Now we are going to create another layer and put some text over our blurred text to create an interesting effect. In your image window, click Dialogues > Layers. The Layers window now appears (Figure 6-6).

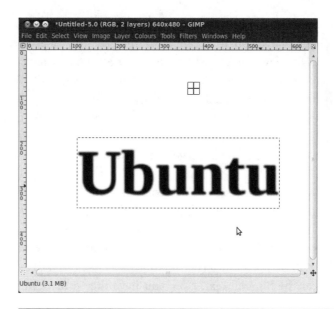

Figure 6-5   Several filters and effects are bundled with GIMP in Ubuntu.

Figure 6-6   Layers are essential when creating complex images with lots of parts.

Layers are like clear plastic sheets that can be stacked on top of each other. They allow you to create some imagery on one layer and then create another layer on top with some other imagery. When combined, layers can create complex-looking images that are easily editable because you can edit layers individually. Currently, our blurred text is one layer. We can add a new layer by clicking the paper icon in the Layers dialog box. Another window appears to configure the layer. The defaults are fine (a transparent layer the size of your image), so click OK.

Now double-click the black color chip in the palette window and select a light color. You can do this by moving the mouse in the color range and then clicking OK when you find a color you like. Now click the text button from the palette and again add the "Ubuntu" text. When the text is added, it will be the same size as before. Now use the move tool and position it over the blurred text. Now you have the word "Ubuntu" with a healthy glow, as shown in Figure 6-7!

The final step is to crop the image to remove the unused space. Click Tools > Transform Tools > Crop, and use the mouse to draw around the Ubuntu

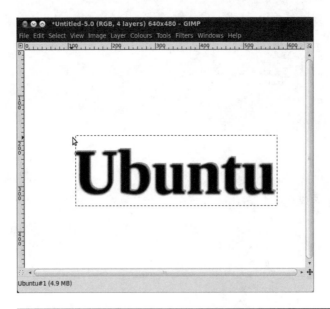

Figure 6-7 Combining steps as we have done can result in interesting effects such as this.

word. You can click in the regions near the corners of the selection to adjust the selection more precisely. Click inside the selection, and the image will be cropped. To save your work, click File > Save, and enter a filename. You can use the Select File Type expander to select from one of the many different file formats.

Further Resources   A great start is GIMP's own help, which is not installed by default, but if you are on the Internet, the help viewer will download it automatically. You can also install it by searching for gimp help in the Software Center. The GIMP's own Web site at www.gimp.org has all the help plus tutorials and more.

Inkscape

package name: inkscape
Windows/OS X equivalents: Adobe Illustrator, Inkscape, Macromedia Freehand

Inkscape is also a drawing and graphic creation tool, much like GIMP, but one that has a slightly different focus. Unlike GIMP, which works with raster graphics, Inkscape is a vector drawing tool. This means rather than a grid of pixels, each assigned a color, drawings are mathematically described using angles and arbitrary units.

To get started with Inkscape, launch it from the Applications > Graphics menu, and very shortly you will see the default window with the basic canvas of either Letter or A4 depending on where in the world you live. At the top of the screen, below the menus, are three sets of toolbars. The topmost contains common tools like save and zoom, the second a series of snapping options, and the third is changeable depending on the tool selected.

All the tools are listed on the left-hand side of the menu, starting with the selection tool and running down to the eyedropper or paint color selector tool. Let's get started by drawing a simple shape and coloring it in (Figure 6-8).

First, select the rectangle tool on the left, just below the zoom icon. Draw a rectangle anywhere on the screen. Now let's change the color of the fill and outside line or stroke.

Figure 6-8 Inkscape's toolbar

NOTE   With any of the drawing tools, the Shift key will cause objects to grow from the center of where you clicked and Ctrl will allow you to constrain dimensions and rotation.

With your rectangle still selected, go to the Object menu and choose Fill and Stroke. Over on the right, you will see the window appear, with three different tabs: Fill, Stroke Paint, and Stroke Style. Let's fill that rectangle with a gradient from orange to white. Immediately below the Fill tab, change from Flat color to Linear Gradient (Figure 6-9).

Look back at your rectangle and see the gradient and a new line running horizontally across the rectangle. Moving either the square or the circle allows you to define where the gradient starts and stops. To change the colors, click the Edit... button. Once the Edit dialog is up, each end of the gradient is called a stop and can be edited separately (Figure 6-10).

Now that we have a rectangle, let's add some text to our image. Select the Text tool, which is right near the bottom on the left, and click anywhere. A cursor appears, and you can start typing. Type "Ubuntu," and then we are

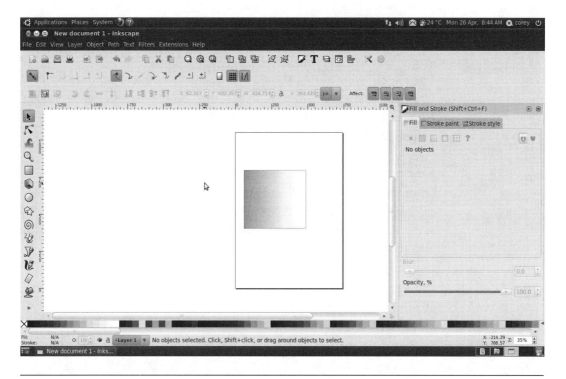

Figure 6-9 Your rectangle, now with gradient-filled goodness

Figure 6-10 Gradient editing dialog

going to change the color and size of the text. Let's make the text 56 points, which can be selected in the upper right, beside the Font name.

The Fill & Stroke dialog should still be open on the right, but if it isn't, reopen it. Change the text color to Red, then choose the selection tool again. Now drag a box around both the text and the rectangle, and you should see both selected (Figure 6-11).

Now open the Alignment dialog, which is right near the bottom of the Object menu. Like the Fill and Stroke dialog, it appears on the right-hand side. To center the text in the box, see the middle two icons with a line and some blue lines on the side of them. Click both the Horizontal and Vertical alignment options, and we are done (Figure 6-12).

By default, Inkscape saves in the SVG or Scalable Vector Graphics format, an open standard for the creation of vector graphics. Inkscape can also save

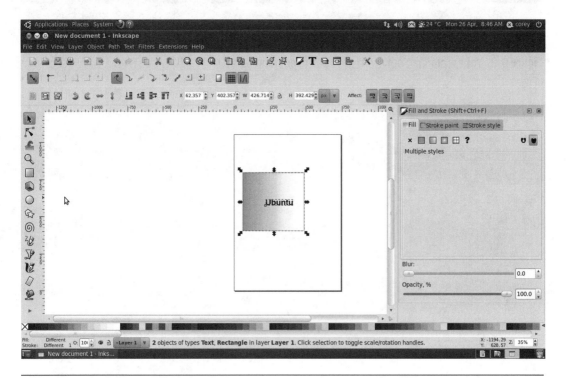

Figure 6-11 Text and rectangle selected

Figure 6-12 Your final drawing

into PDF format, although if you choose to do so, make certain you also save a copy as an SVG so you can edit the image later if you wish. Both SVG and PDF are options in the Save dialog. You can also export your image as a PNG for embedding in a text document or uploading to the Web, although many modern Web browsers such as Firefox and Chrome can display SVG directly. To export, go to File > Export, which allows you to choose to export just the objects selected, the whole document, or some portion.

Hopefully, you have seen just how powerful Inkscape can be. There are many more things you can do with Inkscape, so play around with the various options, dialogs, and shapes.

Further Resources   A good start is always Inkscape's own help, which is in SVG format, so you can see how the original authors created the tutorials. Inkscape's Web site at http://inkscape.org has some great tutorials and articles. If you want a book, Tav Bah's *Inkscape: Guide to Vector Drawing Program, Third Edition*, is a good place to start.

Desktop Publishing with Scribus

Windows Equivalents: Adobe InDesign, Scribus

For more powerful document creation than OpenOffice.org can allow, Scribus is just the ticket. A desktop publishing application, Scribus is built for designing and laying out documents of various sizes and sorts. As such, it makes a few different assumptions that might catch you up if you are used to using OpenOffice.org to create your documents.

When you first launch Scribus, it asks you what kind of document you want to create or if you want to open an existing document. Let's create a one-page document and take Scribus for a spin (Figure 6-13).

The first thing to remember about Scribus is that as a desktop publishing program, it is not designed for the direct editing of images and text. You edit and create your images in applications like GIMP or Inkscape and your text in word processors like OpenOffice.org and then import them.

Figure 6-13 Scribus's opening dialog with lots of options

For starters, let's create a pair of text frames and then import the document Welcome_to_Ubuntu.odt from Example Content. To create a text frame, you need to use the Insert Text Frame tool, which can be found near the middle of the toolbar. After you draw the text frame, you need to add text to it. Right-click on the frame and choose Get Text. A dialog very similar to the Open dialog appears. Choose the Welcome_to_Ubuntu.odt file, and then select OK. You will be asked a few options; for now, accept the defaults. You should see the text appear on the screen (Figure 6-14).

NOTE Scribus currently cannot import Microsoft Word documents, so you will need to open them in OpenOffice.org and convert them to .odt files so Scribus can import them.

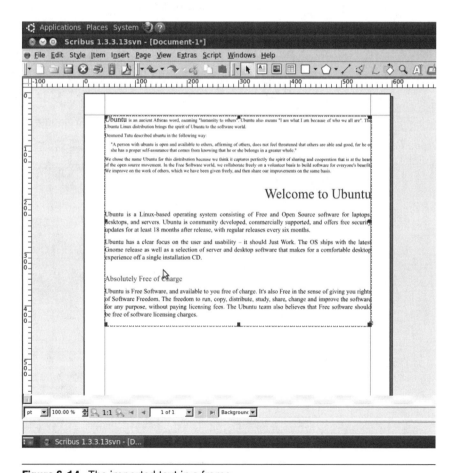

Figure 6-14 The imported text in a frame

But as you can see, the text overflows the frame. In order for the rest of the text to show up, you need to create another text frame and then link the two, allowing the overflow to appear in the second frame. Go up to the toolbar again, select the Insert Text Frame, and draw another frame roughly on the bottom of the page. Then select the first frame and choose the Link Text Frames icon on the toolbar, which looks like two columns with an arrow between them. After you have selected that, click on the second text box and you should see an arrow appear and, more importantly, your text will now flow from one frame to the next (Figure 6-15).

Next let's insert an image at the bottom of the screen. As with text, you need to create an image frame, then add the image to that frame. Draw the image frame below the two text frames, and then right-click and choose

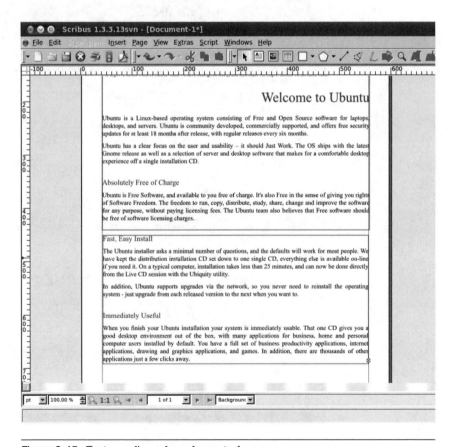

Figure 6-15 Text now flows from frame to frame.

Get Image. Just as with the text import, choose your file, this time an image file, in the Open dialog, and it will appear in the frame. Let's choose the Ubuntu logo, under the Logo folder in Example Content. It will appear in your image frame (Figure 6-16).

NOTE   Scribus can import gif, jpg, png, xpm, psd, tiff, eps, and pdf. It cannot yet import GIMP's XCF, so you will need to save any images in one of the supported formats.

Now that you have added some text and an image, let's export to PDF so you can share your creation with the world. On the toolbar near the left-hand edge, you will see the PDF logo, just to the left of the traffic light icon. Select that, and don't worry about the error about the DPI of the image.

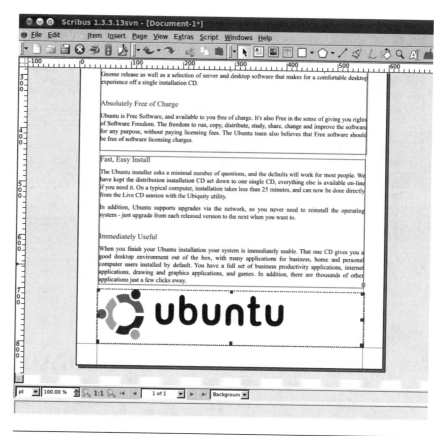

Figure 6-16 Your document with an image added

Select Ignore Errors, and you will see a large dialog with many options for embedding fonts and the like. Don't worry too much about them right now, as the document you have created isn't that complicated. Choose a good name for your document, and then save it to your Documents folder. Now let's take a look at your creation in the Document Viewer. Open the File Manager and load your new document (Figure 6-17).

Now let's go back to Scribus and save the image in Scribus's own SLA format so that you can edit it later if you wish. Enter the name you chose for the PDF name and save it in the Documents folder as well. You have now created your first document in Scribus. There is a lot more to explore, so go and try things out. Just remember to save every now and again.

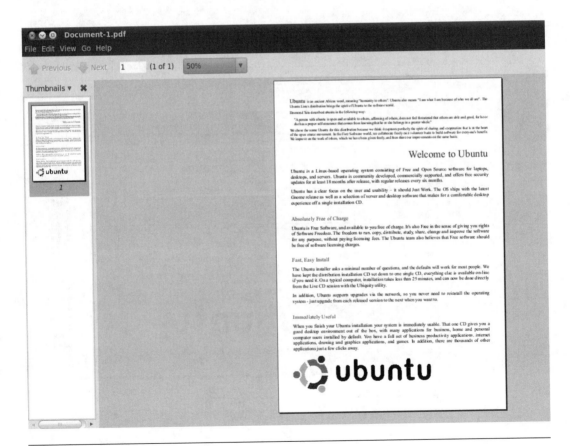

Figure 6-17 Your document as a PDF

Further Resources   As always, Scribus's own help is a great place to start. The Scribus Web site at www.scribus.net has a help wiki, further documentation, and more. There is also an official book, which isn't out as of this writing but should be very shortly. Information about it can also be found on the Scribus Web site.

Playing to Learn with Educational Programs

There are many different educational applications available on Ubuntu. Let's take a look at just a few of them in the Applications > Education menu. You will find a brief summary for all applications here as well as more detailed explanations and screenshots of some of the more advanced packages.

NOTE   Along with the Edubuntu DVD, there is an easy way to install much of the educational software via preselected bundles aimed at different age groups. The bundles are preschool, primary, secondary, and tertiary.

GCompris Administration   This is the administration tool for the GCompris set of tools, which is described a little later. Using this tool, you can create separate profiles for different users of GCompris and enable or disable the list of available activities.

Kalzium   Kalzium presents the pinnacle of periodic table exploration for users of any ages. In its simplest form, it provides a quick and easy reference to the periodic table. Kalzium includes 105 of the naturally occurring elements, many of which are accompanied by sample pictures. If the user hovers the mouse pointer over an element symbol in the periodic table, a balloon appears showing the selected element's name, atomic number, and mass (Figure 6-18).

For more advanced users, Kalzium provides a fascinating way to explore the periodic table. Using the left-hand panel, users have access to the timeline, boiling point, and melting point sliders. When users move these sliders, the elements on the periodic table change color according to their dates of discovery, boiling points, or melting points respectively. Users can

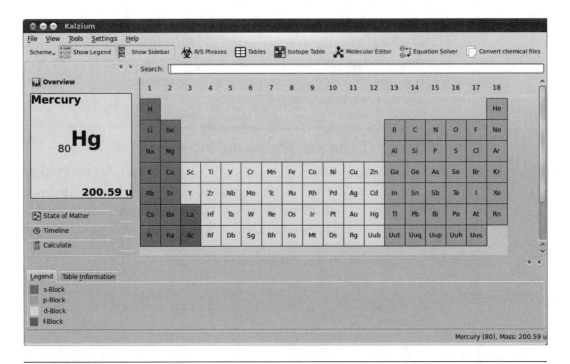

Figure 6-18 Kalzium

then start to see patterns emerging in the periodic table right in front of their eyes.

As well as presenting the basic information, Kalzium provides very advanced statistics on each of the 105 elements present.

Kanagram   Kanagram is a simple package that messes up the letters of a word to create an anagram that children must then unscramble. The package comes with hints, a cheat feature that reveals the word, and built-in word lists, which can be extended.

KBruch   KBruch is a math program to help students practice the use of fractions. It comes with four distinct modes of play.

◼ **Fraction Task:** In this exercise, the user is given a fraction sum that must be solved by adding the numerator and denominator. The difficulty of the sum can be changed by the user, who has control over the number of fractions to use, the maximum size of the main denominator, and the mathematical operations to use, such as addition, subtraction, multiplication, and division.

- **Comparison:** This exercise is designed to test the user's understanding of fraction sizes by making him or her compare two given fractions.

- **Conversion:** The Conversion mode tests the user's skills at taking a given number and converting it into a fraction.

- **Factorization:** Factorization tests the user in calculating the factors of a given number. Factorization is a key skill in using and manipulating fractions.

KHangman   This modern version of a classic game helps children learn to spell and recognize letter patterns in words. KHangman shows a blank base to start; as the user chooses letters, they are entered into the word if correct or placed on the tries list if incorrect, in which case the hangman begins to grow. KHangman comes with three built-in word lists, but these can be extended easily.

Kig   For people wishing to learn about geometrical construction in mathematics, Kig is a must. It is an extremely powerful package but very simple to use. Kig allows users to create complex geometrical abstractions from over thirty simple tools, such as points, parallel and perpendicular lines, arcs, bisectors, circles, and hyperbola (Figure 6-19). When creating abstractions, Kig uses other lines and points already on the diagram to lock onto, making it easy to achieve high precision.

Kig also includes some testing tools. Once a geometrical diagram has been drawn, it is often required to prove a concept by showing that two lines are indeed parallel or perpendicular. Kig offers these tools and more in an easy-to-use manner. Just clicking on the tool prompts the user to choose the item to test against. Then, each time the user hovers over another item while moving the cursor around, Kig will pop up with a message to tell whether or not it satisfies the test case.

KmPlot   KmPlot is a mathematical function–graphing program for Edubuntu. The package has a powerful expression parser built in and can

Figure 6-19 Kig

plot different functions simultaneously and combine their function terms to build more complex mathematical functions. KmPlot also supports functions with parameters and functions in polar coordinates. KmPlot can create graphs to a very high precision, making it excellent for teaching purposes.

KStars   With information on over 130,000 stars and 13,000 deep sky objects, KStars is one powerful package when it comes to space exploration. The main view in KStars follows the time and date to provide the user with a constantly updating view of the night sky. Constellations are highlighted, and star clusters are marked for clarity (Figure 6-20).

KStars has a simplistic user interface, which makes it ideal for amateurs all the way up to astronomy experts. Celestial objects can be right-clicked for more information and can then be tracked and examined in even more detail.

In addition to the huge celestial object database, there are some other fantastic features in KStars. The Calculator, for example, allows the user to

Figure 6-20 KStars

compute coordinates and other figures for a variety of objects and scenarios. KStars can even be hooked up to a telescope to allow real-time tracking of what the screen shows.

The What's Up Tonight? tool provides an overview of what objects will be visible in the sky on that particular night, with the ability to then center on an object and track it in real time. The Altitude vs. Time feature allows users to see how the altitude of a celestial object varies with time during the day. With a built-in scripting language, KStars is the most comprehensive astronomical observation application in the open source community.

KTouch   In this day and age, typing is an everyday occurrence for most people. KTouch is a tutor that gives help and support to those wishing to learn the art of touch typing. With fifteen levels and automatic level progression, KTouch is a fairly advanced tutor program, offering statistics and alternative language options, too.

KTurtle   KTurtle is a Logo programming language interpreter for Edubuntu. The Logo programming language is very easy to learn, and thus young children can use it. A unique quality of Logo is that the commands or instructions can be translated, so the user can program in his or her native language. This makes Logo ideal for teaching children the basics of programming, mathematics, and geometry. One of the reasons many children warm to Logo is that the programmable icon is a small turtle, which can be moved around the screen with simple commands and can be programmed to draw objects (Figure 6-21).

By typing in commands such as `turnleft 90`, `forward 4`, children are using a language native to themselves while also learning procedural logic. KTurtle can even handle simple subroutines, so it's easy to extend the programming onward and upward.

With the introduction of KDE 4, Edubuntu includes a group of brand new educational packages. Following is a brief summary of each new application.

Marble   Marble, the desktop globe, is a virtual globe and world atlas, which can be utilized to learn more about the Earth. With the ability to pan and zoom, click on a label to open a corresponding Wikipedia article, and

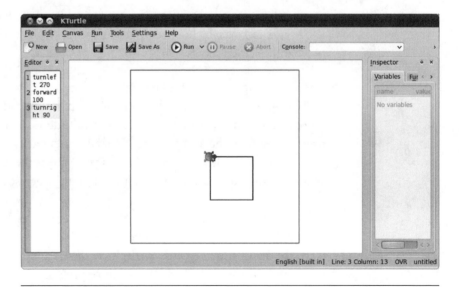

Figure 6-21 KTurtle

view the globe and maps with various projections, Marble is a welcome addition to Edubuntu's educational packages.

Parley   Parley, the digital flash card, allows you to easily remember things utilizing the spaced repetition learning method, otherwise known as flash cards. Features include different testing types, fast and easy setup, multiple languages, the ability to share and download flash cards, and much more.

Step   Step is an interactive physics simulator that allows you not only to learn but to feel how physics works. By placing bodies on the scene and adding some forces such as gravity or springs, you can simulate the law of physics, and Step will show you how your scene evolves.

Blinken   Blinken takes you back, back to the 1970s, as a digital version of the famous Simon Says game. Watch the lights, listen to the sounds, and then try to complete the sequence in order. Blinken provides hours of fun with the added benefit of learning.

Others Not on the Education Menu   Some educational applications are not located in the Education menu. Here are brief descriptions of two of them.

- **Tux Paint:** Applications > Graphics > Tux Paint is a drawing package for younger children. Although geared toward a younger audience, Tux Paint still packs in some of the more advanced features of drawing packages and can draw shapes, paint with different brushes, use a stamp, and add text to the image. The Magic feature allows many of the more advanced tools normally found in full-fledged photo editors to be used, such as smudge, blur, negative, tint, and many more. There is also the facility to save as well as print.

- **GCompris:** Applications > Games > GCompris is a set of small educational activities aimed at children between two and ten years old and is translated into over forty languages. Some of the activities are game oriented and at the same time educational. Among the activities, there are tasks to educate children in computer use, algebra, science, geography, reading, and more. More than eighty activities are available in the latest release. GCompris won a Free Software Award in France in 2004.

Exploring the Future with GNOME-shell and Zeitgeist

Right now is an exciting time to be using GNOME and Ubuntu because of all the new technology on the horizon. Red Hat and others have been working on GNOME shell, a new way of launching applications and managing programs. Coupled with that is Zeitgeist and GNOME-activity journal, the other part of GNOME 3.0. Zeitgeist is a new way of looking at how files are managed—by tags and dates modified rather than by folders. GNOME activity journal is the new user interface to the Zeitgeist daemon.

GNOME-shell is an optional replacement for both the panel and the window manager, offering new ways of manipulating windows, notifications, and other secondary functions of a desktop. Uniquely among desktop applications in GNOME, GNOME-shell is written in JavaScript and rendered with the Mozilla-based gjs. This use of JavaScript and cascading style sheets (CSS) makes adding new effects easy and lowers the barrier for Web developers coming to the GNOME desktop for the first time.

Before you install GNOME-shell on your primary account, it's a good idea to create a new user and try it out there first. This is because GNOME-shell replaces the existing window manager, Compiz, and the panels.

NOTE   To create a new user, see page 124.

After you have created a new user, log out and log in to the new user. You then need to delete the existing panels and launch a terminal session. You will need to run the gnome-shell—replace command. The screen should flicker for a moment and then you will see GNOME-shell (Figure 6-22).

For starters, let's have a quick look at the desktop and see how it is different. At the top of the screen, the extreme left is now a single menu, Activities, rather than the three in the standard GNOME desktop. To the right of that is the currently open window name. In the middle of the panel, you will find the clock, and if you click on it, you will get the calendar, exactly as the old clock worked.

It is in the upper right that you will see the most difference. Because GNOME-shell completely replaces the existing GNOME panel, the new activity indi-

Figure 6-22 GNOME-shell left-hand sidebar

cators and the Me Menu aren't there. What replaces it is a variant on the standard Network Manager menu and a basic presence and logout menu. Hopefully, the Me Menu work will find its way into the GNOME-shell work, as they are aiming for a common standard.

Now let's get into the real power of the GNOME-shell, the overlay mode. To activate that, you need to either click on the Activities menu or run your mouse right into the "hot corner" of the upper left corner of the screen.

Down the left-hand side of the screen, you will see a panel, starting with a search box. That box searches the menu for specific applications and is currently the only way to find programs you have never run before. Below that is an automatically generated list of commonly used applications and selected favorites. You will also see a little arrow beside Applications that shows all recently run applications. Below that are the places and the recent documents, exactly as in the menus of the standard GNOME desktop (Figure 6-22).

One of the core ideas of the GNOME-shell is that of grouping windows together into logical tasks in specific workspaces. By default, you only have a single workspace, but unlike the regular GNOME desktop, adding and removing workspaces is trivial: merely click the + button in the lower right. You can now drag windows to the new empty workspace or launch applications within it. If you want to remove the workspace, move all the windows to another workspace and then click the – key.

The last piece to mention is the new Alt+Tab menu for choosing different windows. As with the standard desktop, you can cycle through the various windows by holding down Alt and clicking Tab multiple times. However, visually, all windows in the current workspace are to the left of the vertical divider and the rest of the windows are to the right. Multiple windows of the same application are also grouped together, so you can select them by holding down the Alt key and using either the arrows or the mouse.

GNOME-shell can be manipulated with the keyboard as well as the mouse, so here are some common keyboard commands to get you started.

- System (Windows) key: Switch between overview and desktop
- Alt+F1: Switch between overview and desktop
- Alt+F2: Pop up command dialog
- Alt+Tab: Cycle between windows
- Alt+Shift+Tab: Cycle in reverse direction in the window cycler
- Alt+`: Switch between windows of the same application in Alt+Tab
- Ctrl+Shift+Alt+R: Start and end screencast recording
- Ctrl+Alt+D: Show desktop and raise windows back
- Ctrl+Alt+Right/Left arrow: Switch between workspaces
- Ctrl+Alt+Shift+Right/Left arrow: Move the current window to a different workspace

There you have it, GNOME-shell in a nutshell. Try it out, see if you like it.

Further Resources   Zeitgeist and GNOME activity journal (GAJ) (http://live.gnome.org/GnomeShell/CheatSheet) are two parts of the same system. Zeitgeist is the part that collects the information, and GAJ displays that information, which means you need Zeitgeist running in order for GAJ to actually display anything.

NOTE   The fastest way to get the latest Zeitgeist and GAJ is the Zeitgeist team's PPA, which is available on Launchpad at https://www.launchpad.net/~zeitgeist/+archive/ppa.

To install Zeitgeist and GAJ, install the gnome-activity-journal package, which will install all the Zeitgeist bits you need too.

After you have installed GNOME-activity-journal, the first thing you need to do is add the two Zeitgeist daemons to your session. Under System > Preferences > Startup Applications, select the add button. The two daemons are called zeitgeist-daemon and zeitgeist-datahub. Log out and then back in again, and the Zeitgeist daemons are now launched. You can check via the System Monitor.

Open a few files just to get some data for Zeitgeist to track and then open the Activity Journal tool under Applications > Accessories (Figure 6-23).

By default, each day is represented by a column, and the various files you have used—be they images, documents or other categories—are broken down by file type. To move forward or backward along the calendar, you can either use the arrows on the right and left of the window or by sliding the calendar bar at the bottom with your mouse.

For even more information about when you used your files, you can click on the Date heading at the top of the column to see when during the day you had that file open. Clicking on the heading again will shrink it back down so you can see the three-day view again. Right-clicking on the same heading bar will show you little thumbnails of all the files, very useful if you are doing a lot of image editing. You can also view a quick thumbnail by mousing over the file name in the regular three-day view.

The calendar bar deserves a little bit of discussion. Clicking anywhere on the calendar bar moves you to that day, and you can see the columns above change to the three days around where you clicked. You can also see that

Figure 6-23 GNOME activity journal main window

the highlighting changes to show you where in the calendar you are. The height of the bar in the calendar indicates levels of file activity that day. Lastly, to quickly return to today, click the Today button in the lower right (Figure 6-24).

Zeitgeist and GAJ are constantly changing, so new ideas, ways of displaying data and data providers are being added all the time. Displaying how you use and view your files in a timeline-style view is quite new, so expect change and have fun.

Further Resources   The Zeitgeist Web site is the best place to start. It can be found at http://zeitgeist-project.com. Because this is a very new project, not many other Web sites or resources have appeared yet, but by the time you read this, there should be plenty more.

Figure 6-24 The calendar allows quick access to files across time.

Getting There Faster with GNOME Do and Docky

GNOME Do, a Quicksilver-like launcher of applications, and Docky, an application dock, share a common heritage and thus are mentioned together here. Like GNOME-shell and Zeitgeist, they are explorations of new ways to use your computer, in this case to launch applications.

To get started with GNOME Do, you need to install the gnome-do package. After it is installed, simply launch it by holding down the Super key (usually the Windows key) and hitting the spacebar.

To launch an application, simply start typing either its name or the command to launch the application, such as Firefox (Figure 6-25).

But GNOME Do can do more, to pardon the pun. You can maximize, minimize, switch to, close, or move an application to another virtual desktop. Just as before, type the application's name, but then hit the tab key to switch to the next box. Now either type the command or press the down arrow for a list of commands (Figure 6-26).

Figure 6-25 GNOME Do's main window

Figure 6-26 GNOME Do's command interface

GNOME Do can also open folders and Tomboy notes via the Open command. Bring up GNOME Do, type "Open," and hit Tab to select the next box. Just as you do to manipulate applications, you can start typing to get a folder name from the Places menu or a Tomboy note name or else press the down arrow to get a list you can scroll though.

If you want to expand GNOME Do capabilities, there are a wealth of plugins available. Launch GNOME Do and then click on the little down arrow in the upper right of the window.

This is also where you can have GNOME Do start automatically, but let's move to the plug-ins tab. There are far too many to talk about, but install a few and try them out. They can easily be turned off through the same menu.

There is a great deal more that GNOME Do offers, but at least you got a little taste. Install it and try it out. You never know—it might be the best thing since sliced bread for you.

Further Resources   As with GNOME-shell, GNOME Do isn't that old, so resources aren't that well developed. The GNOME Do Web site at http:// do.davebsd.com is a good place to learn more and follow the most recent developments.

Docky is a replacement for the bottom panel meant for faster launching and switching of applications. After you have Docky installed, you need to start it. Like GNOME Do, it is not set to start by default.

NOTE   GNOME Do is included in 10.04, but Docky is not. To get Docky, add the Docky PPA from
https://www.launchpad.net/~docky-core/+archive/ppa.

NOTE   You will need to have compositing (also called desktop effects) enabled for Docky to work.
To enable it, open the Visual Effects tab in System > Preferences > Appearances.

If you run your mouse over the dock, icons will grow and shrink as you do
so, exactly as the OS X dock does. This makes it easier to click on the correct icon. Depending on whether or not the program is already running,
you will see two different things. If it is not yet running, the icon will
bounce to show you it is starting before the application itself starts. However, if it is already running, you will zoom to that window.

On the far left of the dock is a brown icon with an anchor on it. This
launches the preferences window for Docky. This is where you can choose
whether or not to launch Docky at startup, various options for how it
appears, and Docklets and Helpers.

Docklets are icons that appear on the dock even though they are not applications. These include a trash icon, a clock, and more (Figure 6-27).

Helpers are small scripts that can add items to the right-click menu of an
icon, such as controlling the playback of music in Rhythmbox. With the
helper enabled, you can start, stop, go back, and go forward without opening Rhythmbox at all (Figure 6-28).

Figure 6-27 Docklets

Figure 6-28 The Rhythmbox helper menu

New helpers are easy to install, either on a per-user or computerwide basis. To learn more, see http://wiki.go-docky.com/index.php?title=List_of_helpers.

Further Resources   The Docky Web site at www.go-docky.com is always a good place to start, and it includes a help wiki if you need a bit more help.

Summary

In this chapter, you've learned how to install and use just a few of the additional applications available for Ubuntu. Although this chapter only scratched the surface of what each application can do, you should have enough of an understanding of each to get started with them, and the Further Resources sections should help you become an expert. But beyond what is in this chapter, the vast universe of new programs is available. Go and explore—try out something new. At worst, you will have wasted a few hours, but you might find something that will change your life.

Always remember that there is a wealth of help and documentation available online. If you ever find yourself stuck, take a look at the Ubuntu Web site at www.ubuntu.com or the Ubuntu documentation at http://help.ubuntu.com and make use of the forums, wiki, mailing lists, and IRC channels.

CHAPTER 7

The Ubuntu Community

- **Venues**
- **Teams, Processes, and Community Governance**
- **Getting Involved**
- **Summary**

COMMUNITY IS A WORD OFTEN used in discussions of Ubuntu. Early articles about Ubuntu bore subtitles asking, "Would you like some community with that?" The earliest press releases and communiqués from the project emphasized a "community-driven approach" to operating system development and distribution. Also, the highest-level governance board in Ubuntu is called the Community Council. Canonical, Ltd. employs a full-time community manager (Jono Bacon, one of the authors of early editions of this book). And we made a very conscious decision to spend an entire chapter of this book describing the Ubuntu community. In fact, every edition has been dedicated to the Ubuntu community!

Still, while the Ubuntu community is important, it is not always easy to succinctly describe it. Ubuntu is, in large part, developed and funded by Canonical, Ltd. The community, almost by definition, extends far beyond Canonical, Ltd. The Ubuntu project has members and self-declared activists (Ubunteros), but the Ubuntu community is more than even those with such explicitly declared relationships. The project contains a wide variety of different venues for participation. But while the community is active in each of these areas, its scope is even wider.

The Ubuntu community is the collection of individuals who build, promote, distribute, support, document, translate, and advocate Ubuntu—in myriad ways and in myriad venues. Most people in the Ubuntu community have never met, talked with, or heard of each other. Members of the community are linked by their contributions, both technical and nontechnical, and by Ubuntu itself. These contributions have built Ubuntu as a distribution, as a social movement, as a set of support infrastructures, and as a project. In short, they have built Ubuntu *as a community*. While any active software development project has a number of people making contributions, not every project has a community.

Community is also a term that represents a promise by the Ubuntu project to remain inclusive. The focus on community means that volunteers are not only welcome but also essential. It means that Ubuntu is a "place" where individuals can come together to create something greater than the sum of its parts. The word *community* gives a nod to the fact that while much development work is paid for by Canonical, Ltd., and while some people contribute more hours, more effort, more code, more translations, more documentation, or more advocacy work to Ubuntu than others, no individual or subgroup can take credit for everything that Ubuntu has become. In Ubuntu, no contribution is expendable. Having a community also reflects Ubuntu's goal to provide a low barrier for entry for these contributions. Anyone who cares about Ubuntu can contribute to the project and can, in whatever ways are most appropriate, become a participant in the Ubuntu community.

This chapter provides a bird's-eye view of the venues and processes in which the Ubuntu community is active. First, it takes a tour through the venues through which the Ubuntu community communicates. It continues by looking at the way the community is organized and the processes by which that organization works. Finally, it walks you through the ways *you* can participate in the Ubuntu community and contribute to its success.

Venues

As we described in Chapter 1, transparent and public communication was an early goal of the Ubuntu project. Technical and community decisions are made publicly and are accessible to all interested parties. When this is impossible (e.g., when there is a face-to-face meeting and it's simply not possible for *everyone* interested to attend), the community attempts to publish summaries and minutes and to provide avenues for feedback. Ubuntu contains no "member only," "developer only," or "decision maker only" back channels except to preserve individual privacy or security—and the Ubuntu community refuses to create them. All work in Ubuntu occurs in places where *everyone* can view the work, and anyone who agrees to engage constructively and respectfully can participate.

Of course, this activity is public only to those who know where to find it. This section tries to document the venues for communication in Ubuntu as completely as possible. It describes the places where discussions of development, support, and advocacy take place. While nobody can engage in communication in *all* of the venues described, knowledge of what exists allows participants to be more informed when they need to choose the right place to ask a question or to make a suggestion.

Mailing Lists

The single most important venue for communication in Ubuntu is the Ubuntu mailing lists. These lists provide the space where all important announcements are made and where development discussions take place. There are, at the time of this writing, more than 300 public e-mail lists. This number is constantly growing.

An up-to-date, full page of mailing lists for Ubuntu can be found at http:// lists.ubuntu.com, where users can see a list of available mailing lists, view archived discussions, and subscribe to lists through a Web interface.

Lists are one of the oldest forms of communication by e-mail. A mailing list provides a single e-mail address that, when mailed to, will then relay the received message to a large number of people. In Ubuntu, lists are topical, and individuals can subscribe to a mailing list if they want to receive information on the list's topic. All mailing lists at Ubuntu are hosted at lists.ubuntu.com. If you would like to send a message to a list, simply e-mail *<mailing list name>*@lists.ubuntu.com, replacing *<mailing list name>* with the name of the list you are trying to mail.

With a few exceptions (e.g., the e-mail lists for the Technical Board or Community Council), *anybody* can subscribe to any Ubuntu list. In most cases, the capability to send e-mail to lists is restricted to list members (membership in lists is, of course, open to anyone). This means that all e-mail sent to a list from someone who is not a member of that list is put into a queue to be reviewed by a human moderator before it is broadcast to list members. This is done as an antispam measure. Users can subscribe to lists and then configure the system to never send e-mail. For several e-mail lists, *all* messages are moderated. This is largely to ensure that lists remain "low volume" or "announcement only."

Ubuntu's mailing lists are run by the popular Mailman software, which may be familiar to some users. Mailman makes it simple to subscribe to lists, to unsubscribe, and to configure any number of options about mail delivery. One popular option is to receive a daily digest of messages rather than a separate e-mail each time a new message is sent. This is all available through a Web interface at http://lists.ubuntu.com. Users can also subscribe to lists by sending an e-mail with "subscribe" in the subject line to <*mailing list name*>-REQUEST@lists.ubuntu.com.

While each list plays an important role in the Ubuntu community, the following central lists warrant a little more detail. You might find it a good idea to subscribe to them.

ubuntu-announce   This fully moderated list relays all important announcements for the Ubuntu project and usually contains less than one e-mail per week. It is the place where new releases are announced and where other important information can be found first. If you use Ubuntu, you may want to consider subscribing to this list. If you subscribe to only one list, this should be it.

ubuntu-devel-announce   This fully moderated list contains announcements related to the development of Ubuntu. It is low volume and contains one to three e-mails per week. If you work with code in Ubuntu, use a development release, or contribute on any technical level, you should be on this list. This is the list that everyone involved in development for Ubuntu is expected to read.

ubuntu-devel-discuss   This list is the primary open list for general-purpose discussion of Ubuntu development. If you are looking to contribute to Ubuntu in any technical way, you should subscribe to this list and begin to follow the discussion. The list has a relatively high volume of e-mails.

ubuntu-devel   This list is a moderated list for discussion of Ubuntu. While subscribing remains free, posting to the list is restricted to those who are Ubuntu developers or chosen other developers. Others may post, but all posts are checked by a moderation team.

Internet Relay Chat

While mailing lists provide the primary venue for asynchronous communication (i.e., not at the same time), there is still an important need for synchronous, or real-time, collaboration. Internet Relay Chat (IRC) fills this niche. While it was designed primarily for group (i.e., many-to-many) communication in channels, it is also equipped with private messaging capabilities that facilitate one-to-one communication—all instantaneously. It is very similar to instant messaging or chat room communication. While time zones and a round globe make it difficult for the global Ubuntu community to meet at the same time, many users and developers take advantage of IRC's capability to let anyone chat about an issue in real time or to ask a question and have it answered immediately.

Like mailing lists, IRC channels provide a venue for a variety of different types of communication in a variety of different subcommunities in Ubuntu. There are many different channels, including channels in a variety of languages.

All official Ubuntu IRC channels are located on the FreeNode IRC network, which also hosts a range of other free and open source software projects. Users can connect to IRC using several pieces of software in Ubuntu, including Pidgin, XChat-gnome (Figure 7-1), and IRSSI. Like the ubuntu-users e-mail list, #ubuntu is designed for help and support. When joining

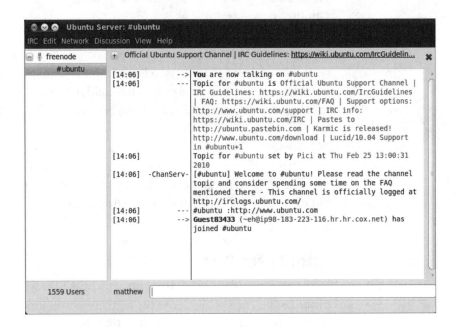

Figure 7-1 XChat-gnome is an IRC client that allows Ubuntu users to connect to the Ubuntu IRC channels.

any channel, users should carefully read the topic as many frequently asked questions are answered there, and moderators of the channel can be annoyed by users who ask questions the moderators have already taken the time to answer in the channel's topic.

Currently the #ubuntu channel is usually the biggest channel on the FreeNode network, with over 1,000 simultaneous users at most times—and it's continuing to grow—especially around releases. Another important channel is #ubuntu-devel, which is reserved for discussion of Ubuntu development. Similarly, Kubuntu users hang out in #kubuntu and developers in #kubuntu-devel. Edubuntu and Xubuntu have similarly named user and support channels. To keep #ubuntu focused on support, all general chatter has been moved to #ubuntu-offtopic, and there are similar channels for Kubuntu, Edubuntu, and Xubuntu. Support for development releases has moved to #ubuntu+1. Maintaining channels with specific purposes has allowed the support community to stay focused and help as many people as possible. A full list of channels can be found at http://help.ubuntu.com/community/InternetRelayChat.

Web Forums

The official Ubuntu forums are the most frequently used venues for communication in Ubuntu. For a number of reasons, many users prefer communication through a Web-based forum or bulletin board over mailing lists. The Ubuntu forums were created to satisfy this group and have done so with amazing success.

The forums are accessible online at ubuntuforums.org and have shown an impressive amount of usage. Statistics as of the time of writing show activity of more than 8 million messages on more than 1 million topics. The forums also boast more than 1 million registered users with around 10,000 online at any given moment. The forums continue to grow explosively. The topics discussed in the forums run the gamut in categories like these:

- Support discussions, including spaces for questions about specific hardware (e.g., Dell computers with Ubuntu preinstalled, or networking and multimedia cards) and specific use cases (e.g., desktop or server users)

- Ubuntu community discussions, including spaces for discussions by people working on art for Ubuntu, those working in science and education, and those developing new documentation and tutorials

- Forum-specific community discussion spaces, including several social spaces and places for administrative and community governance discussions

Each category includes subforums, each containing many threads. Many of these forums provide important spaces dedicated to important community discussions, including:

- A forum to highlight community announcements and news

- A discussion area for support for a variety of third-party projects built on top of Ubuntu that are useful primarily to Ubuntu users or that otherwise serve the Ubuntu community

- Forums for discussion and planning for local community teams (discussed later in this chapter) from across the world

By covering such ground, the Ubuntu forums provide an impressive support resource. They offer an excellent venue for both asking questions and answering questions, both receiving support and making important contributions to the Ubuntu community. If you are interested in any of these, the forums are a good place to begin.

The only caveat regarding the forums worth mentioning is that they are not frequently used by those developing Ubuntu—although there are exceptions to that rule. If users want to send messages directly to the Ubuntu *developers*, the forums may not provide the most effective tool. If users want to get involved in technical contributions to the project, they will, in all likelihood, have to augment their forums' patronage with the use of mailing lists or Launchpad.

The forums were founded by and are moderated and maintained entirely by volunteers and are governed by the Forums Council, which currently contains no Canonical employees. You can find out more in Chapter 11, "Introducing the Ubuntu Forums," dedicated completely to this wonderful resource.

Wikis

Since nearly day one, a large chunk of Ubuntu documentation and support has taken place in the official Ubuntu wiki. In case you don't already know, a *wiki*—pronounced "wik-ee"—is a Web site where any viewer can add, remove, or edit content. The first wiki was created by Ward Cunningham in 1995, and wikis have shown themselves to be an extremely effective tool for collaborative writing in recent years. The term is shortened from *wiki wiki*—Hawaiian for "quick." Many wikis have been created. Most famous among these wikis is the online encyclopedia Wikipedia, which now contains more than 2.3 million articles in the English version alone.

There are several Ubuntu wikis, but two are central to the community. The first is the community support and documentation wiki at http://help. ubuntu.com/community (Figure 7-2). It is edited and directed by the Ubuntu Documentation Team and focuses on issues of community-produced technical documentation for Ubuntu. The second wiki is at http://wiki.ubuntu.com and is meant to be used for everything else. The documentation wiki can be thought of as a project to build an expansive manual through community contributions and editing. The general-purpose wiki is used for specification writing and traffic, conference organization, meetups, pages for teams and individuals involved in Ubuntu, and absolutely anything else that is in written form and relevant to the Ubuntu community. Both wikis can be edited, added to, or reorganized by anyone in the community who creates an account, and edits are unrestricted. Since registration is required, each change can be traced to a particular user.

Unlike other documentation that ships with Ubuntu, anyone can fix an error, inaccuracy, or out-of-date fact in the wiki. As a result, there is no good way to determine whether information in the wiki is correct. It cannot be subjected to the same type of quality assurance workflow that a document such as this book might be. However, it is also *much* more likely to be up to date in the quickly changing world of Ubuntu development, where there is a new release every six months. The wiki provides a venue for this level of up-to-date information with a low barrier to entry and, as a result, acts as an invaluable resource for the community.

The two major wikis each run the Moin Moin wiki software, and the use and operation of the wikis is identical. To use the wikis, you can either

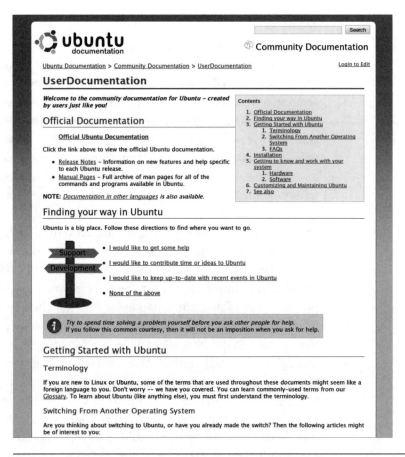

Figure 7-2 Front page of the Ubuntu community support and documentation wiki

search or browse them. Searching is the most common way to get information from the wiki, and users can easily search either titles or the full text of the wiki. To achieve the best results, it is usually best to search titles and then the text to ensure that you look for more relevant information first.

For people who prefer to browse, the general-purpose wiki is divided into a number of categories that include the following:

■ Resources

■ Community

- Events

- Releases

The documentation is browsable in sections that try to serve users at different stages of familiarity with Ubuntu or with particular types of problems. The major divisions in the community documentation wiki include these:

- General help and information for new users

- Help for those switching from Mac OS X, Windows, or another Linux distribution who want a quick guide using analogies they are familiar with

- A large variety of information for people to read after they have installed Ubuntu and have questions about applications or types of use

- Information on maintaining and troubleshooting Ubuntu installs

- Help on connecting and configuring hardware

Most of these categories are relatively self-explanatory. Additionally, the general wiki provides a prominent link to information and support resources in languages other than English. The comprehensive list at www. ubuntu.com/support/local provides both links to pages within the wiki that include documentation and information in languages other than English and links to more than a dozen other wikis that are in another language entirely. Users looking for wiki pages in a language other than English are advised to visit this page.

The Fridge

The Fridge (http://fridge.ubuntu.com) is the quirky community portal for Ubuntu. In many Western cultures, refrigerators provide a central sort of "bulletin board" in a family's home. Because refrigerators are magnetic, children and parents can use magnets to hang pieces of paper that they want to share with the community of people who come in contact with that fridge. For children, this often includes good grades, news reports, or other information that someone is proud of or wants to share. The Fridge tries to create such a shared resource within the Ubuntu community. The Fridge home page is shown in Figure 7-3.

The Fridge is perhaps best described as the community portal for Ubuntu. It is part news site, part grassroots marketing and advocacy site. It hosts developer interviews, news, a picture gallery, a calendar with a list of upcoming events, polls, a list of Ubuntu-in-the-press citations, and much more. The core content on the site is arranged as a Web log. Users frequently set The Fridge as their home page or subscribe to the site via its RSS feed. The Fridge is unique in the community in that it appeals to a wide variety of Ubuntu participants—developers, advocates, translators, users—and provides a venue where each group can share information with others.

Figure 7-3 The Fridge home page

There is a story every two to three days on The Fridge, although this may increase to up to several stories a day with time. Users can comment and discuss each story on The Fridge in an associated forum in the Ubuntu forums.

Anyone can contribute content to The Fridge. If you would like to contribute, you can do so by sending your suggestions for features, articles, or even a piece of original work (such as an article, photo, or event review) to The Fridge editors at fridge-devel@lists.ubuntu.com.

Developer Summits and Sprints

While the vast majority of the work of the Ubuntu community takes place online, Ubuntu contributors do, from time to time, meet face to face. Since Ubuntu was first released, there have been several public developer summits and sprints organized and funded by Canonical, Ltd. Highlights include:

- The Mataró Sessions in Mataró, Catalonia, Spain, in December 2004—the first Ubuntu development summit

- The two named Ubuntu conferences in 2005: Ubuntu Down Under in Sydney, Australia, in April and the Ubuntu Below Zero in Montreal, Canada, in November

- Ubuntu Developer Summit Mountain View at Google Headquarters in Mountain View, California, in November 2006

- Ubuntu Developer Summit-L in Dallas, Texas—in November 2009, the most recent developer summit at the time of writing

With Canonical, Ltd., Ubuntu tries to organize these meetings so that they occur once per release, usually toward the very beginning of a release cycle, so that the specifications and goals for the forthcoming release can be discussed, thrashed out, and decided upon. These meetings move around the globe geographically so that, over a several-year period, a large percentage of the Ubuntu community will be able to attend at least one summit and meet with other developers.

While the format changes slightly each time, these meetings have been between one and two weeks in length. Frequently, a given attendee stays for only one week. At Ubuntu Below Zero, for example, the second week was devoted almost entirely to discussing, implementing, and developing infrastructure related to Launchpad (see Chapter 10). The format of these summits has changed as the attendees have experimented with different methods for structuring the events and maximizing the efficiency of these short periods. One common theme, though, is a process of writing specifications. At UDS-L in November 2009, the entire summit was available for people who could not attend in person to participate remotely. Remote participation enabled off-site attendees to interact via the Internet in designated IRC channels, and many of the sessions were videotaped.

At developer summits, attendees describe features that they would like to see in the next Ubuntu release. At an arranged time or in a series of meetings, a small set of interested community contributors and developers works to draft a written specification. This process of drafting involves brainstorming and ends up with a formal, approved spec that describes a problem or need and provides a detailed description of how it will be fixed or implemented. While these specifications are often technical in nature, they are also used to describe goals that may pertain to localization, documentation, or community building. For example, both The Fridge and the planning of each summit began as a specification. With time, these specifications are categorized in terms of priority for the upcoming release. Later, individuals will claim or be assigned some set of these specs. Paid developers at Canonical, Ltd. frequently take responsibility for the highest-priority technical specs. Each specification is written up and improved as a blueprint on Launchpad so that Ubuntu hackers who cannot attend the summit are still able to participate.

These conferences have, so far, occurred in hotels with conference centers and have been attended by up to several hundred people. The exception was the 2006 conference, which was graciously hosted by Google. The meetings have been wholly organized and funded by Canonical, Ltd., which ensures that its employees attend and also distributes funds for other active volunteers to travel. This funding tends to be divided up based on the contributions of volunteers over the last release cycle and their geographic proximity to the summit location. This is done to minimize travel expenditures and to ensure that users around the world get a chance to attend a conference when it comes near them.

In addition to the biannual summits, Canonical, Ltd. organizes a number of sprints each year. These sprints tend to be one- to three-week intense collocated work sessions that involve a team or subteam tasked with a well-defined goal. They provide a time when team members can write code, write documentation, make plans, or do whatever else is necessary to fulfill that goal. The sprints attempt to squeeze large amounts of work into a short period of time and have earned a reputation for being exhausting, fulfilling, amazingly productive, fun experiences. These sprints are work sessions and are often limited to a small group of Canonical, Ltd. employees but at times may also include volunteer attendees.

User Conferences

Developer summits and sprints are effective but are primarily of interest to technically minded people or individuals who are already very actively involved in the Ubuntu community. Their goal is to accomplish work through high-bandwidth face-to-face interaction among existing teams. User conferences try to provide an alternative space for users who are not yet actively involved in the community. These conferences attempt to bring people up to speed on Ubuntu and to provide a space for community building, support, and networking.

While many local community teams have regular meetings and their own Ubuntu events, there have been several larger-scale Ubuntu user conferences to date, and several more are currently being planned. These conferences fall into two major classes. The first class is a set of laid-back, lightly organized, day-long "unconferences" called Ubucons (short for Ubuntu Conferences). Ubucons have been held many times, the first two at Google headquarters, in Mountain View and in New York City, and others are designed to coincide with the much larger Linux World conferences that many other Ubuntu users attend. The unconference format means that much of the schedule is left up in the air until the morning of the meeting and that many of the attendees are encouraged to come prepared with their own demonstrations, talks, and workshops and with a list of things they would like to learn. Attended by a group of about a hundred users and a handful of developers, Ubucons have provided a simple way for users to connect with each other. Additionally, Ubucons have, to date, also provided space for "installfests" where users can bring computers and have

Ubuntu installed on their machines by other Ubuntu users, developers, and aficionados.

Any active group of Ubuntu users can plan a Ubucon, and Ubucons have taken place in a variety of locations around the world. For example, Atlanta Linux Fest 2009 was accompanied by an Ubucon in conjunction with the main event to test the process of piggybacking. It worked so well that in 2010, several others have permitted an Ubucon to be organized as a smaller part of their larger event. These are becoming more popular because Ubuntu users are already attending the larger events, LoCo teams can afford to organize the Ubucons because the venue costs are quite low and can usually be covered by only one sponsor, they are free events, and popular Ubuntu speakers often are already attending the larger event and are willing and happy to add some participation in the Ubucon to their schedule.

While conferences and summits act as a site for major technical advances in brainstorming and development, they are also fun and enjoyable experiences. They provide a venue for users to put faces to names, IRC nicks, and e-mail addresses, and they provide for enjoyable, humorous, and productive interaction. In addition to work, there are frequent card-playing, eating, drinking, and athletic activities. Many Ubuntu users from the local area who've attended because they were curious have gone on to become some of the community's most important contributors. Attending a conference is like taking a drink from an Ubuntu fire hose. It is frequently overwhelming but can ultimately be a useful, productive, and rewarding experience as well.

Planet Ubuntu

For a window into the people who make Ubuntu what it is, the blog aggregator Planet Ubuntu (http://planet.ubuntu.com) is a great place to start (Figure 7-4). A blog aggregator is basically a blog of blogs that retrieves the latest posts from Ubuntu members who have chosen to add their blogs to the system and then publishes a single blog in reverse chronological order. Although much of the content in Planet Ubuntu is about Ubuntu, as a window into the Ubuntu membership, Planet Ubuntu also includes information from the personal lives of community members. In this way, Planet Ubuntu provides a good way for participants to put their stamp on

Figure 7-4 Planet Ubuntu

the Ubuntu community and for others to see what the Ubuntu community is doing.

Teams, Processes, and Community Governance

Ubuntu operates under the famous hacker mantra of "rough consensus and running code." The project attempts to forge consensus, to make good technical decisions, and to move forward. It attempts to minimize politicization wherever possible and to distribute power to those who are best at getting good work done. Mark Shuttleworth explains, "This is not a democracy, it's a meritocracy. We try to operate more on consensus than on votes, seeking agreement from the people who will have to do the work."

The project attempts to keep disagreements from spiraling out of control by enforcing mutual respect at all times with its Code of Conduct described in Chapter 1. Disagreements, of course, are inevitable and can be technical or nontechnical in nature. The community needs to be able to deal with these and, toward that end, has created a lightweight governance system that aims to ensure that disagreements are resolved carefully and that the project always has a strong, fair, and responsive direction.

The Ubuntu Web site describes the goals of its community governance system as threefold.

1. Ensure that a process is defined that allows people to contribute to decisions regarding the Ubuntu community and distribution.

2. Ensure that decisions regarding the Ubuntu distribution and community are made in a fair and transparent fashion.

3. Ensure that necessary decisions are actually made, even when there is no clear consensus among the community.

With these goals in mind, Ubuntu's system is based on the delegation of decision-making power to small and medium-sized teams. When disagreements arise, they are handled within a relevant team. In the cases of some larger teams, team councils handle a variety of dispute resolutions in a very structured fashion. When teams cannot resolve their own disagreements or when there are disagreements between teams, issues are forwarded to either the Community Council or the Technical Board—depending on whether the issue is technical in nature. As the financier and the project's progenitor, Shuttleworth sits on both boards and occupies a special position as the self-appointed benevolent dictator for life (SABDFL). Users can participate in the Ubuntu governance structure by serving on teams, and as Ubuntu members and maintainers, they have a voice in approving members of both the Community Council and the Technical Board as Ubuntu members and maintainers.

Teams

Most work in Ubuntu is delegated to a set of teams, each responsible for a particular area of work in Ubuntu. A sample of important teams (which is by no means complete) might include the forums, marketing, art, documentation, kernel, server, laptop, and translation teams. Anyone with an interest in a particular aspect of the Ubuntu project can join a team's discussion and contribute to its decisions.

When participants feel that a particular area is under-served, they can go ahead and build a new team by beginning work and writing up a proposal for consideration by the Community Council, which approves the creation of all new teams. Rather than catalyzing work with the creation of a team, the Community Council likes to recognize existing work with official team status. Teams should always involve the participation of several individuals. There are no one-man or one-woman teams in Ubuntu.

Several teams are so large and important that they have built their own more advanced governance structures in the forums of team councils. These councils are appointed by the community council from active members and leaders within the team and act as delegates of the Community Council for that team and its domain in the project. These team councils have regular meetings, resolve conflicts, report to the Community Council, and in some cases even grant membership on behalf of the Community Council. Current large teams with councils include the Forums, Edubuntu, Kubuntu, and MOTU teams.

Local Community Teams

Local community teams, affectionately referred to as LoCos in the community, are an extremely important type of team. Each LoCo is responsible for promoting, supporting, and representing Ubuntu in a particular locale. These locales are usually geographical and frequently countrywide, although in some situations they may overlap geographically. Ubuntu tries to encourage LoCos to work together whenever possible.

LoCos are like Linux User Groups (LUGs) and may often work closely with or be associated with a LUG. LoCos are often involved in localization or translations of Ubuntu into local languages and in advocacy in local schools, public administrations, and communities. The best LoCos meet regularly for social events, talks, and discussion. Often, they meet for installfests, where team members help new users install Ubuntu onto their computers. Representatives of LoCos are asked to assist with localization matters, to speak on behalf of the Ubuntu project at local conferences and trade shows, and to organize a booth or presence at such events.

Canonical, Ltd. provides each team with a mailing list and a domain name (usually in the form of ubuntu-<*CC*>.org, where *CC* is the country's two-letter country code). Canonical also is willing to host LoCo Web pages, wikis, forums, blogs, download areas, and additional mailing lists. LoCos are open to participation by anyone.

MOTUs

Another very special team that deserves an in-depth description in this book is the MOTUs. The MOTUs are the maintainers of Ubuntu's Universe software package repository, and the acronym stands, jokingly, for Masters of the Universe. MOTUs call themselves "the brave souls who try to keep the Universe section of Ubuntu in shape." They are community members who spend their time adding, maintaining, and supporting as much as possible the software found in Universe.

MOTUs are package maintainers. They maintain, as a group, the vast majority of packages in the Ubuntu archive. Several of the packages that have been well maintained by the MOTUs have, with time, migrated into the main component and become an official part of the Ubuntu distribution. Because Ubuntu does not make support or quality promises regarding the packages in universe, the MOTU team provides a way for maintainers to sharpen their teeth and (since it's sometimes unavoidable) make mistakes before jumping into the higher-responsibility packages in main.

The roles and responsibilities of the MOTUs are many. Some important ones are that MOTUs

- understand packaging concepts and have substantial experience uploading packages through a sponsor.
- apply this knowledge by uploading new packages and updating existing packages in the universe component.

- may also contribute to the main component in cooperation with a core developer.

- answer questions of other developers in order to expand their understanding of packaging work.

- provide guidance for prospective Ubuntu developers regarding technical issues.

MOTU contributors are the people who are interested in contributing to Ubuntu and are learning how to package and work in the Ubuntu development community. They primarily work by using MOTUs as sponsors for their work. There are no requirements or exams to pass to become a MOTU contributor, just a willingness to learn and a commitment to the Ubuntu Code of Conduct. Many of these contributors do graduate to full-fledged MOTUs, and many MOTUs eventually are granted full-core developer status. This three-step system is the process by which almost all new maintainers learn to maintain packages in Ubuntu.

The Community Council

The Community Council and the Technical Board are the highest-level governance structures within Ubuntu. The Community Council, as it pertains to all Ubuntu members and activities, is arguably the most powerful team within the Ubuntu project. The Community Council is charged with supervising the social structures, venues, and processes of the project.

The Community Council's day-to-day work involves five major areas in Ubuntu. The first, and the most straightforward, is the maintenance of the Ubuntu Code of Conduct. The Community Council is the only body that can approve revisions to the code. Because the Community Council does not ask each member to "reagree" to the code when it is changed, each of these revisions must be fully within the spirit of the previous drafts.

The second charge of the Community Council is the arbitration of disputes that cannot be handled within a particular team or that arise between teams. These are generally disputes about the Code of Conduct that may require clarification of a part of the Code of Conduct or a description of whether any of the code was in fact violated by a particular action or behavior. However, the Community Council's purview is not limited to Code of Conduct violations, and the Community Council is available to handle disputes in any nontechnical situation. In most situations, the Community Council does not take action against individuals but, rather, helps group members come to agreement or consensus among themselves. If this fails, the Community Council can ask a maintainer or other member of the community to apologize and refrain from particular behavior or to leave the community. The Council promises that nobody will be asked to leave without a substantial review and an opportunity to defend him- or herself.

A third area of council work is the creation and dissolution of teams and the appointment of team leaders. New teams are proposed to the Community Council in the manner described earlier in the section on teams, and the Community Council either approves the request or asks the proposer to wait. Defunct or inactive teams can similarly be dissolved by the Community Council. In cases where team leadership is requested, the Community Council can appoint leaders of teams or shift leadership to different team members. In most situations, the appointment of team leaders is an internal team matter but, when requested, the Community Council is available to intervene.

Fourth, the Community Council is ultimately responsible for approving and welcoming new members to the project. This will be described in more depth in the upcoming subsection on membership.

Finally, the Community Council is responsible for all community-related structures and processes. New types of teams, requirements for membership, and core philosophical documents should first be approved by the Community Council. Community members who wish to suggest new structures or processes can submit their proposal to the Community Council for discussion and approval.

The Community Council meets every two weeks on IRC. Any community participant can submit an item or proposal for discussion by the Community Council. Meetings are open to the community, but the Council seeks only consensus or votes from Council members—although it consults representatives from the team that submitted the proposal and other community members. If an open meeting becomes too noisy, the Council reserves the right to move to a private channel for the duration of the meeting. To date, this has never happened. In all situations, full transcripts of meetings are published immediately following a Community Council meeting. The Community Council at the time of this writing consists of Alan Pope, Benjamin Mako Hill, Mark Shuttleworth, Daniel Holbach, Elizabeth Krumbach, Richard Johnson, Matthew East, and Mike Basinger. Notably, only Shuttleworth and Holbach are Canonical employees. Appointments to the board are made by Shuttleworth and subject to confirmation by a vote among all members. Appointments are for a period of two years.

The Technical Board

The Ubuntu Technical Board is responsible for the Ubuntu project's technical direction. By handling all technical matters, the Technical Board complements the Community Council as Ubuntu's highest rung of project governance. In particular, the Technical Board is responsible for three major areas of Ubuntu policy: package policy, release feature goals, and package selection. Also, the Technical Board is available to arbitrate any technical disagreements or issues within or between teams in a manner similar to the one described earlier in relation to the Community Council.

The Technical Board's first responsibility is Ubuntu's package policy. The Technical Board maintains the policy document, which describes the processes and standards to which all Ubuntu packages are held. Since the policy is constantly evolving, each Ubuntu release is associated with a specific version of the Ubuntu package policy as determined by the Technical Board. Any suggestions or proposals about policy are suggested to and considered by the Technical Board.

Also, the Technical Board is responsible for maintaining Ubuntu's feature goals for each release. During each release cycle, there is a date defined as Feature Freeze, after which no new features are added. The Technical Board sets these dates and decides when and if the rules can be bent for a particular feature or piece of software.

Finally, the Technical Board is responsible for maintaining the *list* of pieces of software (i.e., packages) in Ubuntu. In this capacity, the Technical Board determines which software is installed in the default desktop installation and which packages qualify for full support as part of the main component of Ubuntu. Users and developers can propose a particular piece of software for inclusion in main, the base install, or a desktop install. In all cases, the ultimate decision will be made by the Technical Board.

Like the Community Council, the Technical Board meets at least every two weeks on IRC. Also like the Community Council, any user can submit an item or proposal for discussion by the Technical Board prior to the scheduled meeting. Meetings are open to all interested parties, although decision making and voting is restricted to Technical Board members. Full transcripts and rules about noise, as they pertain to the Community Council, also apply to the Technical Board. The Technical Board at the time of this writing comprises Matt Zimmerman as board chair, Scott James Remnant, and Mark Shuttleworth. Nominations for the Technical Board are considered at the beginning of each release cycle. Like the Community Council, appointments are made by Shuttleworth but are subject to confirmation by a vote among the maintainers instead of all members. Appointments are made for a period of one year.

The SABDFL

Mark Shuttleworth jokingly refers to himself as Ubuntu's SABDFL—self-appointed benevolent dictator for life. He plays an admittedly undemocratic role as the sponsor of the Ubuntu project and the sole owner of Canonical, Ltd. Shuttleworth has the ability, with regard to Canonical, Ltd. employees, to ask people to work on specific projects, feature goals, and bugs. He does exactly this.

Shuttleworth also maintains a tie-breaking vote on the Technical Board and Community Council but has never used this power and has publicly said that he will not use it lightly. In situations where the boards are split and there is no one "right" answer, the SABDFL will provide a decision instead of more debate. The SABDFL exists to provide clear leadership on difficult issues and to set the pace and direction for the project. In exchange for this power, he has the responsibility to listen to the community and to understand that the use of his SABDFL authority can weaken the project.

Ubunteros and Ubuntu Members

Membership in the Ubuntu project is one official way that the project recognizes sustained and significant contributions. The first level of membership in Ubuntu is as an Ubuntero. Ubunteros are Ubuntu activists and can be any person in the Ubuntu community who has explicitly committed to observing the Ubuntu Code of Conduct. Ubunteros are self-nominated and self-confirmed. Using Launchpad, participants can generate a GPG encryption key and "sign" the Code of Conduct as a way of pledging to uphold it within the Ubuntu community. By doing so, that participant automatically gains status as an Ubuntero.

The next, more significant, step is official membership. Official membership is available to any Ubuntero who has demonstrated a significant and sustained set of contributions to the Ubuntu community. These contributions can be of any kind—technical or nontechnical—but need to be of a form that can be represented to one of the Ubuntu membership boards, under the authority of the Community Council. The membership board before which a candidate appears will consider each application individually. A non-exhaustive list of some of the types of contributions that qualify appears in the following section on getting involved. The membership boards try to be flexible in the variety of different types of contributions that will be accepted in consideration of membership.

Ubuntu members are responsible for confirming, by voting, all nominations to the Ubuntu Community Council. They also may be asked by the Community Council to vote on resolutions put to the general membership. In exchange, members gain the right to an @ubuntu.com e-mail address and the right to carry Ubuntu business cards. Membership lasts for two years and is renewable. Members who fail to renew their membership will be marked as inactive but, with renewed activity and a simple procedure that involves approval of the Community Council, can be easily reactivated.

The process to become a member is relatively straightforward and is documented in depth on the Ubuntu Web site. Most important, it requires that users document their contributions on a wiki page that includes links to code, mailing list messages, specific forms of documentation that clearly demonstrate their involvement, and/or other relevant material. Membership applications also need to include testimonials on work and involvement in Ubuntu from current Ubuntu members.

Getting Involved

Users can participate in the Ubuntu community on a variety of levels and in a multitude of ways. The following subsections, adapted largely from a page with links to relevant resources online on the Ubuntu Web site (www.ubuntu.com/community/participate), provides a good list of ways in which people can get a running start in the Ubuntu community. An expanded but unofficial list appears at http://wiki.ubuntu.com/ContributeToUbuntu. Both lists are broken down into the major ways to get involved.

Advocacy

The easiest way for someone to contribute to the Ubuntu community is simply by telling others about Ubuntu. Advocacy frequently occurs in a variety of ways. One good method involves joining or starting a LoCo team. LoCos, described earlier in this chapter, provide a method through which you can get involved in Ubuntu activities. If users do not have a LoCo and do not have the critical mass of users to start one, they might help build support by giving a talk about Ubuntu to a local Linux User Group or other technical group. Ubuntu members and LoCo teams can order CDs at no cost and can distribute them. Through these and other means, advocacy provides a great way to spread the word about Ubuntu and offers a low-barrier opportunity to make contributions to the community.

Support

One of the most meaningful ways that users can contribute to Ubuntu is by helping others use the software. Users can do this by joining the support-oriented mailing lists, IRC channels, or forums, as described in detail earlier in this chapter. By responding to requests for help in each of these venues, users can help other users get up and running on Ubuntu. Even if users are themselves beginners, the knowledge they gain in solving even simple problems enables them to help users who run into the same issues, and as community member and Canonical employee Fabián Rodríguez said at the Jaunty Open Week in April 2009, "Every user is someone's guru."

Ideas and Feedback

Another way to contribute to Ubuntu is by helping steer the direction of the project by describing a vision or providing ideas. This can be done by participating in discussion and brainstorming sessions at conferences and on the Ubuntu wiki. By monitoring specifications as they are written and creating feedback, especially at early stages, users can make meaningful contributions. However, users contributing ideas should remember that talk is cheap. Users are wise to work with others to help turn their visions into reality.

Documentation

When a user is stumped by a problem, chances are good that other users will also be frustrated by it. If users are not in a position to write code to change the situation, they may be able to help others by writing up their experiences and documenting the solution. Ubuntu has a vibrant documentation team and community, and writing documentation is a great low-barrier way to make meaningful contributions to the Ubuntu community.

Users aiming to contribute to Ubuntu's documentation would be advised to take notes as they puzzle through problems and to document solutions when they find them. Before writing, users should also check to see whether documentation for a particular problem already exists. When it does, users would be wise to choose to improve or augment existing documentation rather than write a new document. Similarly, users can also make meaningful contributions by reading through existing documentation and fixing factual, technical, stylistic, spelling, and grammar errors. Users who spend a large amount of time working on documentation may, with time, also want to join the Ubuntu Documentation Team, which can help organize and coordinate this work in terms of Ubuntu documentation goals.

Artwork

For those users who feel that their strengths are primarily artistic, there are many ways to improve the style and feel of the Ubuntu desktop through wholly artistic contributions. For example, Ubuntu is always in need of new ideas for wallpapers, icons, and graphical themes. Inkscape, similar in many respects to Adobe Illustrator, is a great piece of free software in

Ubuntu that proves useful for this type of work. As with documentation, there is an Ubuntu Art Team that helps coordinate artistic work within the Ubuntu community.

Translation and Localization

The discussion of LoCos should have already made it clear that translation is a great way that anyone with a firm understanding of English and another language can contribute to the Ubuntu community. Translation through Rosetta (described in Chapter 10) allows users to translate as little as a single string or as much as an entire application. Through its easy interface and Web-based nature, it provides a low-barrier road to contribution. Serious translators should join a local community team and the ubuntu-translators mailing list so that they can stay in touch with other Ubuntu localizers.

Quality Assurance and Bugs

Quality assurance (QA) is something for which many companies hire special engineers. In Ubuntu, the Development Team relies on itself and the community to test software before it is released to let developers know about problems so that the bugs can be squashed before the vast majority of users ever see it. To test software, users merely need to upgrade to the latest development version of Ubuntu and to upgrade regularly. When users helping out with QA find bugs, they should report them in the Ubuntu bug-tracking system, Malone (see Chapter 10). They can also help by "triaging" bugs, closing or merging duplicates, or verifying bugs and adding information to a bug's description. If you intend to become involved in QA, you should subscribe to the ubuntu-devel-announce mailing list, and you should consider monitoring ubuntu-devel as well.

Programming and Packaging

The final way that users can contribute to the Ubuntu community is through the production of code. Because Ubuntu is free and open source software, users can get access to every piece of software that Ubuntu supports. This allows users to package additional software for inclusion in Ubuntu, to fix bugs, and to add features. Developers, like people testing software, should subscribe to the ubuntu-devel-announce mailing list and should consider monitoring ubuntu-devel, too. The best way to begin making contributions is then through the MOTU team as a MOTU hopeful, as described earlier. Users can also look through a list of specifications to find a project that they find personally interesting. In some situations, there are even bounties available—small amounts of money offered to those who fulfill a small feature goal that has remained unfilled for some period of time.

Summary

Ubuntu is a vibrant and diverse community that is active around the world and in many languages. Its activities happen primarily online in a variety of virtual venues, including mailing lists, IRC, Web forums, wikis, and two special Web-based community portals known as The Fridge and Planet Ubuntu. Ubuntu complements this virtual activity with real-life meetings and conferences. The Ubuntu community is broken down into a variety of teams and processes. At the top of this government structure is the Ubuntu Community Council, the Technical Board, and SABDFL Mark Shuttleworth. Through a variety of ways, this community is designed to facilitate contributions easily. Ultimately, these contributions are recognized through a process culminating in official project membership and enfranchisement.

CHAPTER 8

Using Kubuntu

THE KUBUNTU PROJECT STRIVES to take the best of Ubuntu and the best of the K Desktop Environment (KDE) to produce a great Linux distribution. This chapter covers information ranging from what exactly Kubuntu is to how to manage and keep your Kubuntu system up to date with the latest applications and fixes. The goal of Kubuntu is to provide a graphically beautiful and easy-to-use Linux operating system, an OS that is simple to customize to your desire.

Introduction to Kubuntu

Kubuntu is an official product of Ubuntu—a complete implementation of the Ubuntu OS led by Jonathan Riddell (an employee of Canonical, Ltd.) and an army of developers. However, Kubuntu uses KDE as the graphical user interface instead of GNOME, as in Ubuntu. The main goal of Kubuntu is to be an integrated Linux distribution with all of the great features of Ubuntu, but based on KDE. Since Kubuntu is an official part of the Ubuntu community, it adheres to the same Ubuntu manifesto: Great software should be available free of charge and should be usable by people in their own language and regardless of disability. Also, people should be able to customize and alter their software in ways they deem fit.

Like Ubuntu, Kubuntu makes the following commitments: Kubuntu will provide the very best translations and accessibility infrastructure that the free software community has to offer; Kubuntu will always be free of charge, and there is no extra cost for an "enterprise" version; and Kubuntu will always provide the latest and best software from the KDE community.

Looking for a certain piece of software? Kubuntu has it, with more than 1,000 pieces of software in its repositories, including the latest kernel version and, of course, the latest KDE. The standard desktop applications (Web browsing, e-mail, word processing, and spreadsheet applications) allow Kubuntu to replace any current desktop OS. If you are running servers—whether they're Web servers, e-mail servers, or database servers—Kubuntu can do that as well.

A History of KDE

In 1996, Matthias Etrich posted a now famous newsgroup post that described some of the problems he had with the UNIX desktop.

> UNIX popularity grows thanks to the free variants, mostly Linux. But still a consistent, nice looking, free desktop environment is missing. There are several nice either free or low-priced applications available, so that Linux/X11 would almost fit everybody's needs if we could offer a real GUI. . . .
>
> IMHO a GUI should offer a complete graphical environment. It should allow a user to do his everyday tasks with it, like starting applications, reading mail, configuring his desktop. . . . All parts must fit together. . . .
>
> The goal is NOT to create a GUI for the complete UNIX-system or the System-Administrator. . . . The idea is to create a GUI for an ENDUSER.

With that post, he started building the KDE Project. KDE originally stood for the Kool Desktop Environment but was adapted to be K Desktop Environment. The mascot for KDE is a green dragon named Konqi, who can be found in various applications.

Matthias chose to develop KDE around the Qt toolkit, and by 1997, the first large, complex applications were being released. However, there was much debate because Qt was not licensed with a free software license. Two projects came about from this debate, one named Harmony, which would use only free libraries, and another project called GNOME. In 1998, the Qt toolkit was licensed under a new open source license called the Q Public License (QPL), and in 2000, Qt was released under the GNU General Public License.

KDE is primarily a volunteer effort. However, many companies employ developers to work on this project. Some of these companies include Novell (through the purchase of SUSE Linux) and Trolltech (the company that produces the Qt toolkit).

KDE 4.0 came with a great number of changes to the desktop environment, including the introduction of Plasma, Solid, Krunner, and many other infrastructure changes, most of which are discussed throughout this chapter.

KDE 4.4 is the current version of KDE that ships with Kubuntu 10.04. Significant improvements have been made over the first release of KDE.

For more information on KDE, visit the project's Web site at www.kde.org. The project's home page also provides information on how you can help with the project and contribute to the KDE community.

A History of Kubuntu

When Ubuntu was first being discussed, there were rumors that it would be based only on GNOME and that KDE would be left out. Jonathan Riddell, a KDE developer, posted an article on his blog that soon became the Number 1 hit on Google for Ubuntu Linux. The article states:

> The signs are there that this could be something big, more so than the likes of Linspire, Xandros or Lycrosis. Unlike those companies, they [Canonical, Ltd.] understand Free Software and open development. It is likely to be a GNOME-based job, but maybe there is a KDE developer out there who is working for them without letting on. If not I'm always available.

This post started a flurry of activity for both Riddell and the others who wanted to participate.

A lot of changes needed to be made to get Kubuntu working correctly. The hardware abstraction layer (HAL) and other programs and packages had to be changed to fit the philosophy of Ubuntu. A clean Kmenu had be created, and more people were needed to join the project. It was a conscious decision to keep the default KDE colors and icons in order to remain as close to KDE as possible.

A lot of great releases have come since the first of Kubuntu, and 10.04 will build on them. Kubuntu was the first released distribution to include KDE 4.0 by default, in Kubuntu 8.10.

Like Ubuntu, Kubuntu 10.04 is a long-term release; however, it is only the second long-term release for the Kubuntu team. As mentioned elsewhere in the book, a long-term release means 10.04 will be supported on the desktop for 3 years.

Prior to the 10.04 release, a group of Kubuntu developers got together to discuss what exactly needed to be changed and improved. Out of these discussions came what has been named "Project Timelord" with the goals to focus on translations, marketing, software, user–developer interaction, and recruitment. An example of this is the Firefox Installer, discussed later in the chapter.

Kubuntu 10.04 also includes the first official release of a netbook-specific edition called Kubuntu Netbook Remix.

Kubuntu is quickly building a sizable community of its own. There are more dedicated package maintainers joining the Kubuntu community as well as a growing and equally dedicated documentation team. In addition, many community and enthusiast sites help provide both support and current information. These include sites such as www.kubuntuforums.net. Kubuntu has grown tremendously from just one developer to a large group as it continues to improve the quality of the distribution.

Installing Kubuntu

Installing Kubuntu is just like installing Ubuntu. It is pretty much a snap. Let's start with where you can find it.

Where to Find Kubuntu

Kubuntu is available at www.kubuntu.org/download.php. An image file can be downloaded and then burned onto either a DVD or a CD-ROM. Two different types of Kubuntu images can be downloaded and used. The first is the desktop CD, which allows the user to test and run Kubuntu without changing any settings. The second is the alternate install CD, which provides for a more advanced installation.

The desktop CD of Kubuntu 10.04 is the primary way to install Kubuntu on your system. This CD is a great way to demonstrate the power of Kubuntu to your friends before they install it on their systems. The desktop CD acts as a live CD and allows Kubuntu to run on your system without erasing anything already installed.

Can I Switch to Kubuntu If I Have Ubuntu Installed Already?

If you have installed Ubuntu on your system already, it is extremely easy to install and configure Kubuntu. In Synaptic Package Manager, find the package kubuntu-desktop, which provides all the necessary programs to have your system look and act like Kubuntu. Don't worry—you can still switch between Ubuntu with GNOME and Kubuntu with KDE. Once Kubuntu is installed, you can choose which desktop environment to use, either GNOME or KDE. Also, if you have Kubuntu installed already and wish to install Ubuntu, it is just as simple to switch: Just install ubuntu-desktop through Software Management, and you will be using the GNOME desktop. For those who are switching from Ubuntu to Kubuntu, Software Management performs the same function as Ubuntu Software Center.

Once you have installed the kubuntu-desktop package, end your GNOME session and choose Session from the menu. Select KDE instead of GNOME as your window manager, and then select Make Default. From now on, KDE will start for you when you sign on.

Installing from the Desktop CD

Kubuntu has the ability to install directly from the desktop CD, so there is no need to download separate CDs; simply download the desktop CD and show off to your friends how great Kubuntu is, or give it a test run for the first time. The live installer program for both Ubuntu and Kubuntu is called Ubiquity.

After you start up the desktop CD, an icon called Install appears on your desktop. Choose to install Kubuntu, and Ubiquity guides you through the installation phase (Figure 8-1).

Ubiquity guides you in setting up the correct country and time zone (Figure 8-2).

Once you have answered these questions, Ubiquity prompts you to select the correct keyboard layout (Figure 8-3), create a username and password, configure your disk and its partitions (Figure 8-4), and create your user-name and assign a name to the computer (Figure 8-5).

When everything is all set, click Install to finish the installation (Figure 8-6).

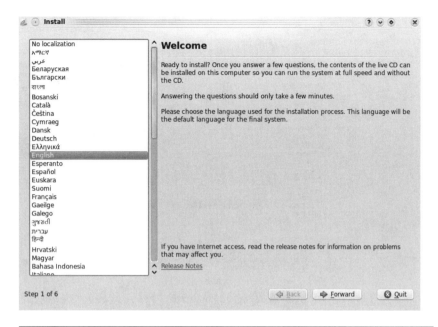

Figure 8-1 Welcome screen of Ubiquity

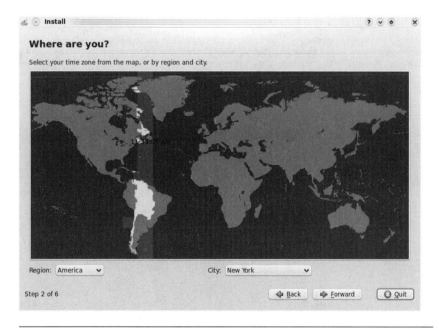

Figure 8-2 Selecting the correct time zone

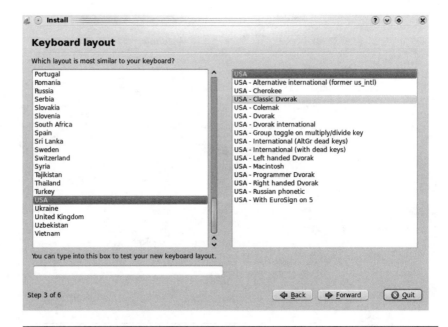

Figure 8-3 Selecting the keyboard layout

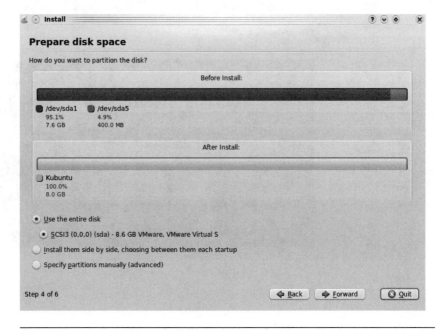

Figure 8-4 Configuring the disk partitions

Figure 8-5 Configuring the username and computer name

Figure 8-6 Finishing the installation

Navigating in Kubuntu

All of the applications in Kubuntu can be accessed through the Application Launcher (Figure 8-7), which is located in the bottom left corner of the Task Manager.

An additional change in KDE 4 to the Application Launcher is how applications are named. Instead of program names (familiar to those who have previously used some version of KDE) such as Konqueror, Akregator, and Kontact, the applications are named after their purpose. For example, Akregator shows up as RSS Feed Reader, and Konqueror shows up as Web Browser.

Once you click on the Application Launcher, you are presented first with Favorites, which is a list designed for applications that are used regularly. You can add any application to the Favorites at any time. Kubuntu 10.04

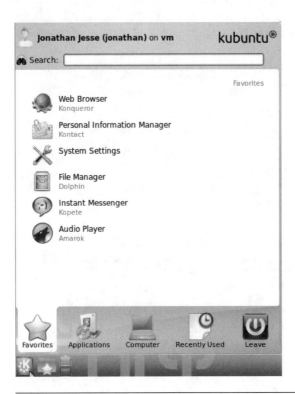

Figure 8-7 KDE4 Application Launcher

ships with Web Browser, Personal Information Manager, System Settings, File Manager, Instant Messenger, and Audio Player already listed in the Favorites section. To remove an application from the Favorites portion of the Application Launcher, right-click on the application and select Remove From Favorites. Likewise, to add an application to the Favorites section, right-click on the application you would like to add and select Add to Favorites.

After the Favorites tab is the Applications portion of the Application Launcher. These applications are organized according to type of program. For example, Instant Messenger (Kopete) is located under the Internet section, while CD & DVD Burning (K3B) is located under the Multimedia section.

The third tab is the Computer tab. This tab provides quick access to different folders within the file system, including the home directory network folders and the CD-ROM drive. The Computer section is divided into Applications (System Settings), Places (Home, Network, Root, Trash), and Removable Storage (Floppy Drive, CD-ROM, and any USB drives).

The fourth tab is the Recently Used section, which is populated by both applications and documents that have recently been used.

One of the best features of the new Application Launcher is the Search Bar at the top of the page (Figure 8-8). The search program searches both menus in the Application Launcher and the Web for information.

Shutting Down Your Computer and Logging Out

To shut down your computer, log out, or switch users, go to the Application Launcher, and under the tab labeled Leave, select the option you would like. This section is divided into two subsections: Session and System. Since Kubuntu is a multiuser system (many users per system), you can easily switch to a parallel session as a different user under the Session subsection. Also under Session, you can Lock the Screen or Logout (ending the current session). Under the System subsection, you can either shut down (Turn off the computer) or restart (Restart the computer). Figure 8-9 shows these options. Also, you can lock the session or Logout by right-clicking on the desktop and selecting the correct option.

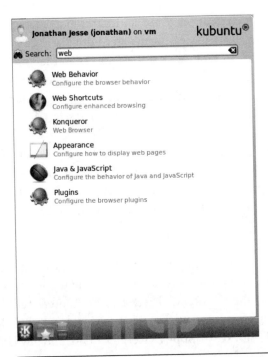

Figure 8-8 Using the Search portion of the Application Launcher

Figure 8-9 Logging out of Kubuntu

Using sudo Instead of a Root Account

A large change for many seasoned users of other Linux distributions is the lack of a root account. Upon installation, you are not prompted to create a root password. The password created with the first user, your password, will allow you to access the administrative functions. You will need the sudo password often when configuring the system or making global changes.

Customizing Kubuntu

A major feature of Kubuntu is the ability to customize almost everything and anything in the system. If you don't like the desktop background, change it. Would you like to remove the new Application Launcher and go back to the old Kmenu style? Likewise, if you would like to remove the new Application Launcher and go back to the old Kmenu style, you can do that as well. Customizing Kubuntu to fit your personal preference is almost effortless.

Customizing Plasma

Continued improvements in KDE 4 have been made to Plasma, the replacement for Kdesktop. A great amount of customization can be done with Plasma, including the addition or subtraction of widgets. From the Plasma Web page (http://plasma.kde.org), Plasma is defined as "the component that is 'in charge' of the desktop interface; the desktop, panel (often referred to simply as the task bar), and related elements."

Widgets allow you to add and remove items from your desktop. A widget can be something from the Application Launcher, for example, or a clock showing a different time zone. Widgets can be added to the desktop only if the Plasma is unlocked by clicking on the Plasma icon on the top left and selecting Unlock Widgets.

To add widgets, either right-click on the desktop and select Add Widgets or click on the Plasma Toolbox located in the top right-hand corner of the desktop (Figure 8-10).

Additional widgets are available through the extragears package (installed via Software Management) and also on kde-look.org under the Widgets section. In fact, in KDE 4, the Application Launcher and Task Manager are both widgets that can be added or removed for complete customization. If

Figure 8-10 Adding Widgets via the Plasma toolkit

the old Kmenu is more your style, remove the Application Launcher widget and replace it with the Application Launcher Menu.

To change the background on the desktop, right-click on the desktop and select Desktop Activity Settings. This opens up the Desktop Settings > Plasma Workspace where you can change the Wallpaper, Activity, and Mouse Actions. New wallpaper can be added through Get Hot New Stuff.

In KDE 4.4, Plasma supports different types of activities; by default, the type is set for Desktop. Another activity type could be Folder View, which holds the contents of a specific folder. In the Kubuntu Netbook Remix Edition, there are two additional activity types: Search and Locate and Newspaper.

NOTE: For more information on Kubuntu Netbook Remix, please refer to Help > Netbook > System Documentation.

Choosing how the desktop looks can help give a personalized feel to Kubuntu. If the appearance seems lacking, you can make further changes by choosing System Settings > Appearance. You can further customize things, such as color, icons, and style. Kubuntu is all about customization, something you may be sick of hearing about, and there are many ways to change the desktop's appearance, which almost guarantees that no two users will have identical desktops.

Get Hot New Stuff

Looking for the latest screen saver, desktop background, or other cool things for your Kubuntu installation? Kubuntu fully supports the Get Hot New Stuff (GHNS) framework of KDE. GHNS allows people to upload templates to a server and have other users download and use that template. In an interview posted on KDE News (http://dot.kde.org/1110652641), Josef Spillner describes exactly how the process works.

> [U]ser A is using a spreadsheet application and modifies a template that comes with it. This template can then be uploaded to a server and eventually be downloaded by user B by checking the contents of the "Get Hot New Stuff" download dialogue.

The GHNS framework (Figure 8-11) shows up in several places throughout Kubuntu.

Figure 8-11 The GHNS framework at work

Different applications have the ability to download information from the Internet and from KDE sites. Throughout applications in Kubuntu, you will find references to Get More, which uses the GHNS framework.

System Administration

Like any computer application or system, Kubuntu occasionally needs administrative support. Do not be afraid of personally administrating your Kubuntu system. While system administration is not completely foolproof, a lot of changes have been made to help make administration easier. Knowledge of command line will go a long way, but the developers have made sure to provide graphical interfaces wherever it makes sense to do so. Everything from changing the IP address (e.g., from DHCP to a static address) to installing packages can be done without having to drop down to the command line. This section focuses exclusively on system administration performed through the graphical interface.

Installing New Packages

As mentioned earlier, Kubuntu is built around some of the same applications and systems as Ubuntu. All applications are installed through packages. Like Ubuntu, Kubuntu uses the Advanced Package Tool (APT), and also like Ubuntu, Kubuntu has a wonderful graphical interface. Kubuntu's graphical installer is called KPackageKit.

In previous versions of Kubuntu, Adept software was used to install and update packages; however, this application was no longer being developed and also was not updated for KDE 4. The developers of Kubuntu switched to KPackageKit, and many improvements to the application were made during the release cycle. The developers of KPackageKit and the Kubuntu developers worked together to make sure this application was up to the quality that Kubuntu users expect.

KPackageKit is found in the Application Launcher under Applications > System > Software Management and can also be launched through Krunner as Software Management.

Upon launching Software Management, you are presented with the KPackageKit application (Figure 8-12).

Figure 8-12 KPackageKit

Three options are available in Software Management: Add and Remove Software (through the Software Management section), Software Updates, and Settings.

In order to add a new piece of software, type the name of the application in the search bar. The screenshots in Figures 8-13 and 8-14 show searching for a chess game and then selecting it for installation.

Once you click on the application to install, more details about the package are displayed, including the description of the package, the file list, other packages that depend on this package, as well as the other packages required by this package. This information allows you to understand what files are being installed and to make sure the correct packages are being downloaded and installed so the application works properly.

To install the application, click on the "+" (plus sign).

This will queue the package to be installed; click on Apply to set up the application on the system. Unlike Microsoft Windows, Kubuntu is great

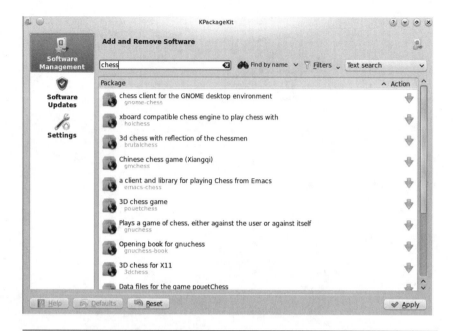

Figure 8-13 Searching for a chess game

Figure 8-14 Selecting 3dchess for installation

about not forcing a system restart in order for the new application to work correctly.

NOTE: A restart could be required if the version of KDE or the kernel is changed, but it is not necessary for the more typical and common update.

Managing Repositories

The Software Management application has the ability to manage the repositories you would like to use. To change which repositories are being used, open Software Management and select settings and the select "Edit Software Sources." After you provide the correct password, a new window will open up (see Figure 8-15).

Software Sources is divided into five sections: Kubuntu Software, Other Software, Updates, Authentication, and Statistics.

Packages are organized into four groups or repositories: main, restricted, universe, and multiverse. The main repository contains applications that are free software, programs that allow for complete distribution and are supported by the Kubuntu team. When you install something from the main repository, you are guaranteed to receive security updates and support through the various venues.

Anything from the multiverse repository contains software that is not free, which is defined by the Kubuntu Main Component License Policy. Software here is used at the user's own risk.

Third-party software is not supported by Kubuntu.

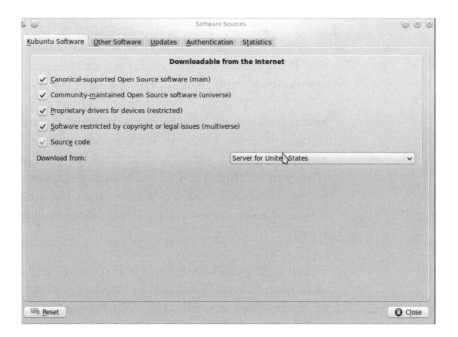

Figure 8-15 Software Source lists

Upgrading Kubuntu

If you are currently using Kubuntu 9.10 and would like to upgrade to Kubuntu 10.04, you can use the update manager to install the new version. There is no need to purchase new software or reload your system; just update from the current version to the latest stable release. From the console, type sudo do-release-upgrade and watch your system upgrade from Kubuntu 9.10 to Kubuntu 10.04.

How to Keep the System Up to Date

Kubuntu will check to see if your system is up to date. Software Management will notify you in the task bar and prompt you to update your system.

In the Settings portion of Software Management, you can change how often the system checks for updates (by default, it is every week). Another setting that can change is whether or not the system will automatically install the updates or prompt you for your updates.

System Settings

System Settings allows users to make changes to the system, including settings for sound, user accounts, mouse behavior, and network configuration. If you are familiar with KDE, you may recognize that System Settings replaces the K Control Center. Figure 8-16 shows System Settings.

System Settings can be found in the Application Launcher, or type System Settings in the search bar of the launcher, or in KRunner. (KRunner is accessed by either right-clicking on the desktop and selecting Run Application or by hitting ALT-F2.) When making changes in System Settings, you will be prompted at times to enter your password. Changes made that require a password are systemwide and will affect all users of the Kubuntu system.

System Settings is divided into two tabs, General and Advanced, and each tab is further divided into sections based on tasks. Under the General tab are the following sections: Look & Feel, Personal, Network & Connectivity, and Computer Administration. The Advanced tab contains two sections: Advanced User Settings and System.

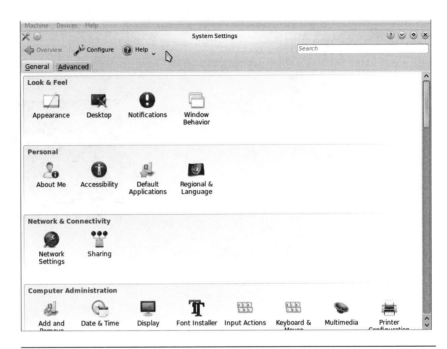

Figure 8-16 System Settings

When moving through the different options, be sure to select Overview to return to the main screen of System Settings instead of clicking on the X. Doing so may take some getting used to.

Look & Feel

The Look & Feel section allows further customization of your Kubuntu system. Sections here include Appearance, Desktop, Notifications, and Window Behavior. One of the options in this section (under the Appearance section) is to customize the splash screen, known as the ksplash (Figure 8-17), displayed after you log in.

Personal

In the Personal section, you can change information about yourself, including your password, settings for your region and language, default applications, and accessibility options.

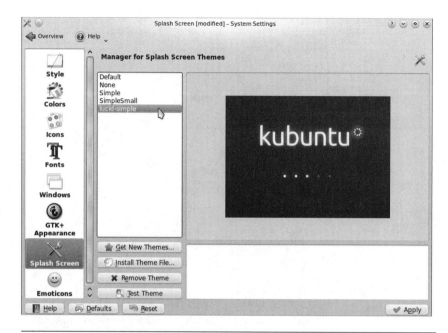

Figure 8-17 Customizing the splash screen

Network & Connectivity

This section allows us to change some network settings and also change items about sharing.

Computer Administration

The Computer Administration section allows you to add or remove software and to change items such as the date and time, display, fonts, input actions, keyboard and mouse settings, and multimedia.

The Display section allows you to change the screen resolution and orientation. If you are using an external monitor or a projector, this is where you would customize those settings. The Power Control Section deals with whether or not the monitor should turn off or go into standby to help conserve power. Figure 8-18 shows the display section of System Settings.

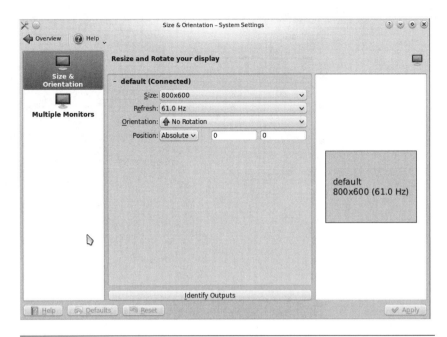

Figure 8-18 Display section of System Settings

Add or Remove Software

New to Kubuntu 10.04 is the addition of Add or Remove Software to System Settings. By opening this portion of System Settings, you open up KPackageKit to install new software. This functions the same way as described under the section Installing New Software.

Printer Configuration

Printer configuration is where users add or make changes to printers. Most printers these days already have drivers available in Kubuntu, and upon detecting a new printer for the first time, the printer configuration wizard will start. The following screenshots show this wizard (Figures 8-19 and 8-20).

Advanced Tab

The Advanced tab of System Settings allows for further customization of user settings. This section is divided into Advanced User Settings and System.

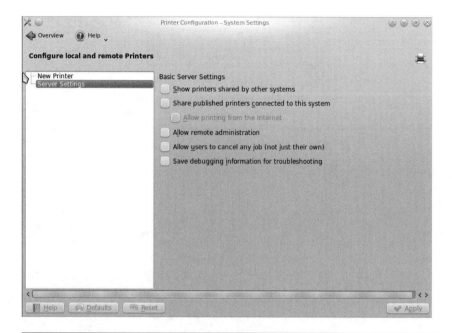

Figure 8-19 Printer Configuration—System Settings

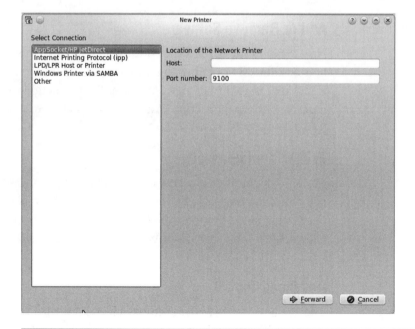

Figure 8-20 New Printer

Advanced User Settings

The advanced user settings portion of the Advanced Tab allows you to customize things such as how Kubuntu handles audio CDs, digital camera settings, file associations, and so on.

The Service Manager, shown in Figure 8-21, is one such Advanced User Setting that allows you to configure what services start during boot up of the computer. In order to make changes, first put in your password and then you can start and stop services that are running.

Also in Advanced User Settings is the ability to configure how Desktop Search works.

"Akonadi is a cross-desktop storage service for Personal Information Manager data (calendars, contacts, email, etc.) and also for the metadata" (http://pim.kde.or/akonadi for more information). Nepomuk can work together with Akonadi and helps you organize the information and metadata on your machine. (For more information, see http://nepomuk.semanticdesktop.org.) Another portion of Nepomuk is Desktop Search (Figure 8-22), which

Figure 8-21 Service Manager

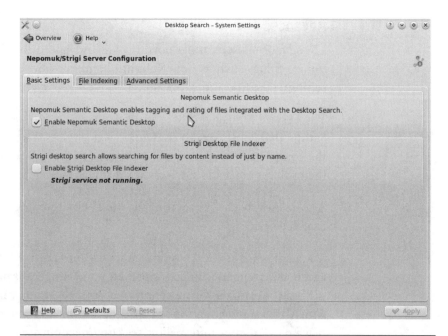

Figure 8-22 Desktop Search: Basic Settings

provides the ability to search for files and applications on your system. These two applications can be configured through System Settings.

The first tab (Basic Settings) of Desktop Search is where you select whether or not the Semantic Desktop is enabled or the Strigi desktop search is running.

The second tab (File Indexing) allows you to select what folders are indexed for searching. This is also where you can exclude file types from being indexed. The third tab (Advanced Settings) sets the maximum amount of memory the database should use.

New to Lucid is the Open Collaboration Services provider management section of System Settings. This is part of the Social Desktop that is being worked on by the KDE developers. OpenDesktop.org is, according to its Web site,

> one of the biggest online communities, social networks, and portals for the free desktop movement in the world where developers, artists, and users can share applications, tools, wallpapers, sounds, icons, themes, and other artwork and stuff for the open desktop.

This module of System Settings allows individual users to log in to or create accounts. The login here will be saved and can be used by different plasmoids within the system.

System

Changes made to the entire system are made in this section. Changes include K3bSetup, Login Manager, and User Management.

K3b Setup   This module in System Settings controls how the CD/DVD burning software works and is configured. Chances are good that you will not have to make any changes to K3b in order to burn CDs or DVDs.

Login Manager   When you launch this module, you will be prompted for your administrative password. The Login Manager is where your username and password is typed in, and it allows you to log in. In this section, you can customize exactly what happens and how it looks when you log in (Figure 8-23).

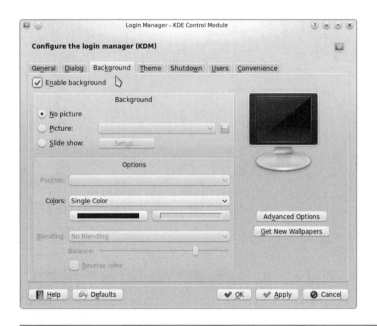

Figure 8-23 Login Manager

One of the items that can be configured is the Auto-login. This is NOT RECOMMENDED because anyone will have access to your machine as soon as it is powered on. Select the user you would like to Auto-login and select Apply.

User Management   The User Management module allows you create new users and even change access rights. To create a new user, click on New and follow the wizard (Figures 8-24 and 8-25).

Managing Files with Kubuntu

Now that you have your system installed and set up the way you would like, it is time to learn how to navigate the different files and access information in Kubuntu. This starts with the default file manager, Dolphin. Konqueror, another application that can be used both as a Web browser and a file manager, is discussed later in the chapter.

Figure 8-24 User Management

Figure 8-25 Create a new user

Introduction to Dolphin

Dolphin was first introduced during the 7.10 release schedule as d3lphin. The KDE 4 version, Dolphin, is now included as the default file manager (see Figure 8-26).

Konqueror, which is also the KDE Web browser, was the previous default file manager. Over time, Konqueror development focused increasingly on the Web browser, while ignoring its file manager functionality. Dolphin focuses only on local files, is built on the Konqueror back end, and should be familiar to many KDE users.

Another key feature of Dolphin is the ability to use a split view to have multiple directories open in the same window, without having to switch tabs.

Dolphin is a very powerful file manager that nicely complements Konqueror. The two programs are often used in tandem.

Changes to the File Structure

Kubuntu 10.04 release utilizes the XDG Base Directory Specification of the freedesktop.org standards.

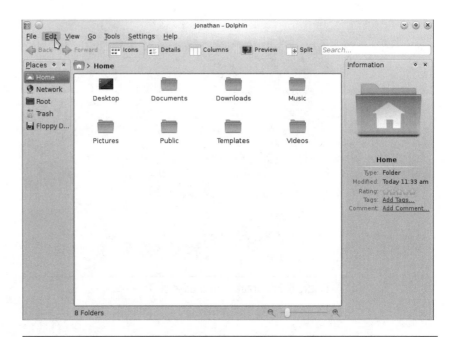

Figure 8-26 Viewing the Home Directory in Dolphin

XDG directories specify a default set of folders within a user's home directory. Some of these folders are Desktop, Downloads, Templates, Music, and Video. The goal is to help create a standard location for files to be stored in a variety of different desktop environments (see Figure 8-27).

Introduction to Konqueror

Konqueror may be the old default file manager in Kubuntu, but it still has a lot to offer. As a file manager, Konqueror can do nearly everything you need (Figure 8-28). You can browse files through either an icon view or a tree view. Copying, pasting, moving, and deleting files are all simple tasks with Konqueror. A nice feature of Konqueror is that directories are automatically updated. This means that if a file is created in a directory currently being viewed, you do not need to refresh the directory to see the changes.

One of the great things about Konqueror is how much you can do within it. Need access to media files? Simply type media:/ and browse your media files. All kinds of other shortcuts, called kioslaves, exist in Konqueror, including

Figure 8-27 Viewing XDG directories in Dolphin

Figure 8-28 Konqueror

ones for searching the Web with Google (gg:/*KEYWORD*) and even browsing files via ssh through sftp://. Need help finding a file on your system? Simply use locate:/ to have Konqueror find it for you. You can visit the different system folders through system:/. Many shortcuts and keywords like this are built into Konqueror, including Google Suggest in the search bar.

Accessing Windows Partitions

A lot of people still have Windows partitions on their hard drives and would like to access the information stored there. Kubuntu can browse these files in read-only mode. By default, Kubuntu mounts the Windows partition in the /media directory. See Figure 8-29 for an example of accessing the Windows drive in Dolphin.

Accessing USB Drives

USB drives are everywhere these days, and Kubuntu handles them quite easily. Simply connect your USB drive, and it will mount automatically. It will then be available under Dolphin through the media folder. Before removing the drive, make sure you unmount it by right-clicking on the device and selecting Eject. The device can then be safely removed.

Managing Music

Amarok is the default application for browsing and managing your music collection. Kubuntu 10.04 includes Amarok 2, which is a large rewrite of Amarok. Amarok is a powerful program that can track your podcasts and music and even provides access to an open music store (Magnatune). Magnatune is a music store that is completely free of DRM (Digital Rights Management) restrictions. Looking for Online Radio stations? Amarok provides access to multiple online radio stations through Cool Streams and also Shoutcast Streams. Amarok can also manage your portable music player (Figure 8-30). Once you have connected your music player, it will show up in the device section. Then feel free to manage your files and playlists.

The first time Amarok is launched, it recommends installing additional multimedia packages from the restricted repository. The recommended packages are for MP3 Tag Reading and Encoding, Flash, Video Codecs, MPEG Plug-ins, and DVD Reading. A notification from Update Notifier will load in the Taskbar, and after double-clicking, you will be prompted to

Figure 8-29 Accessing the Windows partition in Dolphin

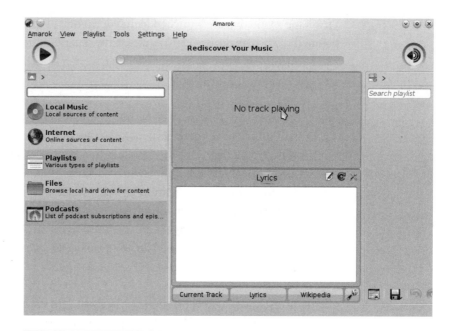

Figure 8-30 Managing your music player in Amarok

select which components to install. To install these packages, you need the administrative password. See Chapter 3's discussion of Ubuntu Multimedia for more information about media codecs and related issues.

Common Applications

Kubuntu comes with a large number of applications preinstalled and configured, including Web browsers, office applications, and e-mail programs. Remember, since choice is a huge feature of Kubuntu, if you do not like the default applications, you can always change them. All of these applications are available through the Application Launcher.

OpenOffice.org

The default office application for Kubuntu 10.04 is OpenOffice.org 3.0.1. This version is an update of the second major release of the suite that includes Writer, Calc, Impress, Draw, and Math; the first three can be launched from the Application Launcher. (Draw and Math are not available from the menu and are launched from within one of the other applications.) Note that the developers of Kubuntu have renamed the applications in the Application Launcher to better reflect what each does. For example, Writer is renamed Word Processor.

Each of these programs is easy to use and can help you switch from the Microsoft Office product line. In fact, the OpenOffice.org suite is included in the desktop CD and can be installed on a Windows system to help you get comfortable and ready for a switch to Kubuntu. Each application corresponds to a similar application in the Microsoft product line. Calc is very similar to Excel, Writer works like Word, and Impress replaces Power-Point. OpenOffice.org can handle all but Microsoft Access files without problems, and the whole suite is ready to be used in a corporate environment as well as for personal use.

To demonstrate the power of OpenOffice.org, let's create a new document. To start OpenOffice.org Writer, open the Application Launcher and navigate to Office and then Word Processor. You can also launch KRunner (Alt+F2), type Word processor, and hit Enter.

Writer resembles any other word processing software you have used. Simply start typing your letter or paper as you normally would, and use the toolbar for formatting options, including changing alignment, setting boldface or italic type, and other needs.

When you are done working on a document, save it by selecting File > Save or by typing Ctrl-S. OpenOffice.org saves documents in the Open Document format. This file format is a standard across the world. You can also save documents in other formats, including Microsoft Office and Adobe PDF. To save as a PDF file, just click the PDF button on the main toolbar (located next to the print icon) and enter a filename.

Web Browsing with Konqueror

As mentioned earlier, Konqueror can function as a Web browser as well as a file manager. To launch Konqueror, open the Application Launcher and navigate to Internet, then Web Browser. Alternately, you can launch KRunner (Alt+F2) and type in Konqueror. Like other modern Web browsers, Konqueror provides tabbed browsing, the ability to have multiple Web pages open in the same window. To do this, select File > New Tab or press Ctrl+T. A new tab will be created in your open Konqueror window. A cool feature is that you can be browsing the Web in one tab, browsing your home directory in another tab, and also browsing network folders in a third tab. All of these functions can help manage your taskbar and keep your desktop looking clean and sharp.

As a Web browser, Konqueror enables you to set bookmarks, change your home page, and use all the other features you would expect from a Web browser.

Navigating around the Internet is no different in Konqueror than in any other Web browser, including Firefox, Opera, Netscape, and Internet Explorer. Just type the Web address into the address bar and hit Enter. For example, type in www.kubuntu.com to visit the home page for Kubuntu.

To search using Google, simply move to the search bar, and directly to the right of the address bar type in what you are looking for. Konqueror will use Google to find it for you.

TIP   If you are using Konqueror in the file manager mode, the Google search bar defaults to locate, which will search your hard drive instead of using Google's search to search the Internet.

Often when browsing the Web, you will see an orange icon at the bottom of Konqueror. This means there is an RSS feed available. To track this feed, simply click on it, and Konqueror will add it to your subscribed feeds in Akregator. We'll talk more about Akregator later in this chapter.

Using Firefox for Browsing the Web

Allowing choice is a key feature of Ubuntu distributions. Kubuntu can use the latest version of Firefox (3.1 as of this writing), which can be installed via the Mozilla Firefox Installer (Figure 8-31).

Figure 8-31 Mozilla Firefox installer

Firefox has taken the Web browser world by storm and is as good as or even better than Internet Explorer. Firefox not only provides better features and a better browsing experience but also adheres more closely to Web standards. Like Konqueror, Firefox includes tab browsing (File > New Tab or Ctrl+T), bookmarks, and everything you would expect of a modern Web browser.

Firefox has many different extensions that can be plugged in to allow greater flexibility for your Web browser. The most common plug-ins are for using Macromedia Flash and Java, which some Web pages require.

Installing a plug-in is as simple as visiting a Web site that requires it. A yellow bar will indicate that you are missing a plug-in. Click on the Install Missing Plug-ins button to install the required plug-in.

Burning CDs—Audio and Data

Another common task is creating or burning audio and data CDs. Kubuntu's default CD creation program, K3b (installed through KPackage-Kit), is a very easy-to-use utility that can help you create backup CDs or even new music CDs. K3b provides a very familiar interface for burning and copying CDs (Figure 8-32).

Simply click on one of the icons from the main Kreator screen that describes the project you would like to create, for example, a new audio CD, a new data CD, or a new data DVD project. You can even copy a CD. After the new project has been started, simply drag the files you want from the top section to the lower section (Figure 8-33).

Once you have moved the files, select Burn, and sit back while your new CD is created.

Instant Messaging

Instant messaging is another feature that we almost cannot live without these days. Kopete, Kubuntu's default instant messaging client, handles this task very well. You can find it under the Internet section in the Application Launcher. You can also launch Kopete from KRunner or the Search

Figure 8-32 K3b

Figure 8-33 Just drag and drop the files.

bar of the Application Launcher by typing Kopete. The beauty of Kopete is that it can connect to all of the major service providers, so you do not have to have multiple programs open. Kopete can handle ICQ, MSN Messenger, Yahoo! Messenger, and AOL Instant Messenger (AIM), and because Google Talk (Google's instant messenger program) is built around the Jabber protocol, Kopete can handle that as well. Kopete also can work with MSN Webcams.

In order to use Kopete, you need to configure accounts. Select Settings > Accounts, and then configure the different accounts you would like Kopete to use. Kopete can save your passwords to these accounts and even automatically connect upon start-up.

Once the accounts are configured correctly, you can change Kopete's behavior to fit your preferences. Many options can be selected, including away settings, what happens when a new message arrives, and even how the system starts up.

Internet Relay Chat

A great place to find support for Kubuntu is Internet Relay Chat (IRC), which can be accessed by using Quassel (Figure 8-34) and the different IRC channels. Join irc.ubuntu.org and then come over to #kubuntu to get many of your support questions answered. Quassel by default is set up to access #kubuntu, but more channels can be added. The people in #kubuntu are full of great knowledge and can help you try to solve any issues that you have.

To launch Quassel, type either Quassel or IRC in the Application Launcher and click on the application.

Kontact

These days almost everyone uses e-mail, and almost everyone uses some form of calendar program to keep track of appointments and schedules. Kontact, Kubuntu's default PIM (Personal Information Manager), takes care of all these tasks plus more.

Figure 8-34 Quassel

To start Kontact, go to the Application Launcher and then to the Internet section. You can also start it from KRunner or by typing Kontact in the Search Bar of the Application Launcher. Figure 8-35 shows an example of the Kontact window.

Looking at the figure, you can see that Kontact has a lot of different features. We cover several of the program's options in the following subsections.

KMail is the program that handles e-mail. It can be run separately from Kontact if you choose. The first step in configuring Kontact is to set up KMail to send and receive e-mail.

Setting Up Your E-Mail Account   You will need several pieces of information to set up KMail. Your ISP or system administrator should be able to provide these details.

- Type of e-mail server (such as POP or IMAP)

- Mail server name (such as mail.domainname.com)

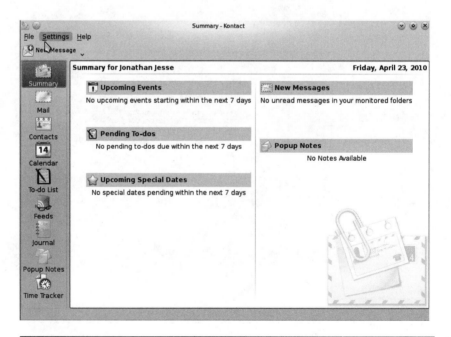

Figure 8-35 Kontact

- Mail account's username and password

- Authentication type (typically password)

- Outgoing mail server name

Configuring Kontact is easier than it may look. Once Kontact is open, select Settings and then Configuring Kontact. From the Configure Kontact panel, select Mail followed by Accounts. Under the tab labeled Receiving, add the information provided from your ISP as the incoming mail information. Once that account has been created, add a new account under the Sending tab that matches the outgoing mail information provided by your ISP.

Using KOrganizer   KOrganizer is included with Kontact. It will track your schedule and provide reminders of your appointments. Upon switching Kontact to calendar mode, you will see a month view on the left and individual days on the right, as Figure 8-36 shows.

Figure 8-36 KOrganizer, Kontact's calendar mode

You can set up two different types of events in Kontact:

- **Meetings:** events scheduled with different people
- **Appointments:** general events

It is easy to add a new meeting or appointment. Find the date for the event in the month view, right-click, and select New Event. In the new window that opens, fill out the Summary, Location, Time, and Description boxes. You can also set up Kontact to remind you when it is time for the appointment.

Using Akregator   Another great application that is part of Kontact (or can be used separately) is Akregator (Figure 8-37), an RSS program that can track your favorite Web feeds. Due to the integration of Akregator and Konqueror, any Web page that has an RSS feed will have an orange icon in the corner of the program that helps you add it to your list.

Simply click on the icon and select Add to Akregator. Akregator will keep your feeds up to date by automatically checking for new content. Another bonus of the integration between Konqueror and Akregator is that Web

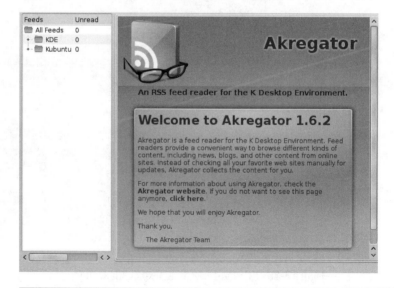

Figure 8-37 Akregator

pages can be opened within Akregator to post comments and view more information than what is provided by the Web feed.

As you can see, Kontact is a great program that helps you organize your life, track your favorite Web sites through RSS, and handle your e-mail.

Kiosk Mode

Kiosk mode allows an administrator to configure KDE and all aspects of the desktop and prevent the end user from changing the settings.

KDE stores all of its configuration information in text files. These files control everything from the default background to whether or not a person can add bookmarks. To see the locations of the configuration files, simply type kde-config -path confi from the Konsole. Note that the order applied is the reverse order of what is displayed. By simply changing one of the files in the highest priority, the last listed in the kde-config statement, you can affect what all users see.

To change the background for all users, simply edit the Wallpaper section found in kdesktoprc, located in /usr/share/kubuntu-default-settings/ kde-profile/default/share/config.

As previously discussed, each user can change the desktop to meet his or her own needs. However, an administrator can make it so some things cannot be changed. Simply insert [$i] at the top of the file for each application you would like to make immutable.

Along with enabling or setting changes, an administrator can remove user access to certain items by simply editing the kde globals file and adding a [KDE Action Restrictions] [$1] section.

There are plenty of additional items that can be limited and changed in Kubuntu.

Exploring the Kubuntu Landscape

Unlike many other operating systems, Kubuntu includes a large number of applications installed by default. These tools have been selected to allow you to install Kubuntu and then just get your work done. Some of the applications installed by default have been covered already. Unfortunately (or fortunately, depending on how you look at it), there are too many applications to discuss in this book due to space restrictions.

To partially solve that problem, here is a quick summary of many programs that are available from the Application Launcher, including how to find them and brief descriptions.

- **Kate:** Application Launcher > Utilities > Kate—This simple and powerful text editor is great for editing documents, making quick notes, and programming. There is a vast range of plug-ins for items such as spell checking, statistics, and syntax highlighting.

- **Calculator (Speedcrunch):** Application Launcher > Utilities > Calculator—Speedcrunch is an extremely powerful calculator that can help you solve both basic and advanced math problems.

- **Konsole:** Application Launcher > Utilities > Konsole—Beneath the desktop is a very powerful command-line core. Konsole allows you to access this command line by putting a nice window frame around it. Konsole is great for command-line junkies, those who prefer to do things with a graphical interface. Konsole can be completely customized to meet your command-line needs.

- **Performance Monitor (KSysGuard):** Application Launcher > System > Performance Monitor—The Performance Monitor provides information about how your Kubuntu system is functioning. Having problems with an application taking too much memory? How would you know? KSysGuard provides this information.

- **System Logs Viewer (KSystemLog):** Application Launcher > System > System Logs Viewer—Interested in what is going on with your system? Kubuntu keeps track of files and access logs that can be viewed through this program.

- **Internet Dial-Up Tool (KPPP):** Application Launcher > Internet > Internet Dial-Up Tool—Need help connecting to your ISP through a modem? KPPP will help take care of this. KPPP can help set up your modem and even set up your dial-up connection.

- **Remote Desktop Connection (KRDC):** Application Launcher > Internet > Remote Desktop Connection—KRDC can help you

connect to remote systems either through the remote desktop
protocol (RDP) or through virtual network connection (VNC).
Simply type in the address and click on Connect. KRDC can save the
settings for each computer you connect to.

■ **PDF Viewer (Okular):** Application Launcher > Graphics > PDF
Viewer—KPDF provides you with the ability to open and view files
saved in the Adobe PDF format.

■ **Screen Capture Program (KSnapShot):** Application Launcher >
Graphics > Screen Capture Program—KSnapShot allows you to take
screenshots and save them in different formats. The great thing about
KSnapShot is that you specify the exact amount of the screen that will
be captured. This program was used to take all of the screenshots for
this chapter.

■ **Image Viewer (Gwenview):** Application Launcher > Graphics >
Image Viewer—Gwenview is the default application for viewing
images in Kubuntu. All different types of images can be opened,
including .png, .jpeg, and .bmp.

■ **KDevelop:** Application Launcher > Development > KDevelop—
While not installed by default, KDevelop is a wonderful integrated
development environment (IDE) that can help you with your coding
projects. This application must be installed via KPackageKit.

■ **Marble:** Application Launcher > Education > Misc > Marble—
Marble is a 3D mapping and globe application. Additional map
information is available through GHNS.

■ **KRandRtray:** Application Launcher > System > Screen Size and
Rotate—This application is used to rotate and resize the monitor. It
also detects and configures external monitors.

Tips and Tricks

The more you use Kubuntu, the more tips and tricks you will learn to help
make your computer experience better and easier. Kubuntu can be configured to do almost anything you would like.

Run Programs Automatically When Kubuntu Starts   You might like to start
some programs automatically every time you log in to your system. For
example, to help you with your Kubuntu work, you might want to access

various channels of IRC every day via Konversation. There are four easy steps to set this up using the session management feature of KDE.

1. Launch all the applications you would like to open automatically.
2. Open up System Settings from the Application Launcher, and click on the User Management section.
3. Click on the Session Manager button on the left, and make sure that the Restore Manually Saved Session checkbox is enabled.
4. Log out, saving your sessions.

Automatically Turn On Numlock When Kubuntu Starts   If you are sick of always having to turn on numlock, the change is very simple to make.

1. Open up System Settings from the Application Launcher, and select Keyboard & Mouse.
2. Under the Numlock on KDE Startup, enable the Turn On checkbox.
3. Click on Apply to save your settings.

Finding Help and Giving Back to the Community
Finding Help

Kubuntu provides a lot of ways to find the information you need to solve a problem. A great place to start is on the IRC channel #kubuntu, which, as we noted earlier, can be accessed through Konversation. There are always wonderful and knowledgeable people in this channel who can answer almost any question. If you prefer to use the Web for answers, the Kubuntu wiki, found at http://wiki.kubuntu.org, has a large amount of information loosely organized with a great search function built in. A third place to find information is the Kubuntu forums at www.kubuntuforums.com. Google is also a great resource. Chances are that someone else has come across your problem before and has written a solution to the issue.

Giving Back to the Community

Kubuntu is built around a great community of people who give back what they learn. There are many ways to get involved and share your love of Kubuntu. A great place to find out how you can make a difference is at www.ubuntu.com/community/participate. Not everyone involved has to know how to create packages, understand how the kernel works, or be a great programmer. Kubuntu also has a place for people to write wiki pages or help with documentation, participate in user advocacy, and give general feedback.

Summary

Kubuntu is a great part of the Ubuntu project and is quickly maturing. From its start as the idea of a single developer to many people working together, Kubuntu is becoming the KDE distribution of choice. However, there is still room for improvement and additions to the setup. A large community of people discuss every day, either through IRC or e-mail, ways to make these improvements. Bugs and other issues are quickly resolved without the additional cost of new programs.

Kubuntu is going to be around for the long haul, and each new release delivers a better, cleaner, and more polished OS. Help spread the word about the project, and get involved by helping out.

CHAPTER 9

Mobile and Netbook Editions

- Installing on a Netbook
- Using the Launcher
- Window Listing
- Maximized Windows
- Switching Back to the Regular Ubuntu Desktop
- Applications to Make Your Netbook Better
- Other Changes from the Desktop Edition
- Summary

NETBOOKS ARE SMALL COMPUTERS, designed for portability and long battery life, that have recently become quite popular. As this has happened, it is logical that many people want to run Ubuntu on them. There are already netbooks on the market that ship with Ubuntu preinstalled, like the Dell Mini 9 and the HP Mini 1000. Most come with other variants of Linux or with Windows. Due to their small screen, netbooks require a custom interface, like the netbook launcher that Canonical has been working on for over two years. Along with some custom software, installing Ubuntu on a netbook is different from installing it on a typical laptop or a desktop. For one thing, most netbooks don't come with internal CD or DVD readers. We outline how to create a bootable USB flash drive to help us get the Ubuntu Netbook Edition (formerly Ubuntu Netbook Remix) installed.

Installing on a Netbook

As with any other flavor of Ubuntu, you need to download the specific image for the Ubuntu Netbook Edition. However, because many netbooks lack a CD drive, you will need to take the downloaded .iso image and copy it to a USB key. Thankfully, there is a special tool in Ubuntu for that. We outline how to begin the process using another computer that is running Ubuntu, but the task can also be done from a computer running a recent version of Windows, Mac OS X, or other modern operating systems.

The Netbook Edition is now officially supported, so it can be downloaded from the same location as the other editions of Ubuntu at http://releases.ubuntu.com. After you have downloaded the ISO, you need to copy it to a USB flash drive. The Create Startup Disk utility in System > Administration is designed to copy an Ubuntu ISO to a USB key (Figure 9-1).

NOTE Prior versions of the Netbook Edition were called the Netbook Remix and were distributed as .img files rather than .iso files as they are now.

WARNING This process will delete anything on the USB flash drive, so make certain you copy any files you need to keep to a safe location before starting this process.

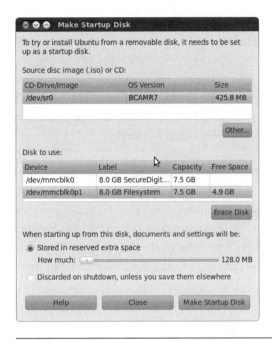

Figure 9-1 Create Startup Disk main window

At the top of the screen is the box showing the source CD or ISO. Click the Other button and select the Netbook .iso file. After it has been added, make certain you select the .iso file you have just added.

The bottom box shows the list of USB keys currently connected to your computer. To prevent accidental data loss, make certain you disconnect any other USB drives from your computer.

Finally, at the bottom is a slider for persistent storage on the USB key. Unless you need the space on the USB key for something else, simply choose the maximum amount by sliding the slider all the way to the right.

After you create the USB key, you need to restart your computer and instruct it to boot from the USB flash drive. This requires either (1) changing a setting in your BIOS to change the boot order to prefer booting from USB before all other methods or (2) holding down a key at startup to choose the device to boot from. Consult your computer's manual to learn how to do this.

Much like a live CD, netbook will work in the same manner as a typical laptop or desktop computer. However, because USB flash drives may be written to as well as read, you can install new packages and download files, and they won't be lost when rebooting.

Once you are ready to install Ubuntu on your netbook, either choose the Install Ubuntu menu option that appears when first booting or launch the installer, called Ubiquity, by pressing Alt+F2, typing *ubiquity*, and pressing enter. When the installation is complete, you can reboot (removing the USB flash drive while the computer is powered off), and you should find your netbook now runs the Ubuntu Netbook Edition. Congratulations!

Using the Launcher

The first and most obvious difference between a regular Ubuntu install and the Ubuntu Netbook Edition is the launcher (Figure 9-2). Instead of a desktop with icons, your menu and desktop are replaced by a launcher that shows installed programs and allows access to files and directories.

The netbook launcher uses the same categories for applications as the standard Ubuntu menu, so finding an application is still easy. For those applications you use all the time, you can right-click the icon and select add to favorites to add it to the Favorites menu (Figure 9-3).

Using the 2D Launcher

If you are finding the 3D launcher a bit slow on an older computer, the creators of Ubuntu Netbook Edition have created something just for you. Designed for use on older computers and the new advanced RISC machine (ARM)-based netbooks, which lack 3D graphics hardware, the 2D launcher uses the Enlightenment Foundation Libraries to emulate the look of the main launcher without the resource issues. To use this version of the launcher, you need to change your session type. On the login screen at the bottom, there is a menu titled Session, which brings up a drop-down list.

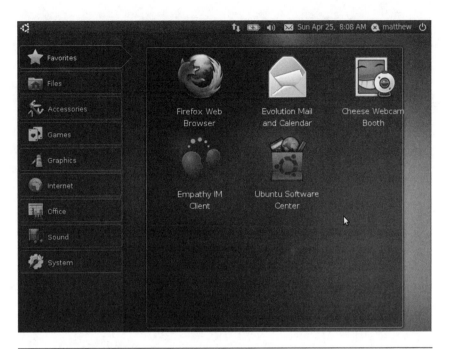

Figure 9-2 Netbook launcher default

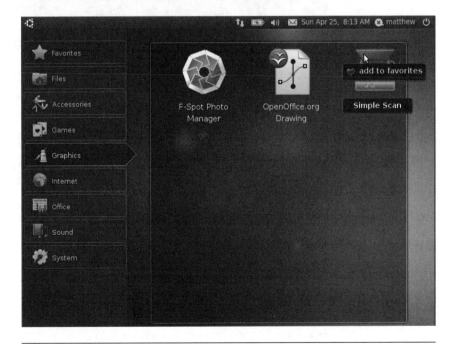

Figure 9-3 Adding an icon to Favorites for easy access later

On that list is the 2D launcher. Select that option, then log in normally (Figure 9-4).

After you log in, you will see a fairly familiar setting with the launcher and the categories but a few differences.

The first major difference is the lack of the go-home applet in the upper left and maximus, which keeps windows maximized. In their place is the standard panel with the drop-down menus. To bring up the desktop launcher, you can use the Show Desktop button in the lower right, just as with the standard Ubuntu desktop.

To add a favorite, right-click on the icon and then select the Add to Favorites option. If it works, you will see a notification in the upper right telling you it has been added (Figure 9-5).

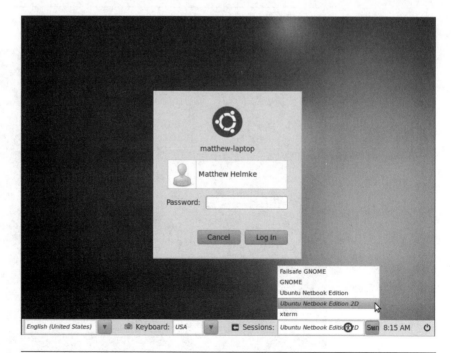

Figure 9-4 The session selection window with 2D launcher selected

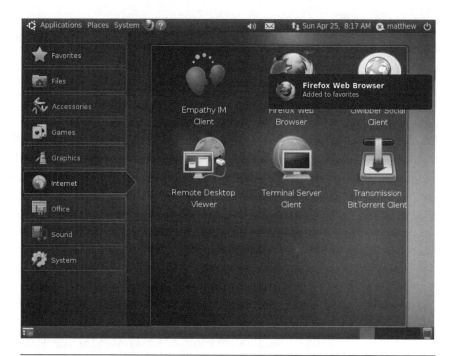

Figure 9-5 Adding to favorites

NOTE You cannot grab the scroll bars to move up and down in a category, but you can scroll anywhere in the menu. This is because the 2D launcher is designed for touch-based computers on which grabbing scroll bars is difficult.

The 2D launcher does two things that the 3D launcher doesn't do. First, it tells you what programs are already running. Look for the little spinning wheel on the upper right of the icon (Figure 9-6). This will show for each running program with a menu entry.

Figure 9-6 Wheel showing running applications

Second, the launcher includes recently used files on the Files view, so you can quickly launch your current work without going through the menus (Figure 9-7).

Window Listing

Instead of a list of named windows on the bottom panel, as in most desktops, in the Ubuntu Netbook Edition, applications are represented by their icons on the upper panel, to the left of the window name, as seen in Figure 9-8. To select an application that is currently running in the background, use Alt+Tab or click on its icon in the upper left. The currently active window will be highlighted with a light gray box around it.

Maximized Windows

Because the Netbook Edition is designed to be used on computers with small screens and the application titles are shown on the panel, a tool to keep all windows maximized was created (Figure 9-9).

Figure 9-7 Files view of the 2D launcher

Figure 9-8 Panel showing currently open windows

Figure 9-9 Window title in the panel

Most applications work just fine with this, but if they don't, there is an easy way to prevent a specific application from being maximized. Launch the GNOME Configuration Editor by starting the Run Applications dialog: Press Alt+F2 and type gconf-editor and enter. After the gconf-editor program has been launched, navigate to apps > maximus. Add the application's name under the exclude_class key, as seen in Figure 9-10, with Totem, which has been added by default.

Switching Back to the Regular Ubuntu Desktop

In Ubuntu Netbook Remix, there was a great tool for switching back and forth between the Ubuntu Netbook interface and the regular Ubuntu one. Sadly, that tool is gone—but you can still switch back and forth. On the login screen is a session switcher, as mentioned earlier, with the new 2D launcher. To switch back to the standard Ubuntu desktop, simply select GNOME, as in Figure 9-11, and off you go. You can even switch every single time you boot if you want.

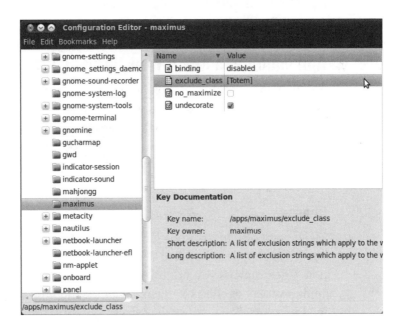

Figure 9-10 Editing the exclude_class key in gconf-editor

Figure 9-11 Session selection to the GNOME option

Applications to Make Your Netbook Better

Although the Ubuntu Netbook Edition has most of the same applications as the standard Ubuntu desktop, and they work great, there are a few applications that can make your netbook even better. These include a webcam or photobooth application called Cheese; an ebook reader, Fbreader; a handwriting recognition tool, Cellwriter; and a note-taking app, Xournal.

Cheese

Many netbooks and laptops have a built-in webcam. For this, a photobooth-type application called Cheese is included in Ubuntu Netbook Edition. Cheese allows you not only to capture photos and video but also to apply a variety of effects to them, including flipping, warping, and changing the colors. You can use the images Cheese takes and upload them to Flickr, use them as your profile picture, or add them to the F-spot library (Figure 9-12).

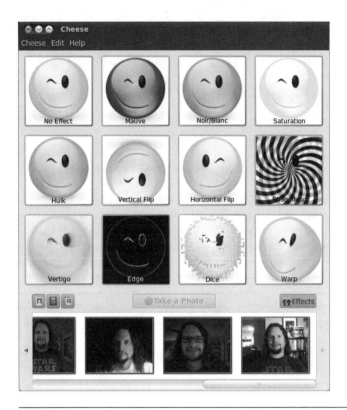

Figure 9-12 Say Cheese!

Fbreader

Because of their long battery life and small size, netbooks make excellent ebook readers. Because of this, Fbreader, one of the more popular Linux ebook readers (Figure 9-13) is included with Netbook Edition. Fbreader can read most ebook formats, including epub and fb2, currently some of the most popular.

NOTE Fbreader cannot read .lit files, a common Microsoft-created format for ebooks. However, it is possible to convert these files to a readable format while using Ubuntu. If you install the convlit package, you can use it to convert most .lit files to HTML and images so they may be read.

NOTE To see the full list of supported and unsupported formats, visit http://www.fbreader.org/doc/formats.php.

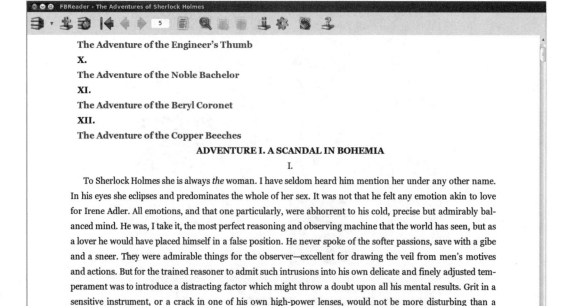

Figure 9-13 Reading ebooks is easy with Fbreader.

Cellwriter

One of the major challenges with touchscreens is character recognition. Because of the increasing number of netbooks shipping with touchscreens, Cellwriter is installed by default. After some basic training of your handwriting (Figure 9-14), Cellwriter can accurately turn writing into text to be copied to a document, to the command line, or elsewhere (Figure 9-15).

Xournal

Also for netbooks with touchscreens, Xournal is a stylus-based note-taking application that can mix drawing, formulas, and text (Figure 9-16). Each journal is organized into pages and can have multiple layers of drawing, allowing annotation of any document. Xournal can be found under the Accessories menu.

Xournal also allows annotating of PDFs (Figure 9-17), which can then be exported to a file or printed. To open a PDF to annotate, choose the Annotate PDF option on the File menu. Choose the PDF you would like to open.

Figure 9-14 Initial training of Cellwriter

Figure 9-15 Once Cellwriter has been trained, entering text is easy.

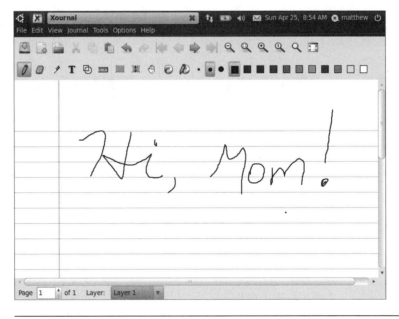

Figure 9-16 Xournal allows for easy note taking.

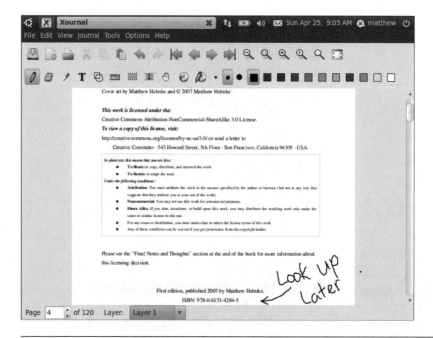

Figure 9-17 Easily annotate PDFs by importing them.

Once you are done editing, the Export to PDF link under the File menu can create a PDF of your notes.

Other Changes from the Desktop Edition

There are a few little tweaks in Netbook Edition that are different from the major interface changes mentioned previously.

Virtual Desktops

Unlike the normal Ubuntu install, the Netbook Edition panel does not show virtual desktops. Only one virtual desktop/workspace is created by default. However, the ability to use virtual desktops still exists, although changing the default takes a bit of work. The default panel lacks any free space, so you will need to remove one of the applets, such as the go home applet in the upper left, and then right click on the free space created and add the workspace switcher applet. However, the applet does not display correctly with the black panel. Change the panel color or use the keyboard shortcuts of Ctrl+Alt+(arrow keys) to move between workspaces.

Summary

The Ubuntu Netbook Edition is a wonderful option for use on today's portable devices. It was developed with cooperation from Intel and several device manufacturers (OEMs) specifically for use with Intel's Atom processors. While it is ready for use today, the project is still in active development and improving continually. To find out the latest information about this remix, take a look here: http://www.canonical.com/projects/ubuntu/une.

CHAPTER 10

Ubuntu-Related Projects

- **Officially Supported Derivatives**
- **Recognized Derivatives**
- **Other Distributions**
- **Launchpad**
- **Bazaar**
- **Summary**

UBUNTU IS NOT MERELY a complete operating system; it is also the center of a growing ecosystem of distributions. Some, referred to as the partner projects, work closely with and within Ubuntu. Others prefer to work outside the project and are considered full derivatives. Often, these projects are created in order to highlight a specific selection of software or use case, such as the Ubuntu Studio project, which focuses on multimedia creation and editing. Others, like the gNewSense project, supported by the Free Software Foundation, exist for philosophical or social reasons.

Still others are created for reasons connected to the international nature of Linux and open source software. While most Ubuntu development happens in English, there are large developer and user communities in other languages and countries. Thus, a derived distribution might spring up to satisfy that need. There are derived distributions targeted at Christians, Muslims, people with slow computers, and people who prefer to have an Ubuntu system optimized for any of several alternative user interfaces or for use in several different schools and government bureaucracies around the world. Should you use any of these over Ubuntu? We can't answer that question for you. Some of these projects are fully within and, as a result, not mutually exclusive from Ubuntu. Others might be more appropriate depending on your preferences or circumstances. You can mix, match, and sample these distributions until you find one that works great for you. As we mentioned in Chapter 1, Ubuntu sees these derivatives as a sign of a healthy and vibrant community. One of the goals of the project is to make it easier for this type of distribution to appear. We can all expect to see more of them in the future.

Officially Supported Derivatives

Officially supported derivatives, formerly called Partner projects, are those projects that work in close relation with Ubuntu. They share a common repository of packages and release in sync with Ubuntu. These derivatives are officially supported by Canonical in both development and security.

Kubuntu

Kubuntu is the first and oldest of all the partner projects. First released alongside Ubuntu 5.04 (Hoary Hedgehog), Kubuntu, which means "toward humanity" in Bemba, builds on the strengths of the K Desktop Environment (KDE) rather than GNOME as Ubuntu does. The project is led by Jonathan Riddell, who now works for Canonical, Ltd.

As with Ubuntu, Kubuntu is a complete desktop, but one built around KDE and Qt. Instead of Ubuntu's brown theme, Kubuntu opts for a more traditional blue and makes only a few other visual changes. Kubuntu is explored in much more depth in Chapter 8 and so is not given a full treatment here.

TIP   **Kubuntu**
Kubuntu can be found at www.kubuntu.org.

Edubuntu

Edubuntu is a version of Ubuntu for use in schools and other educational environments and uses the thin client technology of the Linux Terminal Server Project (LTSP) as well as a number of programs aimed at the educational market, such as GCompris and the KDE Education suite. It is led by a team council that coordinates and participates heavily in its development; the members are listed here:

- Scott Balneaves
- Jonathan Carter
- Jordan Erickson
- Alkis Georgopoulos
- Stéphane Graber
- Richard Johnson

One of Edubuntu's unique features is the inclusion of the LTSP in an easy-to-use, out-of-the-box installer. LTSP uses a different method of deploying clients over a network than is used in traditional computer deployments. Instead of full-powered computers, LTSP uses thin clients, less capable, cheaper computers that connect to a larger server and have it do all the processing work. LTSP is covered in greater detail in *The Official Ubuntu Server Book*, *Second Edition*, also available from Prentice Hall.

Several Ubuntu advocates have leveled the counterintuitive suggestion that the groups of users who have the most problems switching to Ubuntu are those with the most computer experience. For the technically competent, learning Ubuntu often involves *unlearning* something else. For most of those reading this book, Ubuntu is an alternative operating system for an extraordinarily exciting generation of users. No team or project within Ubuntu has done more to target, support, and grow this group of users than the Edubuntu project.

The community-driven Edubuntu project aims to create an add-on for Ubuntu specially tailored for use in primary and secondary education. Edubuntu exists as a platform consisting of tools for teachers and administrators. The real thrust, of course, and the real purpose, is to put free and open source software into the hands of children. In doing so, Edubuntu provides children with a flexible and powerful technological environment for learning and experimenting. Based on free software, it offers educational technologies that are hackable and that can ultimately be used by students and teachers on *their own terms*. Distributed freely, its gratis nature serves an important need for schools where technology programs are always understaffed and underfunded. Fluent in Ubuntu and in free software, the children who, right now, are growing up using Edubuntu are offering the Ubuntu community a glimpse of where it might go and the generation of Ubunteros who may take us there.

While the Ubuntu, Kubuntu, and Xubuntu (another recognized derivative covered later in this chapter) desktops highlight the products of the GNOME, KDE, and Xfce communities respectively, the Edubuntu project aims to provide the best of everything in Ubuntu—properly tailored for use in schools and as easy to use as possible. One thing that made Edubuntu popular was its amazing ability to integrate thin clients, allowing the use of one powerful machine (the server) to provide many very low-powered, often diskless machines (the clients), with their entire OS. This model, while uninteresting for most home or business users using workstations and laptops, is a major feature in classroom settings where it can mitigate configuration and maintenance headaches and reduce the cost of classroom deployments substantially.

In 2008, it was decided that the developers of Edubuntu should focus more on bringing the best educational applications to the desktop rather than trying to maintain an entire distribution of their own. As a result, Edubuntu is no longer a distribution like Ubuntu, Kubuntu, or Xubuntu, but rather an "add-on" for users. What this means is that you can easily install Edubuntu using the Ubuntu Software Center in your Applications menu, selecting Education, and then Educational Desktop for Ubuntu or Educational Desktop for Kubuntu.

TIP   **Edubuntu**
Edubuntu, along with more detailed installation instructions and options, can be found at www.edubuntu.org.

Ubuntu Server Edition

Ubuntu Server Edition was created with the aim of making Ubuntu easy to install and use on servers. The Server Edition was officially launched with Ubuntu 5.04 and initially focused on making certain that the highest quality server applications were available for easy installation and configuration, including MySQL, Apache, and others.

The most recent work has involved improvements to the cloud computing capabilities of Ubuntu Server. This is done via the Ubuntu Enterprise Cloud, powered by Eucalyptus Systems technology, which enables the use and benefits of cloud computing behind a firewall for enhanced security, ease of deployment, and resource allocation.

To learn more about Ubuntu Server Edition, we recommend *The Official Ubuntu Server Book, Second Edition*, also available from Prentice Hall.

TIP   **Ubuntu Server Edition**
Ubuntu Server Edition can be found at www.ubuntu.com/products/whatisubuntu/serveredition with further infomation at www.ubuntu.com/cloud and www.ubuntu.com/partners/Eucalyptus.

Recognized Derivatives

Beyond the officially supported derivatives, recognized derivatives use all the same repositories as Ubuntu and release on the same schedule, but they are not officially supported by Canonical in development or security.

Xubuntu

Xubuntu is a version of Ubuntu built on top of the Xfce window management system. In Xubuntu, Xfce and its associated applications play a role analogous to KDE in the context of Kubuntu. Xfce is small and lightweight compared to the much fancier GNOME and KDE. It uses less memory and fewer CPU cycles than either of the alternatives in a normal configuration. While this means that Xubuntu is often seen as having fewer features or being less user-friendly than Ubuntu or Kubuntu, it also means that it runs faster, is more responsive, and tends to run very quickly on older or less powerful computers, where the weight of either GNOME or KDE may make the system prohibitively slow. As a result, Xubuntu has been used frequently by computer recyclers, by the owners of old computers, and by those who just want to squeeze out better performance from their hardware using a more efficient interface.

Like Kubuntu, Xubuntu is community driven and began outside the project in the universe repository of Ubuntu. In releases 5.04 and 5.10, Xfce 4 was supported by a special Xfce Team in Ubuntu. Due to the great work done on Xfce, Xubuntu was brought into the fold and became Ubuntu's third partner project and a part of the main Ubuntu repository, for release 6.10, where it has remained since.

TIP   Xubuntu
Xubuntu can be found at www.xubuntu.org.

Ubuntu Studio

Ubuntu Studio is a derivative of Ubuntu that is designed and optimized for multimedia production. The system includes a wide variety of applications useful to those engaging in audio and video recording, mixing, editing, synthesis, and production as well as graphics production and manipulation. It contains a modified kernel that allows the system to reduce latency for audio in ways that dramatically improve performance in professional audio recording and manipulation, but the kernel may be inappropriate in other environments. Its first release was based on Ubuntu 7.04.

TIP **Ubuntu Studio**
Ubuntu Studio can be found at www.ubuntustudio.org.

Mythbuntu

MythTV is one of the most popular pieces of home theater software, but it has a bit of a reputation as a beast to set up. Mythbuntu is designed to make that setup easy. Like Xubuntu, Mythbuntu uses Xfce as a desktop environment, has a custom-made Mythbuntu Control Center, and has a LiveCD for easy testing. Mythbuntu's first release was based on Ubuntu 7.10.

TIP **Mythbuntu**
Mythbuntu can be found at www.mythbuntu.org.

Other Distributions

Some distributions generally work outside of the Ubuntu community and usually have their own package repositories. They may not release at the same time as Ubuntu. In the past, several of these derived distributions have been built directly upon other distributions, such as Debian, which is also the base for Ubuntu. The changes that Ubuntu developers make in the process of creating the distribution have been seen as positive and useful as a foundation for others with custom needs or desires. The list of derivative distributions has grown rapidly, and as distributions come and go, the list is constantly in flux. While in the first edition of this book, our list was nearly comprehensive, the size of the derivative distribution community has grown so much that compiling a complete list for this book is no longer possible. Instead, we provide a bit of the flavor of the diversity of derived distributions with some examples of the oldest and most visible derived distributions to give you an idea of the scope of the community.

Guadalinex

Guadalinex is the GNU/Linux distribution developed and promoted by the regional government of Andalusia, the most populated autonomous community in Spain with almost 8 million inhabitants. It is currently one of the largest free software implementations worldwide, with more than 200,000 desktops—and increasing. The project is a consequence of the unanimous support of the Andalusian Parliament on the Information Society and Innovation policies approved in 2002 and 2003, urging all the regional institutions to promote and use free software and open licenses. This makes the Guadalinex initiative unique in the world.

Guadalinex was initially released in 2003, and the first two versions were based on Debian. In 2005 the Guadalinex project decided to develop the third version deriving from Ubuntu. Guadalinex version 3 was released in January 2006 based on Ubuntu 5.10 (Breezy Badger), making it the first major Ubuntu derivative. The project is part of a government plan to implement free software as the default option in the public schools. At the beginning of 2006, this project involved 500 schools and approximately 200,000 desktops equipped with Guadalinex and free software only. These numbers increase every year as new courses start every September and new computers are purchased (about 40,000 in 2006). This initiative alone puts Guadalinex in the top position as the biggest free software implementation worldwide. Additionally, the software is used in public Internet access centers, senior centers, libraries, and women's associations, as well as citizens' homes. Guadalinex is merely one example of many Ubuntu derivatives created by or in cooperation with governments for use in schools and bureaucracies. It is now only one among many massive deployments of Ubuntu in these settings.

TIP   **Guadalinex**
Guadalinex can be found at www.guadalinex.org.

---

gNewSense

While Ubuntu has a strong commitment to free and open source software and software freedom, it makes several compromises for binary-only firmware and drivers whose exclusion renders hardware inoperable. These drivers and firmware are placed in the restricted repository. The multiverse and commercial repositories, while not officially supported, reside in the Ubuntu archive and contain software that does not live up to Ubuntu's standards of software freedom. It is for this reason that the gNewSense project, spearheaded by Irish Ubuntu community members, was launched.

gNewSense is a pun on the word *nuisance*—Richard Stallman, the father of the free software movement and the GNU project, is often jokingly referred to as "chief gnuisance"—but also tries to evoke images of "new sense" that comes from a commitment to software freedom. As a result, the project is primarily reductive.

TIP   **gNewSense**
gNewSense can be found at www.gnewsense.org.

Linux Mint

Because Ubuntu is dedicated to using free software by default as much as possible, it does not come with proprietary media codecs installed. That was the reason Linux Mint was originally created. Over time, it has developed a community that focuses on creating an easy-to-use-and-install Linux desktop that is nice to look at with a focus on making things as simple and enjoyable as possible, especially for newcomers. The distribution is completely compatible with and uses the Ubuntu software repositories. The main differences are in the look and feel as well as choices for software installed by default.

TIP   **Linux Mint**
Linux Mint can be found at linuxmint.com.

Lubuntu

Lubuntu is a new derivative that strives to provide an even lighter and faster desktop by using the Lightweight X11 Desktop Environment (LXDE), by default, in place of GNOME, KDE, or Xfce. It is in active development and seeks to become an official variant. While LXDE can be built on many current Linux distributions, it is the native environment of Lubuntu alone. LXDE is still in active development and has not yet produced its first official stable release, making this a true cutting-edge project.

TIP   **Lubuntu**
Lubuntu can be found at www.lubuntu.net.

TIP   **More Derivatives**
A list of official and recognized derivatives is kept at www.ubuntu.com/products/whatisubuntu/derivatives, and even more are listed at wiki.ubuntu.com/DerivativeTeam/Derivatives.

Launchpad

As we mentioned in Chapter 1, most of Canonical, Ltd.'s technical employees do not work on Ubuntu. Rather, they work on infrastructure. The majority of this infrastructure is a large collection of services that work together to provide the framework through which Ubuntu is built. This superstructure of related applications is collectively referred to as Launchpad. While it has several non–Web-based systems, it is almost wholly accessible over the Web.

While Launchpad is primarily used to develop Ubuntu, the infrastructure was designed to be useful for any free software project and is becoming more popular. It aims to provide these projects with the code-, bug-, and translation-tracking software necessary to more easily and more powerfully collaborate with others and to develop free and open source software. Each of these functions (code, bug, and translation tracking) is highly integrated, making it much more ambitious, and potentially much more powerful, than traditional Web-based solutions with similar goals. Early on, the Launchpad Web page described the project as follows:

> A collection of services for projects in the Open Source universe. You can register your project, and then collaborate with the Open Source community on translations, bug tracking, and code.

That description continues to be valid even as the project has expanded with support and specification modules. In addition to code, bug, and translation tracking, Launchpad provides the ability to deal with code, not just on a per-package or per-project level, but on the distribution level as well. If a bug has been reported against a piece of software in Ubuntu, it is visible to both the upstream and downstream projects. The project can track how its software evolves over time and see, at a glance, whether bugs apply or not. Developers can track translations in a similar way.

The best way to understand Launchpad is to see it in action. This section walks through the individual pieces of Launchpad in more depth. Much of the Ubuntu infrastructure is highly integrated into Launchpad. If you have created an account for contributing to the wiki or ordering CDs at http://shipit.ubuntu.com, you already have a Launchpad account.

Once a source of controversy in the free and open source software world was the fact that the source code to Launchpad was not distributed. This changed on July 21, 2009, when Launchpad and all of its components, including codehosting and Soyuz, were officially made open source using the GNU Affero General Public License, version 3 (AGPLv3).

TIP   **Launchpad**
Launchpad can be found at www.launchpad.net.

Soyuz

Soyuz is the distribution and archive management software integrated into Launchpad. It handles all of the automatic building of software in Ubuntu on each of the architectures and the integration of successfully built software into the archive. Soyuz means "union" in Russian and is the name of the spacecraft that Mark Shuttleworth traveled in during his voyage to space.

Soyuz works almost entirely behind the scenes. It was first activated in early February 2006, but had no initial effect on the way software was uploaded or downloaded in Ubuntu. What Soyuz does is to integrate the process by which software is built and inserted into different parts of the Ubuntu archive. The building of software cannot be tracked using the Launchpad Web infrastructure.

TIP   **Recent Builds**
The status of recent builds in Ubuntu can be found at https://launchpad.net/distros/ubuntu/
+builds.

Launchpad Translations

Translations, commonly called Rosetta, is a Web-based translation system integrated into Launchpad. It was the first piece of Launchpad to be publicly released. It was and is codenamed Rosetta after the Rosetta Stone, the famous piece of dark gray granite with the same text in three scripts that led to the deciphering of Egyptian hieroglyphics.

Rosetta is a Web-based version of a "PO" file editor. In other words, it provides a simple mechanism by which translators can view a list of untranslated phrases or strings and then translate each of them into their language. At the moment, the system works only with translations *from* English. Rosetta's non–Web-based predecessors include Kbabel and Gtranslate, both of which can be downloaded and installed on Ubuntu. By putting this functionality on the Web and integrating it into the archive management scripts, Rosetta lowers the barrier of entry for translation and increases the chance that a translation will make it into the distribution.

Rosetta includes each of the translatable strings contained in every application in Ubuntu. When new software is uploaded into Ubuntu, Rosetta will check to see if any strings have changed or been added. Changes to a string that has previously been translated will result in the translation being marked as fuzzy until a translator can check the translation and the new string, make any necessary changes, and then mark the translation as no longer fuzzy. By tracking new strings, Rosetta can easily prompt translators with new strings to translate as they appear as well as provide statistics on the percentage of strings within a particular application or within all of Ubuntu that have been translated into a particular language.

As users translate strings, they build up positive "karma" within the system—an innovation that has now been deployed to many other parts of Launchpad. Users can also work together in localization teams (called l10n teams because the word *localization* has ten letters between its first and last letters). Rosetta provides a great way for Ubuntu users to get involved in the distribution. Anybody who knows English and another language can begin contributing. Because the system is integrated into Launchpad, users do not need to submit their translations a second time to have them included in Ubuntu—the project already has them. After they are submitted in Rosetta and approved, new translations are automatically pushed out to users who use Ubuntu in those languages.

TIP   **Rosetta**
Rosetta can be found at www.launchpad.net/rosetta.

Launchpad Bugs

Launchpad Bugs, commonly referred to by its codename Malone, is a Web-based bug system like the Mozilla project Bugzilla, which might be familiar to some users. It provides a location where users can file bugs they find in their Ubuntu software by using easily accessible pieces of software such as Bug Buddy, the command-line `reportbug`, or by reporting over the Web. Malone's name is a reference to the gangster movie musical *Bugsy Malone*.

Malone's first role is to provide a location where users can submit bugs. Malone is not just a way to collect complaints, though. Rather, its job is to track and record a bug through its full life cycle, from report to close. Bugs can be assigned to a particular developer or reassigned. If the bug is, in fact, the result of another application, the bug can be reassigned to another package. Bugs can be rated according to severity, or tagged and categorized in any number of useful manners. Information, files, and patches that fix a bug can be uploaded into Malone. When the bug has been resolved, it can be closed. The Malone bug report provides a single venue in which to collect information from the bug submitter, the bug fixer, the upstream maintainer if necessary, and any other involved party.

All of this, of course, is exactly what you would expect from any usable modern bug tracker. Where Malone aims to distinguish itself from its competitors is through its integration in Launchpad. First and foremost, this means that users of Malone can track the status of a bug as it relates to a particular patch or a particular piece of code. Because Ubuntu supports *every* release for 18 months and some releases, such as Ubuntu 10.04 LTS, for much longer, it's important that Ubuntu be able to track which bugs show up in which releases. As derivative works of Ubuntu are created in Launchpad, Malone also allows these derivatives to use Malone to see whether bugs submitted against Ubuntu or other distributions apply to their code and, if so, to quickly grab a fix.

As with Rosetta, Launchpad karma can be built up by fixing, reporting, and interacting with bugs over time. Bug triage that involves closing irreproducible bugs and merging duplicate bugs is one way that users can build up their karma. Of course, simply running developer versions and submitting new bugs is another great way to build good karma.

TIP   **Malone**
Malone can be found at www.launchpad.net/malone.

The Launchpad Blueprint Tracker

The Launchpad Blueprint Tracker, or Blueprint, is Ubuntu's custom specification and feature-tracking system. Blueprint provides a way that users can create specification pages, linked into the existing Ubuntu wiki, for features they would like to see in Ubuntu. Other interested parties can use Blueprint to subscribe to specifications or proposals they are interested in to collaborate on the development of the specification and to track progress. Over time, users working in the wiki and in Blueprint help new ideas through a process that starts with "braindump"—a very rough collection of ideas and brainstorming—and ends with an implemented feature. In Ubuntu, this process involves (1) review by the community and trusted members and (2) approval by decision makers and the Ubuntu Technical Board or by appropriate team leaders and councils. Blueprint provides technology to support this process and ensure that nothing important is dropped on the floor.

In particular, Blueprint helps leaders and decision makers on Ubuntu prioritize features and specifications and ensure that work is progressing on necessary features toward on-time completion for releases. As a result,

Blueprint is used as both the primary specification tracker and the major release management tool for Ubuntu.

While Blueprint is extremely useful for technical specifications, it is also used heavily for developing and tracking community-related proposals as well as for brainstorming stages into implementation. Blueprint also has features designed around sprints and conferences to help organize sessions and coordinate groups to bring forward specifications. As a final bit of trivia, it's interesting to note that Blueprint was also written largely by Ubuntu founder and financier Mark Shuttleworth himself!

TIP   **Blueprint**
Blueprint can be found at www.launchpad.net/blueprint.

Launchpad Answers

Launchpad Answers is a technical support tracker built within Launchpad for use by Ubuntu and other free software projects hosted in the system. It allows community members to file support requests and other community members to help resolve those requests. Unlike most other systems, questions can be asked and answered in a variety of languages. Launchpad Answers tries to complement other forms of community support in Ubuntu by providing a familiar ticketing system that also catalogs answered questions, allowing users to easily find answers to questions that others have asked before. Users can file support requests and communicate with volunteer community support contacts to provide more information, to discuss issues, and to note that their issues are resolved. In addition to storing the answers in a way that makes them searchable, Launchpad Answers helps contextualize support requests by integrating them with other Launchpad features to show the connections and context of relevant bugs, translations, people, teams, and the variety of versions in the variety of releases tracked by Launchpad. Of course, karma can be built by interacting with Launchpad Answers and, in particular, by answering questions.

TIP   **Launchpad Answers**
Launchpad Answers can be found at https://answers.launchpad.net.

Other Functionality

In addition to the visible flagship products within Launchpad just discussed, Launchpad has several other important uses. We've already alluded to the fact that Launchpad handles all the authentication for all the Ubuntu Web sites. If you want to edit or create a Web page in the Ubuntu wiki or even order a CD, you must first create an account in Launchpad. In addition to holding a username and password, a Launchpad account can contain rich information about each individual, including a GNU Privacy Guard encryption key, wiki pages, contact information, and more. More important, Launchpad also contains representations of every team and group within Ubuntu and handles permission within the entire Ubuntu world. For example, the only people who are allowed to upload core packages to Ubuntu are people who are part of the Ubuntu Core Developers Team in Launchpad.

NOTE   The system is also playing an increasingly important role in coordinating sprints and tracking events in a calendar. With time, Launchpad's functionality is only likely to grow, and its help in supporting the new type of development will grow with it.

Bazaar

Bazaar is a distributed revision control system. What does that really mean? First, a revision control system is a program that tracks how the source code of a program changes. It tracks what each specific change was, such as the addition of a new piece of code, as well as who made the change. It also allows a developer to roll back to a previous version or create a branch, or a separate and parallel code version, to try a new idea without forcing the change on the main code.

The second key piece about Bazaar is that it is distributed. Traditional revision control systems have a single place where the code is stored. Only certain people can access this place and change the code there. A distributed revision control system is different in that there is no single place for code storage. Each branch a developer is working on is equal, and they all take code from each other. This system is much like a number of equal merchants at a bazaar, hence the name.

Bazaar started out as a fork of the Arch distributed revision control system. (A fork means that the developers disagree on where to take the program, and they break into different groups to work toward each group's different goals.) However, Bazaar 2 was completely rewritten, as it was found that the then-current code did not work in the long term.

TIP **Bazaar**
Bazaar can be found at www.bazaar-ng.org.

Launchpad Ground Control

Launchpad Ground Control is a new project that aims to make the use of the collaborative features of Launchpad and Bazaar easier for everyday users. To accomplish this, a new package may be installed by users on their computer that integrates Launchpad with their desktop, enabling the use of Launchpad and Bazaar without using the command line. It does so in a way that is completely compatible with all the command-line methods, so it is possible to switch between the methods without harming the project at hand.

TIP **Ground Control**
Ground Control can be found at https://launchpad.net/groundcontrol.

Summary

In addition to building a great OS that many people use, the Ubuntu project has developed an OS that those building other operating systems use as a basis to build from. This has come in the form of both internal partner projects and external derivative distributions. Together, these span languages, continents, and markets. Also, Ubuntu is tightly linked to Canonical, Ltd.'s other projects, Launchpad and Bazaar. While Bazaar provides a compelling version control system, Launchpad provides a one-stop show for bugs, translations, and much more.

CHAPTER 11

Introducing the Ubuntu Forums

- **What Are the Ubuntu Forums?**
- **A Brief History of the Ubuntu Forums**
- **How May I Participate?**
- **Questions, Locations, Conversations, and Activities**
- **Key People in the Forums**
- **Fun Stuff**
- **The Foundation of the Ubuntu Forums**
- **Summary**

THIS CHAPTER INTRODUCES THE Ubuntu Forums by describing what they are, why they exist, and some of the history and fun quirks that make them a place where people come for the tech support and end up staying for the community. Whether you have used Internet forums in the past or not, this chapter will give you a good introduction to an official Ubuntu presence on the Web, a place that is helpful, welcoming, and an enjoyable community in which to participate.

What Are the Ubuntu Forums?

An Internet forum is a Web site where people may sign up for an account and then communicate with one another in discussions of varying types in a casual and free-flowing manner. Most forums are divided into smaller areas, each dedicated to a particular topic or set of related topics. For those who have participated in online activities for a long time, Internet forums are an easy-to-find and easy-to-use equivalent of local dial-up bulletin board systems (BBSs) from the 1980s and early 1990s, as well as a prettier looking version of Usenet news groups.

The Ubuntu Forums were created as a place for people to come and help one another learn how to install, use, and customize Ubuntu. The goal was to create a place on the Internet that was easy to access for those who are not especially adept at or experienced with technology. The site is divided into a number of different topical areas to make finding information easy and to make asking questions and finding answers simple.

In addition, the forums exist in a very informal, sometimes whimsical atmosphere, where the information and tech advice are both solid and useful; the community is kind, gentle, and welcoming; and the spirit is often playful.

A Brief History of the Ubuntu Forums

The Ubuntu Forums were created in October 2004 by Ryan Troy, aka ubuntu-geek (we talk more about forum usernames later in the chapter). The forums were started as a personal project, an unofficial resource provided by one man who was having fun and trying to help people at the same time. Quickly the forums became known as a wonderful place to find other Ubuntu users who are knowledgeable, helpful, and friendly. The forums caught the eye of Canonical very early on, and in November 2004, in recognition of the solid foundation and great atmosphere that had already been established, the forums became the Official Ubuntu Forums. The forums hosting continued to be paid for by Ryan and the occasional donations of forum community members until March 2006, when Canonical graciously offered to host the forums on its own servers. In June 2007, the forums' domain name, license, and assets were all transferred to Canonical, which now maintains sole ownership.

Over the years, the forums have changed their look and feel several times, but one thing has always remained: the feeling of community. The Ubuntu Forums began as a small group of playful geeks (meant in the best of ways) who gathered to have some fun and help one another with a new and interesting Linux distribution in a lighthearted and welcoming atmosphere. As of this writing, the forums have well over one million members, with an average of between eight and fifteen thousand online at any given time, and yet the friendliness and helpful community feeling remains.

How May I Participate?

To browse the forums, read questions and answers, and get a feel for the community, simply point your browser to ubuntuforums.org. You don't need an account to benefit from the information that already exists on the site. You can read and even search the forums to see if others have asked questions about the things you are interested in learning.

However, to really begin to participate in the community, you will want to sign up for an account. Do so by browsing to the main page at ubuntuforums.org and clicking the Register link, as shown in Figure 11-1.

You will be asked to read and agree to the forum rules shown in Figure 11-2. The Ubuntu Forums Code of Conduct is summarized later in this chapter.

After doing so, choose and provide a username and password, along with an e-mail address. You may choose a username that is serious, whimsical, informative, or secretive, almost anything you want as long as it is clean and work/school appropriate. There is also some optional information

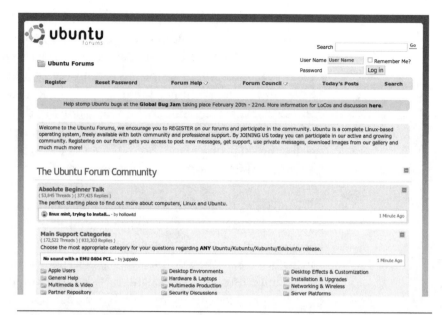

Figure 11-1 UbuntuForums.org Web site front page

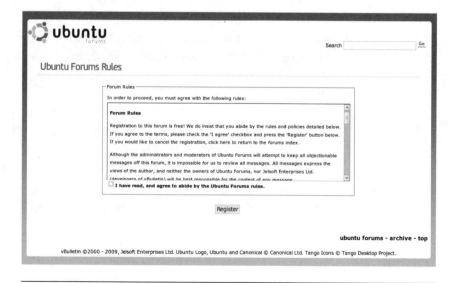

Figure 11-2 UbuntuForums.org rules agreement

that may be included in your registration, such as the username of another forums community member who referred you, and your time zone. When you have entered all the information, click the Complete Registration box, as seen in Figure 11-3. You will receive an e-mail at the address you entered and will need to follow the instructions it contains to complete your registration.

Figure 11-3 UbuntuForums.org account signup page

Now that you have an account, you probably want to ask a question. To do so, pick a category from the list on the front page. For example, if you have a specific issue with multimedia program configuration or your video card not working correctly, you might want to post in the section under Main Support called Multimedia & Video. Click to open that section and click the small box at the top of the list of topics containing the words New Thread, as shown in Figure 11-4.

Topics are called *threads*, and individual comments and contributions within a thread are called *posts*. You will be "posting a new thread" in a specific *subforum*. You will need to give your new thread a proper title and clearly explain your question.

One of our forum staff members, who uses the username aysiu on the forums, wrote a wonderful set of instructions on how to get the best help in Internet forums. You can read his entire guide at http://ubuntucat. wordpress.com/2007/08/06/getting-the-best-help-on-linux-forums/. Following is a basic outline of his helpful advice.

Figure 11-4 UbuntuForums.org posting a new thread example

When posting a new thread with a request for assistance, it is a good idea to follow these steps for the greatest effectiveness:

1. Show that you tried to do some research on your problem. Mention the results of searching the forums or via Google, what you have tried, and the results of your attempts thus far.

2. Come up with a thread title that accurately describes your problem. A title like "help, it doesn't work" is less likely to attract attention and receive quick assistance than one titled "Installing nVidia video driver on laptop with GeForce 9300M GS."

3. State the important facts, but don't ramble. All of the forum community members are volunteers. Not a single one is paid to read or answer questions. You want to keep your post short and to the point, with enough detail to be helpful for understanding the problem but not so long that people get bored or overwhelmed.

4. Focus on the problem you are trying to fix, and stick to one issue per thread. If you have multiple problems, please feel invited to post multiple threads asking questions. If you do this, each issue is more likely to be seen and answered.

5. Be polite to those who help you, and ignore anyone who is rude. Better yet, use the "report post" function to inform the staff of problems by clicking an icon at the bottom left corner of any post that is in violation of the Forum Code of Conduct (discussed later in this chapter). If you aren't sure which icon, hover over each of them with your mouse pointer, and a tool tip will pop up for each one to tell you what it does.

6. When your problem is solved, please say so. If the solution was posted by someone in the thread you started, please acknowledge their help. If you found the answer elsewhere, please post it in the thread where you ask your question. This will help other members in the future who may be struggling with the same problem.

Once you have a feel for the community and for how things work, please know that you are invited to help out as well. One of the pleasures of the Ubuntu Forums is that anyone who knows something is welcome and invited to assist another member. In fact, many of today's most helpful members of the community started out knowing nothing and asking questions. This community is filled with people who are grateful, most of whom are helping others solely because they themselves were once helped and a desire arose to give something back.

With time, many members distinguish themselves as incredibly helpful, friendly, and polite. Many of them are invited to be a part of the forums staff, or members of forum teams with specific goals. A great example of a forum team is the Beginners Team, which searches for threads and questions that have been asked by newcomers and strives to answer their questions as clearly and completely as possible to ease the transition to Ubuntu.

Questions, Locations, Conversations, and Activities

Most community members first visit the forums to find help with adjusting to a new operating system, with understanding how things work and the underlying principles involved, or to ask specific questions regarding hardware or software configurations or problems.

Those first questions are often quite simple, and that is okay. The Ubuntu Forums welcome beginners and beginner-level questions. There is even a special location in the forums called Absolute Beginner Talk that is dedicated to inviting beginners to ask any questions they may have, in whatever way they are able to ask them. This is also a location where the more experienced users work to give their answers in the least technical language possible and to give the most detail in their answers, trying not to assume any prior knowledge while giving the steps necessary to complete a task.

As time goes on and community members learn more of the foundational information they need, they become more confident and tend to gravitate to areas of specific interest, both to learn and often to assist other users with fun and useful items that have been discovered. This is when the Main Support categories start to receive more and more use.

It is also around this time in a member's entry into the community that she may discover a new trick that she hasn't read about anywhere on the forums, and many enjoy sharing those in Tutorials & Tips. Members often discover that those who "hang out" regularly in the forums are fun and friendly people with whom they would like to interact in a less formal style. The Community Cafe, which is kind of like the water cooler at work, exists for just that purpose. People drop in to discuss things that are unrelated to tech support, and the topics are often silly and playful—but still safe for workplace and school.

There is a lot more to explore in the forums. There are sections on gaming, art and design, education and science, running a server, security, multimedia production, and a whole lot more. There are even localized forums for groups based on physical location, called LoCo Teams, most of whom hold regular meetings in the real world as well as conduct some of their business in our forums.

NOTE   LoCo Teams are discussed and described in Chapter 7.

Key People in the Forums

The Ubuntu Forums are led by a small group of people called the Forum Council. The council is currently made up of seven community members, listed here by their usernames on the forums:

- ubuntu-geek (Council Chairman)
- KiwiNZ
- jdong
- Technoviking
- matthew
- bodhi.zazen
- bapoumba

These seven are ultimately responsible for the oversight and operation of the forums. Primarily, ubuntu-geek deals with server and software maintenance and also chairs the council. In addition, he and all the Forum Council members are corporately responsible for maintaining the community atmosphere and dealing with some of the technical aspects of the forums from within the forum software. If a user has a problem, these are the people who will ultimately deal with the issue.

There is an additional group of users who are vital to the smooth running and community atmosphere of the forums. These are the other forum staff. A current list of all staff is available by clicking the "view forum leaders" link on the front page of the Web site. This list includes the extremely important and wonderful community moderators and the leaders of specific teams and LoCo groups.

Fun Stuff

A discussion of the Ubuntu Forums would be incomplete without a mention of some of the more frivolous and whimsical aspects of this community. These exist to remind us that life is about more than technology and that we are doing more than answering tech support questions. Ultimately, we are dealing with people, people who have names and faces and personalities and feelings. We want to give good and accurate information in the forums, and we want to be completely safe for browsing at work or school, but we do not strive for a stark, professional-only sort of atmosphere.

To begin, community members are given the opportunity to express their personality through their forum account. To access the various settings and personalization options, click UserCP and select User Control Panel from the front page of the forums.

From here you may create or edit a signature, a short bit of text that will be added to each of your posts in the forums. Some users put useful information there, others whimsical quotes. You can edit your avatar, which is a small graphic image that you use to identify or represent you to other forum members. You can also add an additional profile picture to be displayed to any user who chooses to view your profile on the forums. There are lots of options for customization, with the opportunity to be as public or private about your real-life identity as you desire.

You will also notice that each user has a few things related to him or her that have some connection to coffee. User titles like "Dark Roasted Ubuntu" and "Ubuntu Extra Shot" are just a fun way to reward community members as they post in the tech support areas. Every time you post in those areas, you earn a bean. As your bean count grows, your coffee-based user title changes, as does your user rank image—the set of coffee-based icons that appears near your username. You will see things like green beans, roasted beans, coffee cups of various styles and fill levels, and more. All of this is done for fun and is not intended to imply that users with high bean counts are any more or less capable than users with low bean counts. Rather, it is an amusing way to say thank you to those who have the time and willingness to hang around and help the community.

There are lots of other surprises in the forums as well. Occasionally forum staff will call a random "tribute" week, inviting users to change their avatars to honor someone or something dear to the heart of the community. There are avatar dress-up times, such as before Halloween, and the staff has been known to change the entire forum look for April Fool's Day.

The Foundation of the Ubuntu Forums

The foundation of the Ubuntu Forums is the Forums Code of Conduct. It is based on the Ubuntu Code of Conduct but is specifically written to cover forum usage, behavior, and expectations. Please refer to the link on the front page of the Ubuntu Forums, under Forum Help, for the most recent version, as this document is occasionally updated.

The basics of the Forum Code of Conduct are simple and are summed up in the first rule: "Be respectful of all users at all times. This means please use etiquette and politeness. Treat people with kindness and gentleness. If you do this, the rest of the Code of Conduct won't need more than a cursory mention."

Summary

This chapter introduced you to the Ubuntu Forums. It began with a little history and then moved on to specifics of usage and the nature of the forums.

CHAPTER 12

Ubuntu One

- What Is Ubuntu One?
- Getting Started with Free Cloud Storage
- Paid Options
- Ubuntu One Music Store
- Summary

FREE SOFTWARE IS NOT created without cost, and while the Ubuntu Foundation that was created to ensure the survival of the operating system and its community has adequate funds for the moment, solutions to help the Ubuntu Foundation fund development for years to come are being put into action. One such action is in the form of a unique service that benefits the community as well as provides income that allows companies like Canonical to pay the large number of developers it employs to work solely on Ubuntu. This service is called Ubuntu One and is actually a collection of several services that are free of cost to any user, combined with some other options that are for profit.

NOTE You can learn more about the Ubuntu Foundation at www.ubuntu.com/community/ubuntustory/foundation and about Canonical at www.canonical.com.

What Is Ubuntu One?

In short, Ubuntu One is a set of online services provided by Canonical. With Ubuntu One, users may store their personal files on an Internet server in a dedicated account and access them from anywhere they have a computer with an Ubuntu One client. The intended use is to mirror content between computers, synchronizing that content at convenient opportunities when the user is online.

For the moment, the service is available only for users of the Ubuntu operating system, but plans are in place to expand access to other operating systems as well, which would mean that you could access your files from a work computer running Windows, from a friend's house and her Mac computer running OSX, or from your own Ubuntu computer at home or wherever you may be using it. Interested Ubuntu users are given access to all of Ubuntu One's features (described in this chapter) and 2GB of storage in their personal cloud at no cost whatsoever.

TIP Cloud computing and storage is a new metaphor and model for dealing with data and programs. In the extreme, personal computers would be limited to providing Internet access, all data would be stored online, and all programs would run in something like a Web browser. Ubuntu One is a middle-road idea, providing the ability to use your computer as is commonly done now but with the added ability to store your files in an online location for easy access anywhere. You can learn more about cloud computing at en.wikipedia.org/wiki/ Cloud_computing. The specific software used for the communication between local computers and the Ubuntu One cloud does not use an existing protocol like FTP or WebDAV, but involves a protocol created in-house called u1storage.

If Ubuntu One stopped there, it would be a pretty neat feature. However, there are other cloud storage options available that are also free and just as easy to use. What sets Ubuntu One apart are the additional capabilities it includes for Ubuntu users—specifically, that it can be directly integrated with programs that many Ubuntu users enjoy every day. For example, an Ubuntu user may synchronize his Firefox Web browser bookmarks between multiple computers, store Evolution contacts, or write notes in Tomboy on his computer, then use this storage as a safe backup or to easily share information between computers and/or people. There are also some capabilities that have just been created and are described later in the chapter, such as the Ubuntu One Music Store.

NOTE   Feel free to skip this paragraph if the technical details don't interest you. This is all possible because Ubuntu One uses CouchDB, a data storage system that is developed by the Apache Software Foundation, whose Apache HTTP Server software is one of the most respected and widely used Web servers in the world and in March 2010 was the server software of choice for over 54 percent of Web sites in the world. CouchDB is free, open source, and designed to enable access to information easily and securely from and to any location with Internet access. It uses a programming interface that software developers appreciate and, despite being quite new, is already very stable. Ubuntu is ahead of the adoption curve and already uses CouchDB on the desktop to synchronize address and bookmark data. This makes integration with Ubuntu One very simple for developers and even easier for users. The added bonus for developers is that they need make very few program code changes to enable the Ubuntu One features within the current Ubuntu desktop, which minimizes the potential for problems.

Getting Started with Free Cloud Storage

To begin, you must sign up for an account. This is most easily accomplished from your desktop menu at System > Preferences > Ubuntu One (Figure 12-1). Clicking this option the first time will take you to the Ubuntu Single Sign On Web site, which is a service used for access to a large number of Ubuntu-related services.

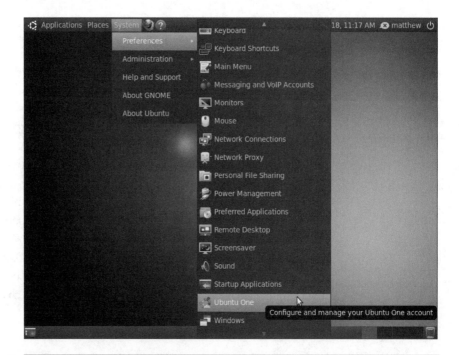

Figure 12-1 Configure and manage Ubuntu One from your desktop menu.

NOTE   You can learn more about Ubuntu Single Sign On at https://login.ubuntu.com/+description.

Let's start by creating an Ubuntu Single Sign On account. Under the Are you new? section of the page, click New Account, as shown in Figure 12-2.

Next, enter your e-mail address and confirm you are a human by entering the words that appear in the box, similar to that in Figure 12-3. Now click Continue.

At this point, you are asked to enter your full name and choose a password, as shown in Figure 12-4. You are required to choose one that is at least eight characters long and includes at least one uppercase letter and one number. If you do not, you will be reminded, as in Figure 12-5.

Figure 12-2 Ubuntu Single Sign On login and signup page

Figure 12-3 Ubuntu Single Sign On e-mail entry

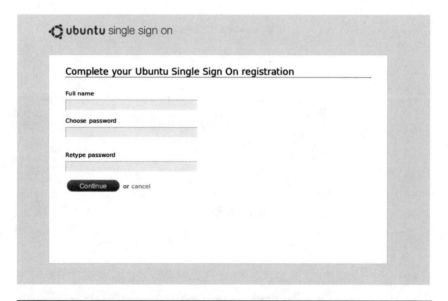

Figure 12-4 Ubuntu Single Sign On full name and password page

Figure 12-5 Ubuntu Single Sign On password error page

Next, you are prompted to look for a registration confirmation e-mail in your inbox. This is to make certain that you are actually the person signing up for the account and that someone else isn't using your contact information for nefarious purposes. If all goes well, you will end up at a page like the one in Figure 12-6. Click Yes, sign me in to access Ubuntu One.

Finally, you will arrive at a first-time startup page for Ubuntu One. Congratulations—your account has been created. You may click any of the tabs on the page (Figure 12-7) to view Files, Notes, and Contacts, all of which will be empty at this point, and you can also access and modify your Account information.

Now we are ready to start using Ubuntu One. Let's begin with where you may upload a file to share. Click on the Files tab at the top of the Ubuntu One Web site, as seen at the top of the Web page in Figure 12-7. This is also the location for the Notes and Contacts tabs we will refer to shortly.

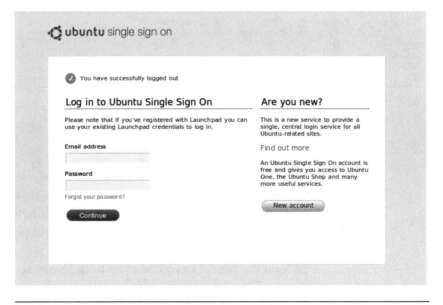

Figure 12-6 Ubuntu Single Sign On sign-in page

Figure 12-7 Ubuntu One's first start page

On the file screen, you may upload files with a single click of the obviously named link: Upload a File. Next to it are links for sharing your files; making them public for others to access; and New Folder, which lets you create folders to organize your files, just as you do on your personal machine.

A click on the Notes tab will take you to the Notes screen where you may add and interact with any notes you may have written using Tomboy. Likewise, a click on the Contacts tab allows you to add and merge contacts from the Web interface.

These described interactions do not appear terribly interesting from the Web interface, but if you use Ubuntu One on your computer rather than the Web interface, you may set it up to interact with this storage site directly, which means that your files, notes, and contacts may be continually and automatically backed up in Ubuntu One every time they are updated locally. That saves a lot of time and effort, and that's where Ubuntu One really shines.

Once you have signed up for an Ubuntu One account, as we did in the first part of this chapter, you may access the online storage center from your panel menu at Places > Ubuntu One. The first time you do this, you will be prompted to allow an application access to keyring. This is necessary for this procedure, and you will want to click Always Allow.

You may also right-click on any folder and choose Share on Ubuntu One to upload from your computer to the cloud storage, and you may specify other people with whom the storage is to be shared using their e-mail address and name. That person will receive an e-mail and will be asked to accept the share by logging in to or creating his or her own Ubuntu One account. You can stop sharing at any time via the Web interface.

If you use Tomboy to write reminders to yourself or other notes, you may store those notes online in Ubuntu One from within Tomboy. Open the program from the panel menu at Applications > Accessories > Tomboy Notes. Within Tomboy, select Edit > Preferences, and under Synchronization, change the service from Local Folder to Tomboy Web and set the server to https://one.ubuntu.com/notes/. Click Connect to Server, and this will have you log in to or create a new Ubuntu One account, confirm that you want to allow access from this specific computer, and then test the connection. If all goes well, you will read a message telling you it was successful, and you can return to Tomboy and click Save back in the Preferences dialog. To synchronize in the future from within Tomboy, click Tools > Synchronize Notes. You will also have access to your notes from the Web interface.

To sync your contacts from Evolution with Ubuntu One, you need to install a package called evolution-couchdb. The first time you do this, you will be prompted to allow an application access to keyring. This is necessary for this procedure, and you will want to click Always Allow. Then, from within Evolution's Contacts menu at the left of the main screen, you should select your Personal address book, and in the Evolution menu, choose Actions > Copy All Contacts To . . ., select Ubuntu One, and click OK. Synchronization will now happen at regular intervals, and you will have access to your contacts from the Web interface as well.

You may also set Ubuntu One as your default address book by selecting it in the Evolution Contacts menu and then clicking Actions > Address Book Properties and choosing Mark as default address book in the dialog box that appears.

NOTE   You can find more documentation and assistance with Ubuntu One at www.one.ubuntu. com/support as well as some wonderful tutorials with specific instructions for use with your Ubuntu desktop at https://wiki.ubuntu.com/UbuntuOne/Tutorials.

Paid Options

You probably noticed in Figure 12-7 that there is a paid option available when using Ubuntu One. If you will only store a couple of gigabytes of information in the cloud, you may do so for free with the 2GB option users receive when signing up for Ubuntu One. However, after testing and working with the service, many users will want to store more data. Those who find themselves needing more storage space may choose to subscribe and access 50GB of storage. The money earned from these subscriptions will help Canonical fund further development in Ubuntu and Ubuntu-related projects like Launchpad.

Canonical has partnered with Funambol, an open source company that specializes in cloud sync for mobile devices, to create a new contact synchronization service to support mobile phones. Paid subscribers to the service will be able to keep their contacts in sync regardless of the device in use: laptops, desktops, mobile phones, and so on. As this is being written, the program is in the alpha stage and is expected to be in public beta testing shortly. By the time this book is printed, the service should be up and running with a full release version available and open to new subscriptions.

NOTE   For more information about Funambol, go to www.funambol.com and to https://wiki.ubuntu.com/UbuntuOne/PhoneSync to learn more about this new partnership and service.

Ubuntu One Music Store

In the Windows and Mac OSX world, the way many people acquire their music is via a program called iTunes. The author, Apple Computers, has stated they have no intention of releasing a Linux version. While that isn't a problem if all you want to do is take the music from your legally purchased CDs and copy it to your computer or buy music from some quality independent artists through wonderful services like Jamendo and Magnatune, it left Linux users with few options for legally purchasing music released by large record labels. This has now changed.

Previously discussed in Chapter 3, Rhythmbox is a powerful music player that integrates podcasts and music purchases from the previously mentioned Jamendo and Magnatune stores that specialize in independent and Creative Commons licensed music, interfaces with most portable music players today, and serves much the same function as iTunes does for users of other operating systems.

Ubuntu 10.04 introduces a new store within Rhythmbox called Ubuntu One Music Store (Figure 12-8). From here you may search for and purchase quality 256 kbps MP3 sound file recordings of songs from thousands of big-name artists with no digital rights management (DRM) restrictions. There are plans to expand the number of Linux music player applications that will support the new store to include other common options like Amarok and Banshee.

A free Ubuntu One account, such as we set up earlier in this chapter, is required to purchase songs. Your Ubuntu One storage may then be used to store your purchased music and make it available to you from anywhere you are able to access the Ubuntu One cloud.

NOTE   You can find more information about the Ubuntu One Music Store at wiki.ubuntu.com/UbuntuOne/MusicStore.

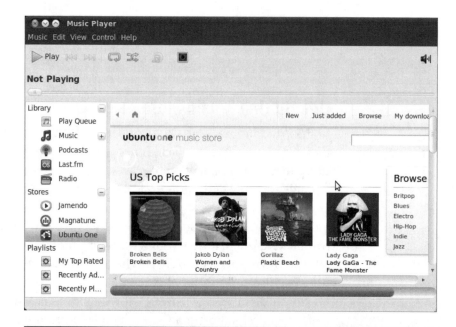

Figure 12-8 The Ubuntu One Music Store is available from within Rhythmbox.

Summary

Ubuntu One provides access to cloud storage with the added benefit of full integration into the Ubuntu desktop. It is easy to use, quick to get started, and there are hints of exciting new features in the queue for future Ubuntu releases. In addition, it is connected to the new Ubuntu One Music Store, which allows Ubuntu users to legally purchase popular music by known artists on major labels—a feature that was previously quite difficult in any distribution of Linux.

Welcome to the Command Line

ONE OF THE MOST powerful parts of any Ubuntu system is the command line. It can also be one of the most daunting to dive into. It seems there is often little help, and that the commands are not easy to find or figure out. If you are willing to learn, the power of the command line will speed up your work and will be a great education that will serve you for years by increasing your ability to do exactly what you want to do with your computer with greater efficiency.

While the command line is a nice addition to a desktop user's life, it is completely invaluable if you run a server. The Ubuntu server installs without any graphical user interface, so the tools explained in this chapter and other books will be absolutely critical to success. And hey, remember to have fun!

Starting Up the Terminal

The terminal can be found under Accessories > Terminal. When it first launches, you will see something similar to what Figure A-1 shows.

You will see a blinking cursor immediately preceded by some letters, and perhaps numbers and symbols, ending with a $. The first word in that string of characters is your username, followed by the @ symbol. After the @, the hostname of your computer is listed, followed by a colon and the name of the directory you are currently in (you always start in your home directory, which is represented by a ~ symbol).

There are many dozens of commands. This appendix presents just a few useful ones in a narrative style to get you started, then lists some more with just a basic description and broken down by category.

Figure A-1 The terminal window

Getting Started

First have a look at the files in your home folder by running the following command:

```
username@computer:~$ ls
```

The ls command lists the files in your current folder. The default command just displays a collection of items that are in your current directory, or location in the filesystem. To make ls more useful, you can type it with options:

```
username@computer:~$ ls -al
```

The -al parts are options that can be passed to the command. In this example, two options, a (list all files) and l (use a long display format to display file permissions, dates, sizes, and more), are used with ls to display all of the files (including hidden files) and their details.

TIP   **To Dash or Not to Dash?**
In many command-line tools, options are added after a dash (-). Some tools, however, don't need the dash. It isn't particularly consistent, so you must pay attention as you learn new commands.

Now move to a different directory:

```
username@computer:~$ cd Desktop
```

The `cd` command changes the directory to the place you specify after the command (in this case, the desktop directory). A nice shortcut that you can use when typing files and folders is to type the first few letters and then press the Tab key to fill in the remainder of the file/folder name. As an example, in the previous command, you could type `cd Des` and press the Tab key to fill in the rest of `Desktop` (with the / added automatically because it is a directory).

When inside a directory, you may want to have a quick look at the contents of a text file. To do this, use the `cat` command:

```
username@computer:~$ cat myfile.txt
```

This command prints the contents of the file on the screen (a more correct way to say this in computer geek jargon would be "outputs to the screen").

Building Pipelines

The power of the command line really comes into its own when you start to pass the output of one command so that it goes to the input of the next, combining commands by using pipelines. A pipeline uses the pipe symbol (|) to string together a number of commands to perform a specific task. As an example, if you use the `cat` command to display the contents of a file to the screen, but the file scrolls past you, create a pipeline and use the `less` command so you can browse the file:

```
username@computer:~$ cat foo.txt | less
```

To see how this works, break the command into parts, each separated by the pipe. The output of the part on the left (cat'ing the file) is fed into the less command on the right, which allows you to browse the file with the arrow keys.

Pipelines can be useful for finding specific information on the system. As an example, if you want to find out how many particular processes are running, you could run a command like this:

```
username@computer:~$ ps ax | grep getty | wc -l
```

Here you count how many getty processes are running (getty is the software that runs a console session). The ps ax command on the left lists the processes on the system, and then the grep command searches through the process list and returns only the lines that contain the text "getty." Finally, these lines are fed into wc, which is a small tool that counts the number of words or lines. The -l option specifies that the number of lines should be counted. Cool, huh?

Running Commands as the Superuser

When you log in to your computer, the account you use is a normal user account. This account is restricted from performing various system administration tasks. The security model behind Ubuntu has you run as a normal user all the time and dip into the system administrator account only when you need to. This prevents accidental changes or malicious installation of unwanted programs and similar things.

To jump to this superuser account when using the terminal, put the sudo command before the command you want to run. As an example, if you want to restart the networking system from the command line, run:

```
username@computer:~$ sudo /etc/init.d/networking restart
```

The command to the right of sudo is the command that should be run as the administrator, but sudo lets you run the command as the current user. When you run the above command, you are asked for the administrator password. This is the same password as the one you established for the first user you added when you installed Ubuntu on the computer. If you are using that user's account, just enter your normal password.

When you have authenticated yourself to sudo, you will not be asked for the password again for another 15 minutes.

Finding Help

Each command on your computer includes a manual page—or man page—that contains a list of the options available. Man pages are traditionally rather terse and intended only for referencing the different ways the command should be used. For a friendlier introduction to using commands, we recommend a Google search.

To view a man page (such as the man page for ls), run:

```
username@computer:~$ man ls
```

The man page command itself has a number of options (run man man to see them), and one of the most useful is -k. This option allows you to search the man pages for a particular word. This is useful when you don't remember the command. As an example, you could find all commands related to processes by running:

```
username@computer:~$ man -k processes
```

The remainder of this appendix gives a brief introduction to some of the more common and useful commands you will encounter and want to learn, organized in categories based on how they are used. We will end with a short list of some other resources for further research.

Moving Around the Filesystem

Commands for navigating in the filesystem include the following.

- **pwd:** The pwd command allows you to know the directory in which you're located (pwd stands for "print working directory"). For example, pwd in the desktop directory will show ~/Desktop. Note that the GNOME terminal also displays this information in the title bar of its window, as shown in Figure A-1.

- **cd:** The cd command allows you to change directories. When you open a terminal, you will be in your home directory. To move around the filesystem, use cd.

  - Use cd ~/Desktop to navigate to your desktop directory.

  - Use cd / to navigate into the root directory.

  - Use cd to navigate to your home directory.

  - Use cd .. to navigate up one directory level.

  - Use cd - to navigate to the previous directory (or back).

  - If you want to go directly to a specific, known directory location at once, use cd /directory/otherdirectory. For example, cd /var/www will take you directly to the /www subdirectory of /var.

Manipulating Files and Folders

You can manipulate files and folders with the following commands.

- **cp:** The cp command makes a copy of a file for you. For example, cp *file* foo makes an exact copy of the file whose name you entered and names the copy foo, but the first file will still exist with its original name.

- **mv:** The mv command moves a file to a different location or renames a file. Examples are as follows: mv *file* foo renames the original file to foo. mv foo ~/Desktop moves the file foo to your desktop directory but does not rename it. You must specify a new filename to rename a file. After you use mv, the original file no longer exists, but after you use cp, as above, that file stays and a new copy is made.

- To save on typing, you can substitute ~ in place of the home directory, so /home/jono/pictures is the same as ~/pictures.

NOTE   If you are using mv with sudo, which is often necessary outside of your home directory, you will not be able to use the ~ shortcut. Instead, you will have to use the full pathnames to your files.

- **rm:** Use this command to remove or delete a file in your directory, as in rm file.txt. It does not work on directories that contain files, which must first be emptied and may then be deleted using the rmdir command. There are some advanced cases where you may use rm to remove directories, but discussing those are beyond the intent of this appendix.

- **ls:** The ls command shows you the files in your current directory. Used with certain options, it lets you see file sizes, when files where created, and file permissions. For example, ls ~ shows you the files that are in your home directory.

- **mkdir:** The mkdir command allows you to create directories. For example, mkdir music creates a music directory.

- **chmod:** The chmod command changes the permissions on the files listed. Permissions are based on a fairly simple model. You can set permissions for user, group, and world, and you can set whether each can read, write, and/or execute the file. For example, if a file had permission to allow everybody to read but only the user could write, the permissions would read rwxr–r–. To add or remove a permission, you append a + or a - in front of the specific permission. For example, to add the capability for the group to edit in the previous example, you could type chmod g+w file.

- **chown:** The chown command allows the user to change the user and group ownerships of a file. For example, sudo chown jim *file* changes the ownership of the file to Jim.

System Information Commands

System information commands include the following.

- **df:** The df command displays filesystem disk space usage for all partitions. The command df-h is probably the most useful. It uses megabytes (M) and gigabytes (G) instead of blocks to report. (-h means "human-readable.")

- **free:** The free command displays the amount of free and used memory in the system. For example, free -m gives the information using megabytes, which is probably most useful for current computers.

- **top:** The top command displays information on your Linux system, running processes, and system resources, including the CPU, RAM, swap usage, and total number of tasks being run. To exit top, press Q.

- **uname -a:** The uname command with the -a option prints all system information, including machine name, kernel name, version, and a few other details. This command is most useful for checking which kernel you're using.

- **lsb_release -a:** The lsb_release command with the -a option prints version information for the Linux release you're running. For example:

```
user@computer:~$ lsb_release -a

No LSB modules are available.
Distributor ID: Ubuntu
Description:    Ubuntu 10.04
Release:        10.04
Codename:       lucid
```

- **ifconfig:** This reports on your system's network interfaces.

- **iwconfig:** The iwconfig command shows you any wireless network adapters and the wireless-specific information from them, such as speed and network connected.

- **ps:** The ps command allows you to view all the processes running on the machine.

The following commands list the hardware on your computer, either of a specific type or with a specific method. They are most useful for debugging when a piece of hardware does not function correctly.

- **lspci:** The lspci command lists all PCI buses and devices connected to them. This commonly includes network cards and sound cards.

- **lsusb:** The lsusb command lists all USB buses and any connected USB devices, such as printers and thumb drives.

- **lshal:** The lshal command lists all devices the hardware abstraction layer (HAL) knows about, which should be most hardware on your system.

- **lshw:** The lshw command lists hardware on your system, including maker, type, and where it is connected.

Searching and Editing Text Files

Search and edit text files by using the following commands.

- **grep:** The grep command allows you to search inside a number of files for a particular search pattern and then print matching lines. For example, grep blah *file* will search for the text "blah" in the file and then print any matching lines.

- **sed:** The sed (or Stream EDitor) command allows search and replace of a particular string in a file. For example, if you want to find the string "cat" and replace it with "dog" in a file named pets, type sed s/cat/dog/g pets.

Both grep and sed are extremely powerful programs. There are many excellent tutorials available on using them, but here are a couple of good Web sites to get you started:

- https://help.ubuntu.com/community/grep

- http://manpages.ubuntu.com/manpages/lucid/man1/9base-sed.1.html

Three other commands are useful for dealing with text.

- **cat:** The cat command, short for concatenate, is useful for viewing and adding to text files. The simple command cat *FILENAME* displays the contents of the file. Using cat *FILENAME* file adds the contents of the first file to the second and displays both on the screen, one after the other. You could also use cat file1 >> file2 to append the contents of file1 to the end of file2.

- **nano:** Nano is a simple text editor for the command line. To open a file, use nano *filename*. Commands listed at the bottom of the screen are accessed via pressing Ctrl followed by the letter.

- **less:** The less command is used for viewing text files as well as standard output. A common usage is to pipe another command through less to be able to see all the output, such as ls | less.

Dealing with Users and Groups

You can use the following commands to administer users and groups.

▪ **adduser:** The adduser command creates a new user. To create a new user, simply type sudo adduser $*loginname*. This creates the user's home directory and default group. It prompts for a user password and then further details about the user.

▪ **passwd:** The passwd command changes the user's password. If run by a regular user, it will change his or her password. If run using sudo, it can change any user's password. For example, sudo passwd joe changes Joe's password.

▪ **who:** The who command tells you who is currently logged into the machine.

▪ **addgroup:** The addgroup command adds a new group. To create a new group, type sudo addgroup $*groupname*.

▪ **deluser:** The deluser command removes a user from the system. To remove the user's files and home directory, you need to add the -remove-home option.

▪ **delgroup:** The delgroup command removes a group from the system. You cannot remove a group that is the primary group of any users.

Getting Help on the Command Line

This section provides you with some tips for getting help on the command line. The commands –help and man are the two most important tools at the command line.

Virtually all commands understand the -h (or –help) option, which produces a short usage description of the command and its options, then exits back to the command prompt. Try man -h or man –help to see this in action.

Every command and nearly every application in Linux has a man (manual) file, so finding such a file is as simple as typing man *command* to bring up a longer manual entry for the specified command. For example, man mv brings up the mv (move) manual.

Some helpful tips for using the man command include the following.

- **Arrow keys:** Move up and down the man file by using the arrow keys.
- **q:** Quit back to the command prompt by typing q.
- **man man:** man man brings up the manual entry for the man command, which is a good place to start!
- **man intro:** man intro is especially useful. It displays the Introduction to User Commands, which is a well-written, fairly brief introduction to the Linux command line.

There are also info pages, which are generally more in-depth than man pages. Try info info for the introduction to info pages.

Searching for Man Files

If you aren't sure which command or application you need to use, you can try searching the man files.

- **man -k foo:** This searches the man files for *foo*. Try man -k nautilus to see how this works.

NOTE   man -k foo is the same as the apropos command.

- **man -f foo:** This searches only the titles of your system's man files. Try man -f gnome, for example.

NOTE   man -f foo is the same as the whatis command.

Using Wildcards

Sometimes you need to look at or use multiple files at the same time. For instance, you might want to delete all .rar files or move all .odt files to another directory. Thankfully, you can use a series of wildcards to accomplish such tasks.

- ▪ * matches any number of characters. For example, *.rar matches any file with the ending .rar.

- ▪ ? matches any single character. For example, ?.rar matches a.rar but not ab.rar.

- ▪ [*characters*] matches any of the characters within the brackets. For example, [ab].rar matches a.rar and b.rar but not c.rar.

- ▪ *[!*characters*] matches any characters that are not listed. For example, *[!ab].rar matches c.rar but not a.rar or b.rar.

Executing Multiple Commands

Often you may want to execute several commands together, either by running one after another or by passing output from one to another.

Running Sequentially

If you need to execute multiple commands in sequence but don't need to pass output between them, there are two options based on whether or not you want the subsequent commands to run only if the previous commands succeed or not. If you want the commands to run one after the other regardless of whether or not preceding commands succeed, place a ; between the commands. For example, if you want to get information about your hardware, you could run lspci ; lsusb, which would output information on your PCI buses and USB devices in sequence.

However, if you need to conditionally run the commands based on whether the previous command has succeeded, insert && between commands. An example of this is building a program from source, which is traditionally done with ./configure, make, and make install. The commands make and make install require that the previous commands have completed successfully, so you would use ./configure && make && make install.

Using Byobu to Manage Your Terminal

One of the challenges of using the terminal is the difficulty of managing multiple screens. If you are in a desktop environment, you can launch another terminal window or use GNOME terminal's tabbed terminals, but that doesn't work everywhere.

Thankfully, such a tool to help you does exist: byobu. Japanese for *screen*, byobu is a set of default configurations for the GNU screen command. Essentially, screen is a window manager for the command line. Since 9.10, this great tool has been installed by default, so all you need to do is launch the byobu command in a terminal.

After it is started, you will notice you are back at a terminal prompt, but with a few differences. At the bottom are two lines of information. The bottom line shows you the version of Ubuntu you are currently running, how long you have logged in, the system load, the CPU speed, the current memory usage, and the current time. The upper bar shows the current logged-in user and, on the right, the list of open windows (Figure A-2).

You can now use your terminal exactly as you normally would, just with a few added pieces of information. Advanced usage of byobu (and screen) is

Figure A-2 Byobu in GNOME terminal

a topic too large for this appendix, but following are a few commands to get you started:

F2:   Open new terminal window.

F3/F4: Move backward/forward through the list of windows.

F6:   Detach from current byobu session. To reattach, use byobu -x.

F7:   Scroll back through the output. Hit Esc to exit this mode and return to the command prompt.

F9:   menu.

Using Byobu by Default in GNOME Terminal

To have GNOME terminal launch byobu by default when it starts, you need to edit the preferences, which can be found at Edit > Profile Preferences under the Title and Command tab. Tick the box "Run a custom command instead of my shell," and enter byobu in the line below. Now when you launch GNOME terminal, byobu will launch with it, and closing byobu will close GNOME terminal as well.

Moving to More Advanced Uses of the Command Line

There are a great number of good books out there for working the command line. In addition, because most of the command line has not changed in many years, a large body of information is available on the Internet. If you need help with something, often simply searching for the command will turn up what you need.

As you can imagine, there are hundreds and hundreds of different commands available on the system, and we don't have the space to cover them here. A number of superb Web sites and books can help you find out about the many different commands.

To get you started, here are some recommendations.

▪ *The Official Ubuntu Server Book* by Kyle Rankin and Benjamin Mako Hill (Prentice Hall, 2009) is an excellent resource for learning all things server related, including the effective use of the command line to accomplish administration tasks.

- *A Practical Guide to Linux® Commands, Editors, and Shell Programming, 2nd Edition*, by Mark G. Sobell (Prentice Hall, 2009) is a good book for any user of the shell in Linux to have on his or her bookshelf.

- **LinuxCommand.org**, found at http://linuxcommand.org, is an excellent Web site designed to help people new to using the command line.

- **The Linux Documentation Project**, found at http://www.tdlp.org, is another excellent and free resource

Index

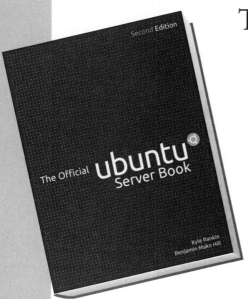

The Definitive, Authorized Ubuntu Server Guide: The Server Companion to the World's Best-Selling Ubuntu Book!

- The complete guide to using the powerful Ubuntu server capabilities that Canonical has been aggressively upgrading and promoting
- Modern, easy-to-use best practices for deploying, managing, and securing any type of Ubuntu server
- Two disks contain the Long Term Support (LTD) Ubuntu Server Edition 10.04 for both 32-bit and 64-bit versions.

The Official Ubuntu Server Book covers everything mere mortals need to know to install, configure, and administer efficient, low-cost Ubuntu servers in any environment. Ideal for both new and experienced Ubuntu and Linux administrators, this book covers a wide spectrum of core admin tasks, including automated Kickstart and preseed installation techniques; package management; security; backup; monitoring; cloud computing; and even virtualization. Readers will also find detailed, step-by-step recipes for installing and configuring each leading type of server, including web, database, DNS, DHCP, file, mail, and many others. Beginning administrators and power users can rely on this book from the moment they decide to install and configure their first Ubuntu servers. Advanced sysadmins and netadmins can save time with elegant, streamlined techniques that fully leverage the major improvements to Ubuntu and Linux administration that have been implemented in recent years.

RENTICE
HALL

DVD Warranty

Prentice Hall warrants the enclosed DVD to be free of defects in materials and faulty workmanship under normal use for a period of ninety days after purchase (when purchased new). If a defect is discovered in the DVD during this warranty period, a replacement DVD can be obtained at no charge by sending the defective DVD, postage prepaid, with proof of purchase to:

Disc Exchange
Prentice Hall
Pearson Technology Group
75 Arlington Street, Suite 300
Boston, MA 02116
Email: AWPro@aw.com

Prentice Hall makes no warranty or representation, either expressed or implied, with respect to this software, its quality, performance, merchantability, or fitness for a particular purpose. In no event will Prentice Hall, its distributors, or dealers be liable for direct, indirect, special, incidental, or consequential damages arising out of the use or inability to use the software. The exclusion of implied warranties is not permitted in some states. Therefore, the above exclusion may not apply to you. This warranty provides you with specific legal rights. There may be other rights that you may have that vary from state to state.

More information and updates are available at:
informit.com/ph